From Practice to Mastery

*A Study Guide for the Florida College
Basic Skills Exit Tests / Reading and Writing*

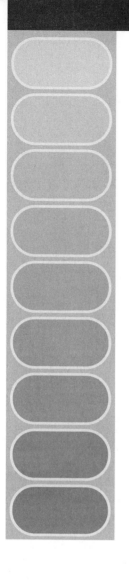

From Practice to Mastery

A Study Guide for the Florida College Basic Skills Exit Tests / Reading and Writing

Barbara D. Sussman

Maria C. Villar-Smith
Both of Miami Dade College

Carolyn Lengel

Bedford/St. Martin's   Boston ◆ New York

For Bedford/St. Martin's

Developmental Editor: Beth Castrodale
Senior Production Supervisor: Dennis J. Conroy
Production Associate: Chris Gross
Project Management: Books By Design, Inc.
Senior Marketing Manager: Rachel Falk
Cover Design: Billy Boardman
Composition: Pine Tree Composition, Inc.
Printing and Binding: Victor Graphics, Inc.

President: Joan E. Feinberg
Editorial Director: Denise B. Wydra
Editor in Chief: Karen S. Henry
Director of Marketing: Karen Melton Soeltz
Director of Editing, Design, and Production: Marcia Cohen
Manager, Publishing Services: Emily Berleth

Library of Congress Control Number: 2004107766

Manufactured in the United States of America

3 2 1 0 9
k l m n o p

For information, write: Bedford/St. Martin's, 75 Arlington Street, Boston, MA 02116   (617-399-4000)

ISBN-10: 0-312-41908-2
ISBN-13: 978-0-312-41908-1

Acknowledgments

Some of the examples and explanations in this book were adapted from the following Bedford/St. Martin's textbooks: *Making It Work: College Reading in Context* and *Putting It Together: Basic College Reading in Context* by Robert DiYanni, *Real Writing: Paragraphs and Essays for College, Work, and Everyday Life* by Susan Anker, and *Writing First: Practice in Context* by Laurie G. Kirszner and Stephen R. Mandell.

Contents

If you're like most people, you don't exactly look forward to taking tests; you might even dread them. The stress, anxiety, and even self-doubt that tests inspire are natural, but they don't have to overwhelm you. In fact, the more you take control of the situation—the more you prepare for an exam—the less helpless you'll feel and the more capable you'll actually be on test day.

This handy book contains all the tools you need to take control of your preparation for the Florida College Basic Skills Exit Tests in reading and writing. Full of practical instruction and plenty of examples, the book includes

- Two tests each (pre- and post-tests) for reading and writing. These tests, consisting of the same types of questions you will encounter on the exit tests, will give you valuable practice and help you diagnose problem areas. (See the section **"How to Use This Book"** for more details.)

- Detailed yet clear instruction in all the skills covered in the reading and writing tests— from identifying a passage's main idea to correcting grammatical errors. *From Practice to Mastery* provides a simple three-part program for mastering each skill. Specifically, the book (1) *explains* a skill or concept through a brief introduction and definition, (2) *shows* you how to apply the skill, with plenty of examples, and (3) *gives you plenty of practice* to master the skill—using the same types of questions that are on the exit exam. Be aware that unlike some exams that cover specific subjects, there's no way to memorize correct answers for Florida College Basic Skills Exit Tests; the only way to succeed is through practice, practice, and more practice.

- Charts, handy lists, and other learning tools to help you understand and master concepts readily.

- An appendix that will help you produce a successful writing sample—another component of the exit exam.

How to Use This Book

You may use this book on your own, or your instructor may ask you to work through specific sections. If you are being directed to this book by your instructor, follow his or her directions carefully. If you are using this book on your own, we recommend this process:

1. Take the relevant pre-test(s) (reading, writing, or both), using the answer forms on pp. 283 and 285.

2. Check your answers against the answer key on pp. 240–42, marking an *X* on the key by numbers of answers that you missed.

3. Review the questions that you answered incorrectly. For each question, this answer key includes references to sections of the book where you can get more help. If you've marked an *X* by a question number, visit the relevant section of the book, where you'll find helpful explanations of the topic being tested, followed by practice questions.

4. Complete the practice questions, using the answer forms on pp. 287–95. (If you need more of these forms than we provide in this book, you may duplicate the forms or just use notebook paper.)

5. Check your work on the practices using the explanatory answer keys on pp. 243–82. These keys give detailed explanations of the answers and note why certain questions might be tricky or confusing, so you can avoid being tricked by similar questions on the test. If you still don't understand a question or general topic, try additional practices or get help from your instructor or writing-center tutor (if one is available).

6. Take the relevant post-test(s), using the answer forms on pp. 297 and 299, after you've become more comfortable with challenging topics.

7. Check your answers against the keys on pp. 276–82. These answer keys provide both explanations and references to sections of the book so you can understand why you missed a question and get more help.

8. Consider doing additional practices and even retaking the pre-tests or post-tests until you feel more comfortable with difficult topics.

9. Review the appendix about succeeding on the writing sample.

The more you practice, the more confident and adept you will become. If you still feel confused about any question or topic, see your instructor or a writing-center tutor. They are there to help you, and they want you to succeed!

Other Helpful Strategies

By using this book to prepare for the exit exam, you're taking a big step toward success on test day. But there are other things you can do—both before and during the test—to improve your performance. We asked instructors who help prepare students for the reading and writing tests to offer their top tips, and here's some of the advice they shared:

- Promise yourself some type of reward for completing the test—a phone call or visit with a good friend, a favorite meal, some relaxation time … anything that will be a welcome treat after hard work.

- Get plenty of rest the night before, and have a healthy breakfast or lunch beforehand. A tired or poorly nourished brain won't function at its best. However, avoid drinking too much liquid before the test; you might not be allowed to leave the room during the exam period.

- Dress appropriately on exam day. Test rooms can be hotter or colder than is ideal, so consider dressing in layers that you can remove as needed. Wear comfortable clothes so you will not be distracted by them (e.g., a belt that is too tight).

- Make sure to bring several sharpened no. 2 pencils (with erasers) and a watch, which will help you pace yourself. Do not assume the test room will have a pencil sharpener or a clock. **A note about erasers:** Test them beforehand to make sure they don't leave smudges. Scantron machines used to grade the tests will read smudges on Scantron forms as answers.

- Arrive at least a few minutes early. Arriving late—or too close to the start of exam— may leave you flustered and distracted at the time the exam begins. Use the extra time to relax and focus your mind. Breathe deeply, rub your own shoulders or temples, or try other relaxation techniques.

- Check the time at the beginning of the exam, and aim to complete at least half of the questions by the time that half of the exam period has elapsed. If possible, aim for a faster pace so that you'll have a few minutes at the end of the exam to check your answers or revisit difficult questions.

- When you are asked a set of questions about a passage, read a few questions (not answer choices) before reading the passage. This will help you focus your attention and locate answers without wasting time. When reading any question or set of instructions, make sure you understand what's being asked of you.

- On the reading test, skim passages to get an overview of the content. This will help you answer questions about main ideas. Once you determine the main idea, it is often easy to determine the author's overall organizational pattern, purpose, and tone.

- Answer *all* the questions on the reading and writing tests. If a question stumps you, put a light dot next to it, in the margin of the answer form, so that you can come back to it later. However, be sure that when you skip a question, you don't put answers to later questions in the wrong place on the answer form. Also, be sure to erase dots in the margins of your answer form before you hand it in.

- Later, answer any questions that you did not answer the first time. Try to eliminate answers that are clearly false or illogical or that seem less plausible than others. Remember: *Don't leave any question unanswered.*

- If you have finished the exam with some time remaining, quickly check your answers and make sure you've marked answers in the proper place on the answer form. Resist the urge to change answers unless you are certain, or nearly so, that you made an error. Your first instinct is often correct, and second-guessing can be counterproductive.

- Take that reward you promised yourself. After all, you worked hard to prepare for and complete the exam!

We hope that these tips—and all the resources in this book—will help you on your way from practice to mastery, and on to greater successes.

Diagnostic Pre-Tests

1.1 Reading Pre-Test

Read the passages and answer the questions that follow each one. (An answer form is included on p. 283, and pp. 240–41 provide answers to this pre-test, as well as references to sections in this booklet where you can get help.)

What environmental choices are worth worrying about? Should consumers be concerned about getting paper bags at the supermarket and about choosing cloth diapers over disposables? Many Americans who want to make good environmental decisions consider these efforts worthwhile. But environmental experts argue that people should not agonize over judgment calls that make little differ- 5 ence in the overall quality of the environment. Instead, consumers should concentrate on decisions that have a real environmental impact.

Many concerned Americans mistakenly believe that relatively unimportant consumer choices make a critical difference to the environment. For example, having heard that disposable diapers are making landfills overflow, new parents 10 may feel obligated to avoid disposables. Instead, they may turn to a cloth diaper service. But disposable diapers are getting smaller all the time and thus taking up less room in the nation's dumps; in addition, diaper services require gasoline-using, exhaust-producing trucks to make pickups and deliveries, and washing the diapers uses additional electricity and water. Clearly, both disposables and cloth 15 diapers offer environmental trade-offs.

Similarly, some environmentally conscious consumers object to plastic grocery bags because the plastic is petroleum based, while paper bags are made from trees, a renewable resource. However, grocery bags also involve trade-offs: plastic bags take up less space than paper bags in landfills, and the manufacture of 20 plastic bags requires relatively little energy. Ultimately, most experts agree that the difference in the environmental impact of paper and plastic grocery bags is very slight. People with a strong preference for paper (or for plastic) bags should feel free to use their favorite, and everyone else can stop worrying about the whole question. *(continued)* 25

Does this mean that an individual's choices don't really affect the environment? No, a single person or household can indeed make a difference—for better or for worse. Cars, for instance, affect the environment dramatically every step of the way from the manufacturing plant to the scrap heap, yet automobile owners rarely demand fuel-efficient, clean-running vehicles or make a conscious decision to reduce their reliance on driving. Gas-powered lawn mowers and weed cutters also have a greater impact than many people realize; their inefficient engines emit many more pollutants per gallon of fuel used than cars do. And the chemical fertilizers and pesticides carelessly applied to many lawns cause increasing problems for the nation's water supply. In many cases, a consumer's decision to do without certain high-impact products, or to use them as little as possible, can significantly conserve resources and reduce pollution.

The bottom line for consumers who care about the environment is that they should use their limited time and energy effectively. If a choice matters little to the environment, people should not waste time trying to decide one way or the other. But when an individual choice can make a real difference, anything consumers can do to make the right decision—and to persuade others to do the right thing as well—is probably worth doing.

1. Which of the following statements best expresses the main idea of the passage?

    a.   Consumers should concentrate on decisions that have a real environmental impact.

    b.   Many concerned Americans mistakenly believe that relatively unimportant consumer choices make a critical difference to the environment.

    c.   Disposable diapers are getting smaller all the time and thus taking up less room in the nation's dumps.

    d.   Environmental experts argue that people should not agonize over judgment calls that make little difference in the overall quality of the environment.

2. The implied main idea of paragraph two is that

    a.   disposable diapers are usually a better choice to protect the environment.

    b.   cloth diapers are considerably more expensive to consumers than disposable diapers.

    c.   landfill overflow is not a significant environmental issue, so consumers should not be concerned.

    d.   consumers can pick a type of diaper without worrying that they could have made a better environmental choice.

3. The author's primary purpose is to

    a.   illustrate ways in which consumers should protect the environment.

    b.   explain the significance of important and unimportant decisions relating to consumer choices that affect the environment.

    c.   persuade consumers not to worry about the environmental effects of their choices.

    d.   list environmental responsibilities for the average consumer.

4. What is the relationship between the parts of the following sentence?

> "If a choice matters little to the environment, people should not waste time trying to decide one way or the other."

    a.   comparison

    b.   addition

    c.   cause and effect

    d.   spatial order

5. According to the passage,

    a.   a single person or household can make an environmental difference.

    b.   choices individuals make rarely affect the environment.

    c.   few consumer choices should be based on environmental concerns.

    d.   automobiles have no direct effect on the environment.

6. As used in line 31, the word *reliance* most nearly means

    a.   love.

    b.   dependence.

    c.   interest.

    d.   dislike.

7. Identify the relationship between these two sentences from the first paragraph.

> "Many Americans who want to make good environmental decisions consider these efforts worthwhile. But environmental experts argue that people should not agonize over judgment calls that make little difference in the overall quality of the environment."

    a.   addition

    b.   cause and effect

    c.   time order

    d.   contrast

8. In this passage, the author is biased in favor of

    a.   consumers avoiding use of all chemical fertilizers and pesticides.

    b.   consumers not wasting time considering environmental effects of their decisions.

    c.   consumers avoiding disposable diapers.

    d.   consumers considering the environmental effects of their choices.

9. For this passage, the author uses an overall organizational pattern that

    a.   contrasts the environmental factors concerning disposable and regular diapers.

    b.   explains that consumers should understand that only some decisions have an environmental impact and gives examples.

    c.   analyzes the importance of protecting our environment.

    d.   discusses that consumers should not be worried about any environmental decisions.

Although spelling reform has a long and distinguished history in the United States, it has enjoyed only minimal success. Many notable Americans have promoted at least some changes in the way American English words are spelled. Over time, and with governmental help, the spellings of some words have been simplified. However, spelling reformers who have pushed for broad changes have 5 not found much popular support.

Few would deny that English spelling and English pronunciation often seem very distantly related. One sound can often be spelled in many ways. Guessing the spelling of an unfamiliar American word is therefore notoriously difficult, as spelling-bee contestants recognize. Conversely, a single combination of letters— 10 for example, *ough*—might have multiple pronunciations, as in the words *cough, though, through,* and *bough*. These difficulties explain why proposals to simplify American English spelling have claimed supporters, including some influential and famous ones.

Among well-known reformers, the first was Noah Webster, whose 1828 dic- 15 tionary standardized American spelling. Webster proposed a number of changes to American spellings, many of which were adopted. He argued for eliminating many silent letters, for example, changing such British spellings as *colour* and *traveller* to the now-familiar American versions, *color* and *traveler*. Later in the nineteenth century, Mark Twain wrote a piece defending simplified spelling, and 20 Andrew Carnegie donated money to the cause. In the biggest twentieth-century success for spelling reform, President Theodore Roosevelt ordered the U.S. Government Printing Office to adopt some simpler spellings, such as *catalog* for *catalogue*; this official recognition ensured the eventual popular acceptance of such changes. 25

But organizations that agitate for bringing the spelling of every American word into line with its pronunciation have not won over many people. First, such changes would alter the spelling of more than half of American English words, according to some estimates, and the adult public is likely to resist such dramatic changes. Second, the fact that a word may be pronounced differently by different groups implies either that the new spelling of certain words would have to vary from dialect to dialect or that the spelling of such words would still strike some people as arbitrary. 30

Spelling reform has counted a few successes. However, even as English spreads more widely around the world as the most common language of business, the idea of spelling reform has weakened. In fact, most people are not even aware that serious advocacy of spelling reform exists. While die-hard reformers continue to argue against the idea that English spelling must always be difficult to master, most Americans remain more or less content to look up confusing words, rely on computer spell-checkers, and hope that their writing doesn't contain too many spelling errors. 35 40

10. Which sentence best describes the main idea?

a. Few would deny that spelling and pronunciation in English often seem very distantly related.

b. Webster proposed a number of changes to American spellings, many of which were adopted.

c. Spelling reform has counted a few successes.

d. Spelling reform has a long and distinguished history in the United States, but it has enjoyed only minimal success.

11. The word *advocacy* (line 37) means

a. support.

b. dislike.

c. confusion.

d. mystery.

12. According to the passage, which famous person was involved in spelling reform?

a. Andrew Carnegie

b. Noah Webster

c. Theodore Roosevelt

d. All of the above

13. For this passage, the author uses an overall organizational pattern that

a. makes a statement about spelling reform and then clarifies it with examples and explanation.

b. classifies reasons to support spelling reform.

c. contrasts the spelling reform movement with the movement to change pronunciation.

d. lists steps, in order of importance, to successfully bring about spelling reform.

14. The author's primary purpose is to
   a.   persuade the reader to fight for spelling reform.
   b.   criticize the spelling reform movement.
   c.   explain the history of efforts to reform spelling.
   d.   define spelling reform.

15. Identify the relationship between these two sentences from paragraph 1.

> "Over time, and with government help, the spellings of some words have been simplified. However, spelling reformers who have pushed for broad changes have not found much popular support."

   a.   time order
   b.   comparison
   c.   cause and effect
   d.   contrast

16. What is the overall tone of this passage?
   a.   optimistic
   b.   ironic
   c.   objective
   d.   nostalgic

17. In paragraph 4, the author expresses a bias
   a.   against spelling reform.
   b.   in favor of spelling reform.

18. "Among well-known reformers, the first was Noah Webster, whose 1828 dictionary standardized American spelling."
   This is a statement of
   a.   fact.
   b.   opinion.

Scientists can be carried away by a fondness for their own hypotheses. Wanting an idea to be correct, they may be unable to recognize evidence that proves it wrong. For this reason, skeptical analysis by other scientists without a personal investment in the outcome of an experiment is essential to the scientific method.

The century-old story of Clever Hans dramatically illustrates the necessity   5
of scientific skepticism. Clever Hans was a horse owned by a retired German schoolteacher, Wilhelm von Osten, who believed that horses possessed intelligence equal to that of humans. To prove his point, von Osten began tutoring Hans as he had taught children. Hans, who obviously could not speak, learned

to count and indicate letters of the alphabet by tapping his hoof. After four years 10 of lessons, the horse astounded von Osten by appearing to correctly answer questions about history, geography, literature, mathematics, and other subjects.

Von Osten invited scientists to come and observe his remarkable horse. In front of audiences, Clever Hans answered both spoken and written questions, even when the questioner used a language that the horse had not been taught. Hans an-15 swered correctly when von Osten was not present, putting to rest the suggestion that the teacher was secretly signaling the animal. Von Osten never accepted money for Clever Hans's performances. Many observers—among them zoologists and psychologists—arrived with the expectation that von Osten was a charlatan but left convinced that he had actually taught a horse to read and reason. 20

But one psychologist, Oskar Pfungst, refused to accept that Clever Hans was anything other than a well-trained animal. Pfungst designed experiments in which Hans was blindfolded or in which no one observing the animal knew the correct answer to the question. In such cases, Hans stood silently. Pfungst was eventually able to prove that Clever Hans's previous questioners had inadver-25 tently signaled the horse, giving him cues when they expected him to tap his hoof and again when they expected him to stop. The cues, which included facial expressions and nods, were so subtle that no observer had noticed them before Pfungst described what he saw. No one, including von Osten, had realized that Clever Hans was clever only at figuring out what people wanted him to do. 30

Had Pfungst not maintained a skeptical attitude toward Clever Hans, people might still believe that a horse could understand human language and logic. Such a belief might give some people pleasure, but knowing the truth— that humans can unwittingly fool themselves—is infinitely more important. Pfungst's 1911 study explaining the mystery of Clever Hans is now commonly 35 cited in psychology texts. The story of von Osten's horse clearly shows the need for dispassionate analysis of scientific claims—especially extraordinary ones.

19. The implied main idea of paragraph 3 is that

 a. Wilhelm von Osten was a fraud who was making every effort to trick the scientists.

 b. Von Osten honestly wanted scientists to convince themselves of Hans's intelligence.

 c. Clever Hans was a unique horse and no other horse would be capable of his achievements.

 d. scientists who came to observe Clever Hans were convinced beforehand of his amazing abilities.

20. According to the passage, the story of Clever Hans has been told for

 a. four years.

 b. twenty years.

 c. fifty years.

 d. one hundred years.

21. The word *skeptical* as used in line 3 means

    a.   open.

    b.   doubtful.

    c.   professional.

    d.   convinced.

22. The author's primary purpose is to

    a.   persuade.

    b.   inspire.

    c.   inform.

    d.   evaluate.

23. Identify the relationship between these two sentences from paragraph 4.

> "Pfungst designed experiments in which Hans was blindfolded or in which no one observing the animal knew the correct answer to the question. In such cases, Hans stood silently."

    a.   addition

    b.   spatial relationship

    c.   contrast

    d.   cause and effect

24. The tone of this passage can best be described as

    a.   humorous.

    b.   pessimistic.

    c.   informative.

    d.   reverent.

25. A conclusion that can be drawn from this passage is that

    a.   Wilhelm von Osten was not very intelligent.

    b.   Wilhelm von Osten intended to mislead his colleagues.

    c.   Wilhelm von Osten loved horses.

    d.   Wilhelm von Osten sincerely believed Clever Hans was an intelligent horse.

26. The author's claim that "skeptical analysis by other scientists without a personal investment in the outcome of an experiment is essential to the scientific method" is

    a.   adequately supported by factual evidence.

    b.   inadequately supported based on personal opinion.

27. "Had Pfungst not maintained a skeptical attitude toward Clever Hans, people might still believe that a horse could understand human language and logic."

This is a statement of

a. fact.

b. opinion.

Until the second half of the twentieth century, people with schizophrenia could count on little sympathy and no effective treatment in the United States; instead, most of them were isolated in institutions. Today, much remains unknown about schizophrenia, but scientists are working to uncover the causes of the disease and to develop more hopeful treatments for its sufferers. 5

Some risk factors for schizophrenia are biological. Indeed, researchers are in basic agreement that the disease has a hereditary aspect. Having close relatives with schizophrenia clearly increases a person's risk: according to research, 46 percent of people with two schizophrenic parents became schizophrenic themselves. Furthermore, in one study of identical twins in which one twin was schiz- 10 ophrenic, the other twin also developed the disease in 48 percent of the cases. Yet genes alone do not cause the illness, as the twin study demonstrates, since identical twins share identical genes. Nonhereditary biological factors that might also affect the development of schizophrenia include prenatal viral infections, birth trauma, and imbalances in brain chemistry. 15

Nonbiological factors seem to increase the possibility of schizophrenic illness in people who are genetically vulnerable to the disease. A Scandinavian study indicates that people in families with highly emotional communication styles may have a greater risk of schizophrenia than people in families that communicate more calmly. Some specialists also believe that negative views of family 20 members toward a patient with schizophrenia can make the person less likely to recover—but other researchers argue that negative attitudes may be a result, rather than a cause, of a long illness. So far, scientists have not determined exactly what pushes a person toward schizophrenia, but many are hopeful that the clues they are now uncovering will someday help families to reduce the risk of a 25 member's falling ill with this disease.

Treatments for schizophrenia have improved over the past decades, but no one solution works for all patients, and nothing can yet guarantee recovery. Antipsychotic drugs that affect brain chemistry can treat the worst symptoms of schizophrenia. Unfortunately, many of these drugs cause such severe side effects 30 that patients refuse to take them. Even more disturbingly, some studies suggest that antipsychotic drugs can make patients less likely to recover completely from the illness. On the other hand, schizophrenia sufferers often thrive when they are taught social skills so that they can live outside of hospitals. Some researchers argue, therefore, that schizophrenia is less crippling when those with the disease 35 can contribute to and participate in the larger society. *(continued)*

A diagnosis of schizophrenia remains a severe blow to the patient and to family members. No longer does schizophrenia require sufferers to be locked away from the world, and research may someday make such diagnoses less common. Finally, many scientists hope that recently developed and forthcoming treatments will offer schizophrenics a chance for a normal life. 40

28. The tone of this passage can best be described as
   a. nostalgic.
   b. optimistic.
   c. pessimistic.
   d. reverent.

29. According to the passage we can assume that
   a. nondrug treatments appear more promising than treatment with antipsychotic drugs.
   b. schizophrenics are never able to participate in society.
   c. antipsychotic drugs are the preferred course of treatment for most schizophrenic patients.
   d. schizophrenia is the most serious mental illness.

30. "Yet genes alone do not cause the illness, as the twin study demonstrates, since identical twins share identical genes."
   This is a statement of
   a. fact.
   b. opinion.

31. According to the passage,
   a. prior to 1950 there was no effective treatment for schizophrenia in the United States.
   b. a Scandinavian study shows the relationship of income and schizophrenia.
   c. the treatments for schizophrenia have declined in the past ten years.
   d. antipsychotic drugs are panaceas for schizophrenic patients.

32. The author's primary purpose is to
   a. educate.
   b. persuade.
   c. criticize.
   d. satirize.

33. The primary form of organization for paragraph 4 is
   a.   illustration.
   b.   contrast.
   c.   time order.
   d.   classification.

34. What is the relationship between the parts of the following sentence?

   "No longer does schizophrenia require sufferers to be locked away from the world, and research may someday make such diagnoses less common."

   a.   contrast
   b.   clarification
   c.   addition
   d.   spatial relationship

35. The author's claim that "no one solution works for all patients and nothing can yet guarantee recovery" is
   a.   adequately supported by factual evidence.
   b.   inadequately supported by opinions.

36. The author shows a bias
   a.   in favor of exclusive use of antipsychotic drugs.
   b.   against exclusive use of antipsychotic drugs.

Each sentence in the following passage has a number. Read the passage carefully and then answer the questions, which refer to the sentences by number. (An answer form is included on p. 285, and pp. 241–42 provide answers to this pre-test, as well as references to sections in this book where you can get help.)

1. _____. **2.** Miyazaki's films, which create magical imaginary worlds, push animation into the realm of art. **3.** The films are visually spectacular, using subtle lighting effects and stunning—if impossible—scenery. **4.** *Spirited Away* (2002), for example, depicts a windswept abandoned theme park in the pale light of late afternoon; after dark, the place becomes a lantern-lit bathhouse on an island served by both a riverboat and a train that hums along an underwater track. **5.** Along with their painterly look, the dreamlike story lines allow Miyazaki's films to avoid the juvenile excesses of some conventional Japanese animation. **6.** Although the filmmaker has a cult following in the United States, he remains relatively unknown to mainstream American audiences. **7.** His current obscurity may not last long, _____. **8.** *Spirited Away* won the 2002 Academy Award for Best Animated Feature, and now Disney has plans to release new English-language versions of Miyazaki's other films. **9.** *Spirited Away* also holds the record as Japan's top box-office hit of all time. **10.** The Japanese master's immense talent will not disappoint the wider American audience that his movies are beginning to attract.

1. Which sentence if inserted in the blank labeled 1 is the best main idea, or topic sentence, for the selection?

   a.   Although Miyazaki's films are well-known in some places, in others, no one has even heard of him.

   b.   Miyazaki's films are known worldwide.

   c.   Hayao Miyazaki is a filmmaker born in Japan.

   d.   Hayao Miyazaki's brilliant animated feature films deserve a larger American audience.

2. Which of the numbered sentences is not supported by specific evidence?

   a.   1   b.   4   c.   5   d.   9

3. Which arrangement of sentences 2, 3, and 4 provides the most logical sequence? Choose A if no change is necessary.

   a.   Miyazaki's films, which create magical, imaginary worlds, push animation into the realm of art. The films are visually spectacular, using subtle lighting effects and stunning—if impossible—scenery. *Spirited Away* (2002), for example, depicts a windswept abandoned theme park in the pale light of late afternoon; after dark, the place becomes a lantern-lit bathhouse on an island served by both a riverboat and a train that hums along an underwater track.

b. The films are visually spectacular, using subtle lighting effects and stunning—if impossible—scenery. Miyazaki's films, which create magical imaginary worlds, push animation into the realm of art. *Spirited Away* (2002), for example, depicts a windswept abandoned theme park in the pale light of late afternoon; after dark, the place becomes a lantern-lit bathhouse on an island served by both a riverboat and a train that hums along an underwater track.

c. *Spirited Away* (2002), for example, depicts a windswept abandoned theme park in the pale light of late afternoon; after dark, the place becomes a lantern-lit bathhouse on an island served by both a riverboat and a train that hums along an underwater track. The films are visually spectacular, using subtle lighting effects and stunning— if impossible—scenery. Miyazaki's films, which create magical imaginary worlds, push animation into the realm of art.

d. *Spirited Away* (2002), for example, depicts a windswept abandoned theme park in the pale light of late afternoon; after dark, the place becomes a lantern-lit bathhouse on an island served by both a riverboat and a train that hums along an underwater track. Miyazaki's films, which create magical imaginary worlds, push animation into the realm of art. The films are visually spectacular, using subtle lighting effects and stunning—if impossible—scenery.

4. Which sentence is least relevant to the passage?

a. 1   b. 9   c. 10   d. 4

5. Which transitional word or device, if inserted in blank 7, would show the relationship between 6 and 7?

a. since   b. in addition   c. hence   d. however

In the following sentences, you will need to do one of three things to answer the questions correctly: (1) choose the most effective word or phrase in the given context, (2) determine if the underlined portion of a sentence is incorrect and select the option that corrects the error, or (3) choose the correct version of a sentence (from a selection of three).

6. The door, with its creaking hinge and loose knob, needed to be _____.

a. bought   b. replaced   c. handled   d. torn

7. Since your library book is _____, you will have to pay a late fine.

a. remiss   b. delayed   c. overdue   d. old

8. The new grocery store buy our home has been sold by a real estate agency; the
                                     A   **B**

agency will buy old buildings too.
               C

a. by   b. bye   c. by   d. No change is necessary.

1

9. What <u>effect</u> did that medicine have on <u>you're</u> headache? It did not <u>affect</u> me very well.
         A   **B**   **C**

    a.   affect   b.   your   c.   effect   d.   No change is necessary.

10. a.   Hanging in the window of the shop that sold my favorite shoes, I found a "closed" sign.

    b.   I found a "closed" sign hanging in the window of the shop that sold my favorite shoes.

    c.   In the window of the shop that sold my favorite shoes, I found a "closed" sign hanging.

11. The concert tickets go on sale Friday at 10 in the morning, _____ I can't make it until 1 p.m.

    a.   so   b.   but   c.   and   d.   for

12. Our new puppy was up all last night, _____ he slept this afternoon.

    a.   and   b.   yet   c.   for   d.   so

13. a.   Even though Patrick has many hobbies, his favorite daily activities are sunbathing, hiking, and to take long walks.

    b.   Even though Patrick has many hobbies, his favorite daily activities are to sunbathe, hiking, and taking long walks.

    c.   Even though Patrick has many hobbies, his favorite daily activities are sunbathing, hiking, and taking long walks.

14. a.   On our last trip to Saint Augustine, Florida, we took a trolley tour, ate Spanish food, and learned interesting facts.

    b.   On our last trip to Saint Augustine, Florida, we took a trolley tour, eating Spanish food, and learning interesting facts.

    c.   On our last trip to Saint Augustine, Florida, we took a trolley tour, ate Spanish food, and it was fun to learn interesting facts.

15. The <u>pastor and priest</u> both knew a lot about the <u>Bible but neither</u> could answer the
                     A   **B**

Sunday school <u>class's</u> questions.
              C

    a.   pastor, and priest   b.   Bible, but neither

    c.   classes   d.   No change is necessary.

16. I have not <u>been</u> to a drive-in movie in a long <u>time, nor have</u> I wanted to <u>go to one</u>.
                   A   **B**   **C**

    a.   been: to   b.   time nor have   c.   go, to one   d.   No change is necessary.

17. Mr. Greene taught six <u>sections of</u> the philosophy <u>class. With</u> forty <u>students attending</u> each group.
                            A   **B**   **C**

    a.   sections. Of   b.   class, with

    c.   students, attending   d.   No change is necessary.

18. My aerobics <u>instructor has</u> another <u>job across town,</u> it takes her thirty minutes <u>to drive</u> there.
                       A   **B**   **C**

    a.   instructor, has   b.   job across town. It

    c.   to: drive   d.   No change is necessary.

19. This brace <u>keep</u> my leg straight, and it <u>helps</u> me walk, as you can <u>see</u>.
                  A   **B**   **C**

    a.   keeps   b.   help   c.   saw   d.   No change is necessary.

20. Tammy <u>go</u> everywhere with her poodle, even to the mall.

    a.   have gone   b.   has went   c.   goes   d.   No change is necessary.

21. There <u>were</u> a few slices of pizza left after the raucous party.

    a.   was   b.   have been   c.   are   d.   No change is necessary.

22. One of the three deaf students <u>recognizing</u> that learning to write will take time.

    a.   recognize   b.   have recognized

    c.   recognizes   d.   No change is necessary.

23. Last night, Pedro <u>went</u> to the store and <u>picked up</u> some dessert. Then he <u>brings</u> it to his
                      A   **B**   **C**

brother's house.

    a.   goes   b.   picks up   c.   brought   d.   No change is necessary.

24. Alice told Myrna that <u>she</u> needed to set up the meeting room.

    a.   she, Alice,   b.   her   c.   it   d.   No change is necessary.

25. The attorney asked <u>me</u> to keep the information about the suicide between <u>her and I</u>, and
                           A   **B**

I agreed.
C

    a.   I   b.   her and me   c.   me   d.   No change is necessary.

26. All the partygoers should have <u>his</u> tickets ready.

    a.   theirs   b.   them   c.   their   d.   No change is necessary.

27. At first I really didn't like using the computer. You can waste valuable time
　　　　A　　　　　　　　　　　　　　　　　　　　　　B

looking up insignificant facts, and I was having to strain my eyes.
　　　　　　　　　　　　　　　　　　　　　　　C

　　a.　you　　　　b.　I wasted　　c.　I'm　　　　d.　No change is necessary.

28. No one likes to have their picture taken without permission.

　　a.　them　　　　b.　his or her　　c.　theirs　　　d.　No change is necessary.

29. I tried to convince them, but you knew how stubborn they could get.
　　　　　　　　　　　　A　　　　B　　　　　　　　　　C

　　a.　their　　　　b.　I　　　　c.　theirs　　　d.　No change is necessary.

30. The experiment conducted by the engineers worked perfect.

　　a.　more perfect　b.　perfectly　c.　most perfect　d.　No change is necessary.

31. The movie was _____ than the book.

　　a.　worser　　　b.　badder　　c.　worse　　　d.　No change is necessary.

32. The trial lawyer made the jury members beleive that the victim was courageous.
　　　　A　　　　　　　　　　　　　　　　B　　　　　　　　　　　C

　　a.　tryal　　　　b.　believe　　c.　couragious　d.　No change is necessary.

33. After listening to the classical music station all day, a myriad of emotions flooded me.
These included grief, despair, and inspireation.
　　　　　　　　A　　　B　　　　　C

　　a.　greif　　　　b.　despare　　c.　inspiration　d.　No change is necessary.

34. The article in *American Traveler* magazine stated that Summer provides the best driving
　　　　　　　　　　　　A　　　　　　　　　　　　　　　B

conditions for travel in the East.
　　　　　　　　　　　　C

　　a.　American traveler　　　　　　　b.　summer

　　c.　east　　　　　　　　　　　　　　d.　No change is necessary.

35. Many Europeans are not familiar with the Gettysburg Address, which was discussed in
　　　　　A　　　　　　　　　　　　　　　B

May's conference.
　　C

　　a.　europeans　　　　　　　　　　b.　Gettysburg address

　　c.　may's　　　　　　　　　　　　d.　No change is necessary.

36. a. Before I even applied, I knew the colleges regulations would be stringent.

   b. Before I even applied, I knew the college's regulations would be stringent.

   c. Before I even applied, I knew the colleges' regulations would be stringent.

37. a. The Garcias have donated children's toys every holiday season.

   b. The Garcias have donated childrens' toys every holiday season.

   c. The Garcias have donated childrens toys every holiday season.

38. Many of the incoming <u>freshmen</u> had heard about <u>professor Dika's</u> class, but few
              A   **B**

   registered for his <u>course.</u>
                         C

   a. Freshmen   b. Professor Dika's

   c. Course   d. No change is necessary.

39. a. This weeks' special item in the store has attracted many customers.

   b. This weeks special item in the store has attracted many customers.

   c. This week's special item in the store has attracted many customers.

40. Lee always goes to the beach <u>early. To</u> make sure he gets a good spot.

   a. early: to   b. early; to   c. early to   d. No change is necessary.

2 Mastering the Reading Test

2.1 Main Idea, Support, and Purpose

2.1A IDENTIFYING THE MAIN IDEA

What Is a Main Idea?

The **main idea** of a paragraph or an essay is the most important point the author is trying to get across. However, it can be easier to identify the main idea if you think of it as the most general idea the author is making about a topic.

The main idea of a paragraph occurs in the **topic sentence**, to which all the other sentences in the paragraph relate directly. The main idea of an essay is the **thesis statement**; all the topic sentences (and their related paragraphs) support the thesis.

The main idea of a piece of writing may be stated directly in a single sentence, but sometimes a writer uses two or more sentences to convey the overall point. In other cases, the main idea is implied; the author includes a series of details that suggest the point without saying it directly.

EXAMPLE OF DIRECTLY STATED MAIN IDEA

In the following example, the main idea is expressed in a thesis statement. Then several paragraphs, each with a topic sentence, offer support for that idea.

More and more smokers are aware of the serious risks smoking poses for themselves and for the nonsmokers around them. Many smokers would like to quit but just do not think they can. However, several strategies can help them achieve this goal.

Thesis statement

The first and easiest strategy is to substitute something for the cigarette that they have become used to holding. Some people use a pencil, a straw, or a coin. I have a friend who started using a Japanese fan. There are even special products available to keep people's hands busy, such as worry beads and small rubber balls. Almost any small object can work.

Topic sentence

Next, people who quit smoking need to substitute something for the stimulation they get from cigarettes. They might chew a strongly flavored sugarless

Topic sentence

5

10

(continued)

gum, for example, or take fast, short breaths. Other people splash their faces with ice cold water or do some light exercise. Some even claim that standing on their heads has helped. The point is to find something that gives a physical jolt to the system. 15

Topic sentence — A third strategy is to change habits associated with smoking. For example, people who associate cigarettes with drinking coffee might temporarily switch to tea or another beverage with caffeine, and people who generally smoke while talking on the telephone might try sending e-mail instead. Unfortunately, some smoking-associated activities are difficult to eliminate. People who associate 20 smoking with being in their cars obviously cannot give up driving. The point, though, is to alter as many habits as possible to eliminate situations in which one would normally reach for a cigarette.

Topic sentence — Finally, most people who successfully quit smoking prepare themselves to resist temptation in moments of stress or discomfort. Rather than reach for a cig- 25 arette, they have another sort of treat ready for themselves. Some people, understandably, choose candy or sweets of some kind, but these are not the best alternatives, for obvious reasons. A better idea is to use the money saved by not buying cigarettes to purchase something to pamper oneself with, such as expensive cologne or a personal CD player. 30

No one would say that it is easy to quit smoking, but this fact should not keep people from recognizing that they can kick the habit. These four antismoking strategies have worked for many ex-smokers, who recommend them highly.

EXAMPLE OF IMPLIED MAIN IDEA

In the following example, the main idea is implied rather than directly stated. Can you identify the main idea?

Humans generally eat several meals a day. A lion may eat once in several days. A boa constrictor may eat once a month. Hibernating animals may go five to six months without eating.

The implied main idea is that different animals can go without eating for different lengths of time.

How Do You Identify the Main Idea?

To find the main idea of a passage, look for the most important point the author is making. Or you might ask yourself, "What is the general idea the author is presenting about the topic or subject?"

Remember that (1) other material in the passage is likely to be more specific than the sentence or sentences that contain the main idea and (2) other sentences will support, rather than simply state, the author's most important point. Ask the following questions about any sentence that seems to express the main idea:

- Does this sentence state the most important point about the topic or subject?

- Is it the most general statement in its paragraph?

- Do the other sentences in the paragraph provide more information to support the main idea or topic sentence?

If the main idea is implied rather than directly stated, first identify the topic of the passage, then figure out what the author seems to be saying about the topic.

EXAMPLE

Genetically modified crops, created by adding a desired trait from one plant to another, can be very beneficial. "Golden rice," for example, was created when scientists took genes from daffodils and other small plants and put them into a strain of rice. These genes gave the rice a golden color. More important, the new genes enabled the rice to produce beta-carotene, or vitamin A. The Swiss scientist who created golden rice wanted to produce a product that contained this vitamin because he knew that about three hundred million people in China suffer from vitamin A deficiencies. The lack of vitamin A can cause a person to become sick easily or even to go blind, but in China vitamins are not easily available, and they are expensive. So, if the rice the Chinese people depend on already contains a vitamin that they need, eating the rice might solve a number of medical problems.

5

10

- Does the main idea appear to be stated directly or implied? *stated directly*

- Which sentence seems to state the most important point in this paragraph? *first sentence*

- Is it more general than the other sentences in the paragraph? *Yes, the rest of the paragraph describes a specific example — "golden rice."*

- Do the other sentences provide support for this sentence? *Yes, they give details that support the main idea.*

EXAMPLE

Economists, financial advisers, and policy makers in government and business study the latest data on unemployment and inflation. Physicians must understand the origin and trustworthiness of the data that appear in medical journals. Business decisions are based on market research data that reveal consumer tastes. Engineers gather data on the quality and reliability of manufactured products.

5

- Does the main idea appear to be stated directly or implied? *implied*

- What is the topic of this paragraph? *data*

- What does the paragraph imply about the topic? *People in many professions rely on data to do their work well.*

Note: Be aware of the difference between the main idea of a passage and a *detail* supporting that idea. In the previous example, the fact that engineers gather data on the quality and reliability of manufactured products is a detail supporting the main idea that people in many professions rely on data.

Practice Identifying the Main Idea

Read the following passages and answer the questions about the main idea. Answers and explanations appear on p. 243.

Twice in the 1970s, a female athlete competed one-on-one against a male athlete in a heavily promoted sports match. For many people, both events symbolized the era's battle over women's rights. Thousands of ticket holders and millions of television viewers wanted to know whether female champions could hold their own, or even triumph, against male competitors. However, while observers of the 5 first event—a tennis match—enjoyed a comedy that permanently raised the status of women players, observers of the second—a horse race—witnessed a tragedy that offered no solace to any supporters of the sport.

In September 1973 the first competition, a tennis match between aging Wimbledon champion Bobby Riggs and rising star Billie Jean King, left everyone 10 except Riggs laughing. Riggs had boasted loudly that "any half-decent male player" could beat any female tennis champion. After challenging and defeating a top-seeded woman, Riggs took on Billie Jean King. He tried to intimidate her by sending flowers and making insulting pronouncements, but King maintained a sense of humor about the event. Riggs arrived at the Houston Astrodome 15 flanked by women in bikinis. Not to be outdone, King arranged to be carried in on a sedan chair borne by musclemen. Unable to win a psychological victory, Riggs, who was fifty-five, was trounced in straight sets by the female champion as millions who had never before cared about tennis watched. Analysts believe that this huge publicity stunt set women's tennis on the course to its present popularity. 20

The second contest involved two athletes in their prime: a pair of three-year-old racehorses. Like the Riggs-King match, the Foolish Pleasure–Ruffian race in July 1975 pitted an able female champion who had competed only with other females against a male competitor. Ruffian had not only triumphed in the Filly Triple Crown but had won each of her ten races with obvious ease. She had 25 never even been passed by another horse on a racetrack, and she had broken track records set by such great horses as Man O'War and Secretariat. Foolish Pleasure, her opponent, was the 1975 Kentucky Derby champion. At the start of the race, Foolish Pleasure nosed ahead for a few seconds, and then Ruffian began to pull in front of him. The two horses had run less than a mile when Ruffian's 30 anklebone suddenly snapped. Foolish Pleasure finished the race alone, and Ruffian had to be euthanized later that day when surgery failed to save her. The unexpected catastrophe left some stunned viewers—many of whom had been drawn to the match as a symbolic battle of the sexes—unwilling to watch another thoroughbred race. 35

The contests between Billie Jean King and Bobby Riggs and between Ruffian and Foolish Pleasure both symbolized the battle of the sexes in the 1970s.

King's triumph over Riggs provided comic relief and a boost to one women's sport. The tragic outcome of the horse race, however, left few with the heart for any additional symbolic matches.

40

1. The implied main idea of this passage is that

    a. the defeat of the male tennis player Bobby Riggs proved that women athletes are superior to men athletes.

    b. due to the sad outcome of the Foolish Pleasure–Ruffian race, the battle of the sexes has yet to be won.

    c. two very different outcomes had very different effects on viewers of athletic gender battles.

    d. no one who observed the Foolish Pleasure–Ruffian horse race now enjoys viewing horse races as a result of the tragedy that occurred.

2. What is the implied main idea of paragraph 3?

    a. Due to the sad outcome of the Foolish Pleasure–Ruffian race, the race lost its significance as a symbolic battle of the sexes.

    b. Thoroughbred racing is no longer popular as a spectator sport.

    c. Ruffian would have been the champion if she had not broken her anklebone.

    d. Like the Riggs-King tennis match, the Foolish Pleasure–Ruffian race pitted an older male athlete against a younger female athlete.

Many medical tests are very effective at assisting doctors in diagnosing ailments and diseases early, when they can still be treated effectively. Some of these tests are recommended for most adults at certain stages of life—tests for certain cancers, for example. One new type of test, the full-body scan, has been heavily promoted as a way for patients to discover problems in any part of the body before symp- 5 toms arise. But experts argue that full-body scans may do more harm than good.

In a full-body scan, radiation provides detailed images of the body's interior organs and systems. The procedure is painless and noninvasive. Many people who are concerned about their health are eager to undergo full-body scans to set their minds at ease, and the procedure is becoming increasingly common. Pa- 10 tients often seek out scans without being referred by a doctor; in this case, they pay for the scans, which are rarely covered by insurance.

Patients obviously want the results of the scan to be negative. If the scan does discover some problem, they want to find out all that they can about the problem so that it can be resolved. However, the results of full-body scans are 15 often false positives—indications of health problems that turn out to be nothing. Before the frightened patient learns that she doesn't have a tumor, she has to suffer the trauma of believing that she may be about to die; then she must undergo uncomfortable, possibly dangerous procedures to discover that there is no tumor

2.1A—Identifying the Main Idea   **27**

Unnecessary surgery, like necessary surgery, always carries the risk of serious 20
complications including death. In addition, it is expensive. For people covered by
insurance, the out-of-pocket expenses may not be high, but the insurance companies pass the higher costs on to other customers in the form of increased rates.

Medical professionals also point out that high doses of radiation are involved in any scan. A full-body scan, which affects much more tissue than a typi- 25
cal CAT scan, exposes a body to considerably higher amounts of radiation than a
standard X-ray does. Thus, a man who undergoes an annual scan may actually
increase his risk of developing a tumor. Even though the full-body scan procedure may not cause problems for patients, health experts urge all people to limit
their voluntary exposure to radiation. 30

Patients should take responsibility for keeping an eye on their health, most
doctors agree. But according to many physicians, undergoing a full-body scan
merely gives people the impression that they are taking charge of their lives. A
better, and cheaper, alternative is to follow the recommendations of a doctor the
patient knows and trusts. 35

3. What is the implied main idea of this passage?

   a.   Full-body scans are foolproof diagnostic tests that everyone who can afford them
should have.

   b.   Full-body scans should be avoided because they emit excessive amounts of radiation.

   c.   Full-body scans are becoming more popular as diagnostic tools.

   d.   Patients should rely on a trusted doctor's advice regarding necessary medical tests
rather than self-prescribe full-body scans.

4. What sentence best states the main idea of paragraph 1?

   a.   But experts argue that full-body scans may do more harm than good.

   b.   Many medical tests are very effective at assisting doctors to discover ailments and
diseases early, when they can still be treated effectively.

   c.   Some of these tests are recommended for most adults at certain stages of life—tests
for certain cancers, for example.

   d.   One new type of test, the full-body scan, has been heavily promoted as a way for
patients to discover problems in any part of the body before symptoms arise.

5. What is the main idea of paragraph 4?

   a.   Medical professionals also point out that high doses of radiation are involved in
any scan.

   b.   A full-body scan, which affects much more tissue than a typical CAT scan, exposes
a body to considerably higher amounts of radiation than a standard X-ray does.

   c.   Thus, a man who undergoes an annual scan may actually increase his risk of
developing a tumor.

   d.   Even though the full-body scan procedure may not cause problems for patients,
health experts urge all people to limit their voluntary exposure to radiation.

What kind of driver are you? If you're like most Americans, you think you're a pretty good driver—better than average. Unfortunately, it's statistically impossible for a majority of people to be better than average at anything, so some "better-than-average" drivers are kidding themselves. Maybe you're one of the following types of better-than-average drivers; if so, you might want to try to change your ways behind the wheel. 5

If you're a better-than-average-but-angry driver, you tailgate to let other drivers know that they're moving too slowly. You honk your horn a fraction of a second after the light turns green to let other drivers know that it's time to move. You swerve ostentatiously around slower traffic, making dangerous lane changes, because the other cars are in your way. 10

If you're a better-than-average-but-distracted driver, you're changing the CD, cheering the home run, and talking on the cell phone while you're supposed to be watching the road. You're thinking about what to cook for dinner or deciding just to pick up some pizza instead of focusing on the traffic. When the angry driver tailgates you as you speed up and slow down, apparently at random, you don't notice. You almost hit him because you're drifting into the next lane as he passes, but you don't notice that, either. 15

If you're a better-than-average-but-tired driver, you're the one dozing off at the traffic light. You have slow reaction times when the distracted driver in front slams on the brakes in response to something a deejay has said. You may have a terrific excuse—you were up late changing the newborn's diapers, or you had to get up early to study for the midterm—but you are dangerous to yourself and others on the road. 20

Which one are you? At different times, you've probably been all of the above—and so has every other driver. Everyone gets angry; after all, most of those other drivers are so much worse than average! Everyone gets distracted. Everyone gets tired. The trick is to notice these states. If another driver makes you angry, take a deep breath and let it go. If you are often distracted, force yourself to concentrate on the task at hand: driving. If you're tired, get more rest, and in the meantime, take public transportation where you can safely close your eyes. Maybe the thing genuinely better-than-average drivers know is that nobody can always be better than average—and they try to drive safely even when they aren't at their best. 25 30

6. Which sentence best describes the implied main idea of the passage?

   a.   Studies have shown that most Americans think they're better-than-average drivers.

   b.   Some better-than-average drivers tailgate to let other drivers know that they're moving too slowly.

   c.   Many drivers incorrectly believe that they are better-than-average drivers.

   d.   It is statistically impossible for a majority of people to be better than average at anything.

7. The implied main idea of paragraph 3 is that

    a. a driver who is not paying attention will unknowingly be a serious hazard on the road.

    b. drivers should not listen to music while driving because it can cause them to become distracted and that can lead to a bad accident.

    c. drivers should decide on dinner plans or food arrangements before driving.

    d. all drivers tend to be distracted at some time in their driving experiences.

The ice cream social, once an American summer ritual, has now gone the way of the black-and-white television screen. A few people still make ice cream at home, it's true, but most modern Americans who buy ice cream freezers choose a kind with an electric motor. What could they be thinking? Making ice cream ought to be a social event, and to ensure that it is one, people should invest in old- 5 fashioned hand-cranked ice cream freezers to do the job right.

    Making ice cream by hand requires planning and sweat. Ice cream makers must procure good cream and cook it gently with sugar and vanilla beans (and, if they must, other flavorings like ripe peaches or even chocolate). Then they have to lay their hands on rock salt and plenty of ice. When the cream has been 10 chilled, it's time to gather strong-armed and strong-willed volunteers for the cranking, and then additional cranking, followed by more cranking. (This part of the process is best done out of doors because the melting ice trickles salty water down the sides of the machine.) After an eternity, when even the strongest muscles have been defeated by the task of turning the handle, the ice cream is fin- 15 ished—and, fittingly, the hard work comes with a just reward: the best-tasting dessert on the planet.

    In contrast, an ice cream freezer with a motor is child's play. One person alone can pour the ice cream mixture into the freezer. Then this lonely gourmet probably watches television in air-conditioned comfort while the infernal ma- 20 chine whirs away unattended on the kitchen counter. Where is the fun in that? "It tastes the same," some deluded food critics have been known to declare, but they are wrong. Everyone knows that a prize that is earned is always more appealing than a prize that comes after little or no effort.

    So let Americans everywhere pull the plugs on their sad electric ice cream 25 freezers. Instead, they should be encouraged to get the real thing and gather friends to celebrate one of the best warm-weather rituals there is. If they don't have enough friends to crank an ice cream freezer, they've probably been spending too much time alone—but anyone who invests in a hand-cranked ice cream freezer will assuredly attract a few more friends. 30

8. What is the implied main idea of this passage?

    a.   Opportunities for socialization and a better product are reasons why ice cream should be made by hand.

    b.   It is significantly easier to produce ice cream with a modern motorized ice cream freezer.

    c.   More people are making ice cream at home than ever before because of modern technology.

    d.   Ice cream made by hand has a superior taste compared with ice cream produced mechanically.

9. What is the implied main idea of paragraph 2?

    a.   The process of making ice cream by hand can be messy and the proper precautions should be taken to avoid damage.

    b.   Only people with strong muscles should attempt to use a hand-cranked ice cream freezer.

    c.   It is a known fact that ice cream is the most popular summer dessert in the United States.

    d.   Although making ice cream by hand is difficult, it is well worth the effort.

> Limiting competition among rivals limits the choices available to consumers. If only one fish-shaped cheese cracker is allowed on the market, the price may be higher than it would be if the cracker had a close competitor, and consumers are denied the decision of which cracker is more appealing to them. If one yoga master controls the use of a technique, consumers may have to pay dearly for classes 5 under instructors who have paid for a license from the original master; in addition, yoga teachers might be prevented from introducing changes to the technique that would appeal to some customers.

10. What is the stated main idea of this passage?

    a.   If only one fish-shaped cheese cracker is allowed on the market, the price may be higher than it would be if the cracker had a close competitor.

    b.   Yoga teachers might be prevented from introducing changes to the technique that would appeal to some customers.

    c.   Limiting competition among rivals limits consumers' choices.

    d.   Cheese crackers would be more successful if marketed by a variety of companies.

What Are Supporting Details?

Supporting details are specific examples, reasons, and facts that show, explain, or prove the author's main point. Supporting details make up the largest part—the body—of a paragraph or an essay. Without appropriate and convincing supporting details, the thesis statement or topic sentence can make a claim, but it will not convince many readers.

Supporting details may include both major supporting evidence—examples and reasons that directly support a topic sentence or topic sentences that support a thesis statement—and minor supporting evidence, the details that expand on and clarify the major support.

On the reading portion of the test, you will need to understand this kind of support so that you can answer questions about meaning.

EXAMPLE   *Topic sentence*

Major support followed by supporting details

There are four main modes of transporting food to one's mouth. The oldest and most widespread is the use of the hands. All peoples use the hands to some extent, but Indian, Arab, and most African traditions employ this primary mode of eating. Second, some people modify hand eating by adding an edible sheet, pieces of which are torn off and used to envelop loose food. Examples are in Ethiopia, where a supple bread called *injera* is used, and Mexico, where corn tortillas serve the same purpose. Third, some peoples use chopsticks, slender rods serving as extensions of the fingers to grasp chunks of food; their traditional use is in East Asia. Finally, the knife-fork-spoon toolkit of Europe can be used to cut, spear, and scoop food. The spoon has been used by most societies, although sometimes only as a serving implement. (Lanny B. Fields, Russell J. Barber, and Cheryl A. Riggs, *The Global Past*)

How Do You Identify Supporting Details?

Supporting details are more specific than the general idea they develop. Supporting details, both major and minor, include whatever evidence the writer introduces to back up the main point. Major supporting details usually introduce an example, an idea, or a reason that relates directly to the topic sentence of a paragraph or the thesis statement of an essay. Minor supporting details explain and clarify the major supporting details.

To find supporting details, ask yourself the following questions:

- What statements relate to the main point?

- What statements contain details—specific examples, facts, reasons, or statistics to convince the reader that the main point is true? (Note that transitions such as "for example," "for instance," and "the reason that" may introduce support.)

In the reading portion of the test, questions about support might not use the word *support*; often, they begin with "According to the passage." However, you will need to understand a passage's support to answer such questions.

Topic
sentence

Major
support
followed
by sup-
porting
details

EXAMPLE

A **conditioned reinforcer,** also called a *secondary reinforcer*, is one that has ac-
quired reinforcing value by being associated with a primary reinforcer. The clas-
sic example of a conditioned reinforcer is money. Money is reinforcing not
because those flimsy bits of paper and little pieces of metal have value in and of
themselves, but because we've learned that we can use them to acquire primary   5
reinforcers and other conditioned reinforcers. Awards, frequent flyer points, and
college degrees are just a few other examples of conditioned reinforcers. (Don H.
Hockenbury and Sandra E. Hockenbury, *Psychology*)

A test question about this passage might be:

1. According to the passage,

   a. awards, frequent flyer points, and college degrees are primary reinforcers.

   b. money is a conditioned, or secondary, reinforcer because it does not have value in
itself but is associated with things that do.

   c. a conditioned reinforcer can eventually become a secondary reinforcer.

   d. money is a primary reinforcer, unlike awards, frequent flyer points, and college
degrees.

To answer this question, look back at the support in the passage and check the answer
options against that support. Option A is not supported—the passage tells you that awards,
frequent flyer points, and college degrees are conditioned reinforcers. C is incorrect because the
passage says nothing about conditioned reinforcers eventually becoming secondary reinforcers.
D is also incorrect because the passage indicates that money, awards, frequent flyer points, and
college degrees are conditioned reinforcers. B is the correct answer because it is clearly supported by the details in the passage.

Practice Identifying Supporting Details

Read the following passages and answer the questions about supporting details. Answers and
explanations appear on p. 244.

Coal fires require little oxygen to smolder, and those that ignite veins of ore in
underground mines are notoriously difficult to put out. Underground coal fires
may burn for years and do extensive damage. The fires are surprisingly common
in coal-mining parts of the United States; thirty-six are currently burning in
Pennsylvania. The worst of these fires is under the town—or former town—of   5
Centralia.

    Centralia had about eleven hundred residents in 1962, many of whom
worked in the coal mines nearby. When the town burned its garbage at the local
dump that May, the fire surprised everyone by burning for a month. Then, workers

(continued)

clearing away the debris discovered that the trash fire had ignited a coal vein 10
near the surface. An underground coal fire was under way.

According to Centralia's current mayor, Lamar Mervine, no one did anything about the fire for several months. Later, locals used material on hand—fly
ash from burned coal—to try to smother the fire. It didn't work. Coal fires are
hard to smother because mines usually have many airways and tunnels, and coal 15
needs only about a tenth as much oxygen as is found in air in order to keep burning. Coal fires in mines also tend to burn hottest in the ceilings of the tunnels,
meaning that the entire tunnel needs to be filled to the brim to smother the fire.

The arrangement of Centralia's coal veins, which veer down from the surface at angles as steep as sixty degrees, also worked against the firefighters. Dig- 20
ging a hole deep enough to get underneath the fire was simply not possible after
it had been burning for some time. Locals eventually dug a trench to try to contain the fire, but it had spread faster and farther than anyone realized and had already moved beyond the trench.

The blaze continued unhindered for twenty-one years. Then, in 1983, part 25
of Route 61—a major roadway south of Centralia—collapsed from the effects
of the fire under it. The cracked and smoldering section of road was permanently
closed. On investigation, the U.S. Office of Surface Mining determined that
putting out the fire would cost 663 million dollars. The government chose the
cheaper alternative: it paid the people of Centralia to leave the area. Only about 30
twenty citizens remain in town today.

The biggest thing in Centralia now is the coal fire. It covers about 1.8
square kilometers, above which the ground is hot to the touch. Some geologists
estimate that the coal near the fire takes up another twelve square kilometers.
With that much fuel, the fire is expected to burn for another 100 to 250 years. 35

1. According to the passage,

   a. Lamar Mervine was the mayor of Centralia when this passage was written.

   b. Lamar Mervine was the mayor of Centralia from 1962 until the present.

   c. Lamar Mervine was not the mayor of Centralia when the coal fire began in 1962.

   d. Lamar Mervine has been the most concerned mayor in Centralia's history.

2. According to the passage,

   a. the Centralia coal fire lasted for twenty-one years.

   b. the Centralia coal fire will last until at least 2083.

   c. coal fires last indefinitely.

   d. the Centralia coal fire was initially neglected for several years.

3. The coal veins in Centralia

   a.   are found in natural trenches.

   b.   are filled with fly ash from burned coal.

   c.   are often at sixty-degree angles from the surface.

   d.   measure 1.8 square kilometers.

4. According to the passage, the town of Centralia

   a.   originally had a population of more than one thousand residents.

   b.   was totally closed down in 1983.

   c.   was the site of one of two dozen coal fires that burned in Pennsylvania.

   d.   has recovered from the coal fires and is a thriving town today.

On August 27, 2003, the planet Mars had a close encounter with the planet Earth. The two passed within a mere fifty-six million kilometers of each other in a phenomenon known as a perihelic opposition. This event brought the planets closer than they had been since Neanderthal times, but other perihelic oppositions—including the most recent—have been almost as impressive. 5

Planets have elliptical, or oval, orbits as they travel around the sun. This means that they are much closer to the sun at some periods in the orbit than they are in others. The point when a planet is closest is known as the perihelion, and in August of 2003 both Mars and Earth were perihelic. The two planets were also in opposition then. In astronomical terms, opposition occurs when two planets line 10 up with the star they orbit; in perihelic opposition, Earth lies between Mars and the sun. During the event, Mars appeared as a very bright reddish glow in the sky, clearly visible to the naked eye. Anyone with even a small telescope could view Mars in great detail during its close-up. Many amateur astronomers caught glimpses of the red planet's polar ice caps and other surface markings. 15

Perihelic oppositions with Mars occur only rarely; few people see more than one in a lifetime. The most recent happened on August 23, 1924. In each such event, the planets pass within varying distances of each other, depending on how much their orbits are distorted by the gravitational pull of other planets. Although the 2003 perihelic opposition brought the planets closer than they had 20 been seventy-nine years earlier—probably closer, in fact, than they had been for sixty thousand years—astronomers point out that the approximate distance between Earth and Mars in every perihelic opposition is roughly the same. From a distance of fifty-six million kilometers, viewers on Earth don't see any significant differences when Mars is a few kilometers closer or farther away. 25

Those who missed the perihelic opposition of 2003 will have to wait some time for the next one, which is due in about 280 years. Fortunately for anyone who would still like a glimpse of Mars passing by only fifty-six million kilometers away, astronomers on Earth took plenty of photographs.

5. According to the passage, the orbits of planets traveling around the sun are

    a.   circular.

    b.   diagonal.

    c.   rare.

    d.   elliptical.

6. The next perihelic opposition will occur

    a.   in 2283.

    b.   in sixty thousand years.

    c.   never again.

    d.   when Mars orbits the sun.

7. During past perihelic oppositions between Mars and Earth, the astronomers' view of Mars has

    a.   remained basically the same.

    b.   differed depending on the distance between the planets.

    c.   improved vastly when the planets were closer to each other.

    d.   often been obscured by other planets.

The Coriolis force, named for the nineteenth-century French mathematician Gaspard de Coriolis, refers to the way Earth's rotation influences moving objects. Coriolis first described the force to explain why prevailing winds on Earth move in curved rather than straight lines. The Coriolis force also explains why hurricanes above the equator rotate counterclockwise and those below the equator move clockwise. Because it works only on a large scale, however, the Coriolis force has almost no effect on one phenomenon with which it is often incorrectly linked: the direction water circles before flowing down a drain. [5]

Here's the myth: in the Northern Hemisphere, water always circles counterclockwise before draining out of the bathtub, sink, or toilet and water in the Southern Hemisphere moves clockwise. The same myth claims that water does not circle at all when the toilet, tub, or sink is directly over the equator. (To make matters even more confusing, some of these false claims even get the direction of the Coriolis force wrong, stating that the tub or toilet in the Northern Hemisphere is the clockwise one.) The physical facts are not nearly as intriguing or as simple as this false "fun fact," which makes it difficult for scientists to convince the public that the toilet-water story has been definitively known to be false for several decades. [10] [15]

In any case, here's the truth: the size of the Coriolis force is so negligible in a sink, toilet, or bathtub that other forces have much more power to influence the direction of water going down the drain. The direction of water flowing out of a relatively small container is affected most by the direction the water was travel- [20]

ing as it entered. If water flows in clockwise, it is likely to retain the clockwise motion as it swirls out, and vice versa. The direction can also be influenced by the movement of pulling out the plug and by the shape of the container. 25

Since the general public has no monopoly on wondering why water swirls out of toilets in a certain direction, scientists have, not surprisingly, studied the Coriolis force in small containers. However, in a 1962 experiment at the Massachusetts Institute of Technology, researcher Ascher Shapiro filled a six-foot circular tank six inches deep with the water entering clockwise. He covered the tank 30 to prevent disturbances from outside, kept the temperature constant, and waited. When he pulled the plug after two hours, the water drained out clockwise, presumably because it retained some of the motion from the clockwise filling. However, after twenty-four hours the water swirled completely counterclockwise as Shapiro drained it, in keeping with the direction of the Coriolis force in the 35 Northern Hemisphere.

Shapiro's experiment more than forty years ago and people's general observations of the drains they encounter daily have not yet laid to rest the myth that water always drains counterclockwise in the Northern Hemisphere and clockwise in the Southern Hemisphere. The Coriolis force is real, but it shows up most 40 readily in hurricanes, not in toilets.

8. When a container is small, the direction of the water flowing out if it is most directly affected by
   a. the Coriolis force.
   b. the direction the water was traveling as it exited.
   c. the direction the water was traveling as it entered.
   d. many factors including the pressure of the water.

9. According to the passage, the French mathematician, Gaspard de Coriolis, was famous in the
   a. 1900s.
   b. 1800s.
   c. 2000s.
   d. 1700s.

10. Ascher Shapiro's experiment at MIT involved
    a. a hurricane.
    b. a tank that was six inches high.
    c. a rectangular tank that was six feet high.
    d. a tank that was six feet high and six inches deep.

2.1C IDENTIFYING THE AUTHOR'S PURPOSE

What Does Purpose Mean?

The **purpose** of a piece of writing is the reason the author had for writing it, that is, what he or she wants to accomplish by writing it. The three basic reasons for writing are to inform, to persuade, and to entertain, although sometimes these categories are broken down further: writers may intend, for example, to evaluate, to praise, to criticize, to inspire, to analyze, to clarify, to illustrate, to define, or to serve some other purpose.

EXAMPLES

Writing to Inform

In any case, the camera crew has just five or ten seconds in the life cycle of a TV Whopper to capture good, sizzling, brown beef on film. After that the hamburger starts to shrink rapidly as the water and grease are cooked from it. Filming lasts anywhere from three to eight hours, depending upon the occurrence of a variety of technical problems—heavy smoke, grease accumulating on the camera equip- 5 ment, the gas specialist's failure to achieve a perfect, preternaturally orange glowing flame. Out of one day's work, and anywhere between fifty and seventy-five hamburgers, the agency hopes to get five seconds of usable footage. Most of the time the patties are either too raw, bloody, greasy, or small. (Joey Green, "Beauty and the Beef") 10

Writing to Persuade

The vigor of our nation's creativity must be protected. No government can spare its citizens the job of being good parents. If you don't want your kids watching, turn the darn thing off. Just as, if you don't want them reading the Iliad because it's violent or the Decameron because it's gloriously, openly erotic, you would put the books on a high shelf they can't reach. These days the public, goaded on by 5 politicians, seems like it's warming up for a book burning, and the idea of holding a book burning in the halls of Congress is truly violent and obscene. And it's the most un-American thing anybody has thought of in a long time. (John Romano, "It's a Job for Parents, Not the Government")

Writing to Entertain

You are now ready to begin carving. Sharpen the knife on the stone and insert it where the thigh joins the torso. If you do this correctly, which is improbable, the knife will almost immediately encounter a barrier of bone and gristle. This may very well be the joint. It could, however, be your thumb. If not, execute a vigorous sawing motion until satisfied that the knife has been defeated. Withdraw the 5 knife and ask someone nearby, in as testy a manner as possible, why the knives at your house are not kept in better carving condition. (Russell Baker, "Slice of Life")

How Do You Identify the Author's Purpose?

An author may write to inform or explain, to persuade readers to think a certain way or to follow a particular course of action, or to amuse or entertain readers. To identify what the author wants to accomplish with the piece of writing, ask the following questions.

- Does the writing aim mainly to present information, to analyze how something works, to illustrate a point, to clarify a concept, or to define a term or an idea?

- Does the author maintain a neutral tone instead of taking a clear position in favor of or against something?

If you answered *yes* to both of these questions, the author's purpose is primarily to inform or explain. Within these categories, the writer may *analyze* (look at how something works or is put together or how something happened), *illustrate* (offer examples), *clarify* (make a difficult idea understandable), or *define* (explain the meaning of a concept).

- Does the writing argue for or against a position, argue that a certain action should be taken, or otherwise aim mainly to express the author's views of the topic? Is the main idea of a paragraph or passage an opinion?

If so, the author's purpose is primarily to persuade. Persuasive writing may aim to *evaluate* (come to a conclusion about the relative worth of two or more similar things), *criticize* (express a negative viewpoint about a topic), *praise* (express a positive viewpoint), or *inspire* (to influence, usually to a higher order of action, thought, or feeling).

- Does the writing seem intended mainly to amuse readers?

If so, the author's purpose is primarily to entertain.

Certain terms and characteristics are associated with writing that informs, persuades, or entertains, as the following lists show. Keeping an eye out for these terms and characteristics can help you determine the purpose.

Inform	Persuade	Entertain
Describe	Praise	Amuse
Define	Criticize	Dramatize
Illustrate	Inspire	Tell a joke

EXAMPLES

Informative and Explanatory Writing

I went to South Africa for three weeks in May 2000 to write about the AIDS epidemic there. AIDS is caused by the HIV virus, which is passed from person to person through sexual fluids, blood, or blood products, or from mother to unborn child in the womb or through breast-feeding. The virus destroys the immune system, which protects the body from infectious diseases. A person may live for ten years or longer with HIV and have no symptoms, but eventually his immune system begins to disintegrate and other viruses, bacteria, and fungi,

(continued)

which a healthy immune system would normally fight off, take hold. AIDS is the name given to the syndrome in which the patient slowly rots alive from these opportunistic infections.

Persuasive Writing

GlobalCall provides the lowest rates of virtually any calling card—just 5 cents a minute within the United States. It also offers some of the lowest international rates you can find—as low as 10 cents a minute. In fact, compared to other calling cards, you could save up to $500 a year on phone charges using GlobalCall. And GlobalCall delivers crystal clear connections to anywhere you call.

Entertaining Writing

Our hotel was located in the charmingly named town of Horseheads, a good 30 miles beyond Ithaca. Apparently, what with graduation, all the local hotels named after equine anatomy were booked solid.

However, "Where do you think you are, the Horseheads Holiday Inn?" is a phrase I derisively asked myself many times the next day, when a hair dryer, comforter, or hot bath would have been welcome indeed. I'd forgotten to bring a jacket, and upstate New York rewarded my lack of respect with late-May weather as cold as any day in Boston last winter. It snowed. James Earl Jones was the commencement speaker, and in one part of his speech, he bellowed, "The reason that we are all here today is . . . (trying futilely to turn the page with his frozen hands) . . . my hands are very cold." I don't remember any other nuggets of wisdom, but I think that other colleges considering his services should stipulate in his contract that he has to say "Simba," "Luke, I am your father," and "Welcome to 411" at least once.

Practice Identifying the Author's Purpose

Read the following essays, then answer the questions about the author's purpose. Answers and explanations appear on pp. 245–46.

The question of who owns intellectual property such as literature, symbols, images, and ideas frequently ends up being answered in court. Does Pepperidge Farm own the idea of fish-shaped, cheese-flavored crackers? Does the yoga master who invented a method of teaching yoga in a very hot room own the technique? These and other questions have been the subject of recent legal discussion. As a result of intellectual property disputes, certain ideas and symbols become unavailable for public use—a trend that ultimately punishes all Americans.

The cases of the cracker company and the yoga teacher share a theme: the originator—or at least popularizer—of an idea, image, or symbol wants to limit or prevent others' use of it. Pepperidge Farm wants to restrict competitors from selling a similar product, and the yoga master wants to prevent rivals from benefiting from his idea. The benefits to Pepperidge Farm and the yoga teacher are clear if courts rule in their favor, but it is equally clear that consumers will gain nothing from allowing corporations and individuals to copyright such intellectual property.

Limiting competition among rivals limits the choices available to consumers. If only one fish-shaped cheese cracker is allowed on the market, the price may be higher than it would be if the cracker had a close competitor, and consumers are denied the decision of which cracker is more appealing. If one yoga master controls the use of a technique, consumers may have to pay more for classes under instructors who have paid for a license from the original master; in addition, yoga teachers might be prevented from introducing changes to the technique that would appeal to some customers.

This last effect is, in fact, the worst problem with granting ownership of ideas and images to one company or individual: if one party owns them, others are prevented from building on them or using them in innovative ways. The result may be a limit on creativity. The point of competition, after all, is to ensure that the best ideas win. If only one corporation or person is allowed to compete in a given area, there is no way for the best idea to succeed and no incentive to improve an idea.

For the good of American consumers, artists, entrepreneurs, and others, ideas should remain free. If ideas and symbols are owned by anyone with enough money and legal clout to copyright them and order others not to use them, everyone suffers.

1. The author's primary purpose in the preceding passage is to
   a. entertain the reader with anecdotes of intellectual property.
   b. inform readers of the importance of intellectual property.
   c. list different types of intellectual property.
   (d.) persuade readers that intellectual property should be public property. ✓

Gardeners refer to any plant that they dislike, or that is simply in the wrong place, as a weed. But in biological terms, *weed* has a specific meaning. Weeds are plants—and animals, or even microbes—that reproduce quickly, take advantage of new surroundings, and thrive in a variety of habitats. Once they have been transplanted to new locations, they are very hard to get rid of. Weedy species often compete with less hardy varieties of living things for limited resources; the result is that weeds severely pressure or kill more fragile plants and animals in the region. In biological terms, fast-growing vines like kudzu are weeds; so are rats, cockroaches, crows, certain viruses—and humans. *(continued)*

Many plants and animals cause no problems in their original habitats; they become weeds only when they disperse to new areas, where other species lack defenses against them and allow them to take over. In modern times, human mobility has allowed many organisms to turn into weeds now that global travel and commerce ensure that plants, animals, and viruses move around the world along with humans. Sometimes people disperse a species intentionally, as when gardeners import nonnative plants. Sometimes humans simply act as unwitting transportation.

However weed organisms arrive in their new homes, they all adapt quickly and aggressively to new surroundings. Most weed plants grow quickly, spread seeds easily, and return year after year; dandelions are just one example of an aggressive, fast-spreading weed that was once cultivated as an ornamental flower. Weed animals often either eat other local creatures—coyotes are one such species spreading rapidly across the United States—or consume much of the food available, thereby starving out less hardy species. Weed microbes adapt easily to new hosts, perhaps crossing species or leaping from birds or small mammals to humans.

In many cases, weed organisms actually change the ecosystem as they drive out former competitors and increase their own numbers. The mark of a truly successful weed species is its ability to continue to adapt as its environment changes. By this definition, no other weed can compare to humans, the most innovative users of the environment—and the ones most likely to change their habitats and kill much of the varied but fragile life found there.

Established weeds are notoriously difficult, but not always impossible, to eradicate. Like dandelions and coyotes, humans are survivors whose population continues to grow, and people seem to be in no danger of losing their ability to exert at least some control over most habitats and living things. But human beings should remember one important fact about weeds: no one knows when the next aggressive and highly adaptive species will take advantage of a lucky chance.

2. The author's primary purpose in the above passage is to
   a. define and provide examples of weeds.
   b. convince the reader that weeds are dangerous.
   c. argue for the elimination of all weeds.
   d. inform the reader of the importance of weeds.

Many Americans spend their healthiest and most vigorous years working very hard toward a time in the future when they will be able to relax and enjoy life. All too often, however, people in this situation discover that the imagined leisure time never arrives. Trying to get a higher-paying job, many workers feel that they must put in longer hours; once the good job arrives, people feel trapped into trying to pay for ever-larger houses and cars or increasingly elaborate vacations. Instead of looking for ways to make more money, many people would be happier if they tried to make more time for things that really satisfy them.

The first step in avoiding the cycle of earning more and spending more is for families and individuals to think about what would really bring them happiness. Is the ultimate goal of life to devote more time to a hobby? to spend more time with family or friends? to have children? to travel? Some may think at first that the goal is simply to make as much money as possible—but these people should ask themselves what the money is for.

After identifying goals, each person needs to figure out how to reach them. Most overworked Americans find that more free time is the luxury item they most covet. These people should try to find a way to cut down on hours at work. In most cases, deciding to work less means accepting less money; wages drop when someone works fewer hours, and chances for advancement dwindle for an employee who does not seem to make the job a high priority.

Working less and earning less need not mean a lower quality of life, however. The next step for the person determined to keep off the earning-and-spending treadmill is to figure out how to be satisfied with less money. Simplification is often the key. How big does a house have to be? Which expenses are essential and which are not? Can simpler items substitute for more luxurious ones—a smaller car instead of an SUV, for example? Simplifying life can also mean learning to enjoy less expensive pleasures, such as taking a walk or visiting a park instead of relying on technology for entertainment. Using creativity—and spending time interacting with people instead of a computer—might be a novel and immensely satisfying experience for many Americans.

Those who stop trying to earn as much as possible often become much more pleased with their lives. Many people find working long hours unsatisfying. Perhaps they shouldn't try so hard to be on top. Instead, they might want to stop, think, accept less money, and see if they will be content with more time.

3. The author's primary purpose in the preceding passage is to
   a.   list the ways Americans spend money.
   b.   inspire Americans to evaluate and change their values regarding money.
   c.   convince the reader to seek jobs with the highest income.
   d.   describe the spending habits of Americans.

When is communication not really communication? This may sound like a joke, but the answer—"when it tries to conceal rather than to convey information"—isn't very funny. Communication that is really a cover-up aims to confuse or even intimidate an audience. If you can recognize communication cover-ups, you will be less likely to be taken in by incomprehensible or misleading language.   5

One type of misleading communication is bad academic writing. In fact, academic jargon probably sets the gold standard for the most incomprehensible writing anywhere. If you ask a roomful of English teachers to explain the meaning of a sentence in another English professor's article and no one can define either the point of the sentence or the meaning of words in it without a dictionary,   10 then the sentence in question isn't brilliantly analyzing literature—it's just plain bad. The purpose of this kind of cover-up is simple: to disguise mundane ideas as innovative and to prevent readers from recognizing what is really being said.

Another type of confusing communication is business language, which slips into mindless jargon far too often and at other times is used to cover up bad   15 business practices and greed. Whether or not you've ever worked for a corporation, you have probably encountered clichés like "on the same page" and "vision statement." This kind of bloated, self-important jargon serves no purpose other than making insiders feel like insiders (and outsiders feel like outsiders). Even worse are new creations such as "rightsizing" (another word for "downsizing"),   20 which gloss over the fact that employees are losing their jobs while implying that the jobs were unnecessary in the first place. When businesses use language to hide things, let the listener beware.

The final, and most important, type of misleading communication is political and military jargon. Political leaders manipulate buzzwords designed to   25 make the policies of their political party look good and those of the other party look foolish or evil. When you develop the critical ear to recognize these attempts to use emotional language to confuse and mislead, you take the first step toward being able to resist and think for yourself. More disgusting is the deliberate use of bland or meaningless phrases to describe horrors, as when officials   30 report "collateral damage" to disguise the deaths of innocent civilians. Whether the language is hiding terrible things with boring phrases or whipping up emotions to confuse listeners, the best defense is recognizing the cover-up for what it is.

English is a complex language that offers speakers and writers many ways   35 to say something. Some people choose to communicate clearly, and some deliberately choose not to. If you become aware of the common types of misleading communication, you will be less likely to fall for mindless and confusing constructions—and less likely to mangle the language by using them yourself.

4. The author's primary purpose in the preceding passage is to

a. illustrate good communication techniques.

b. discuss methods to improve communication techniques.

c. teach the reader how to overcome weaknesses in communication skills.

d. criticize poor, misleading, and destructive communication tactics.

Before his first major nervous breakdown in 1888, Vincent van Gogh, the great Dutch painter, was living in southern France. During the summer, he painted bright landscapes that many experts see as reflecting the artist's optimistic mood. In September, however, depression struck. Van Gogh's misery is clear in the first painting he completed after the onset of his illness. 5

The Night Café depicts a harshly lit room and the unhappy-looking people who gather there. The viewer's eye first falls on the central object, a large green billiard table casting a shadow over the pale yellow floor. To the right of the table stands a man in pale clothing. His hair, reflecting the ceiling, appears green. He is the only one of the several people present who is definitely awake. Farther 10 to the right, the blood-red wall of the café slants sharply toward the foreground. The table at the far right of the painting is occupied by two seated men. One has his back to the viewer and his head covered with a large yellow hat while his companion, facing front, props his head drunkenly on one hand. Behind the second man is a long table on which an empty bottle and glass sit abandoned by an 15 earlier solitary drinker.

Moving counterclockwise, toward the red rear wall of the café, the eye comes to the top of the painting, where a bile-green ceiling clashes sharply with the dominant yellows and reds of the room. Hanging lamps that resemble squinting eyes radiate yellowish light, painted in the thick, wavy lines typical of van 20 Gogh's brushwork. Farther left, a half-open curtain reveals the café's back room, also lit with a yellow glare. The other patrons appear along the left side of the painting: a man and woman hunch dejectedly side by side in the rear left corner of the room, while the table in front of theirs is occupied by a solitary man who is either asleep or dejected, with his head resting on his folded arms. Two more 25 tables on the lower left are littered with debris from departed guests. At the bottom of the painting is an empty expanse of pale yellow floorboards leading back to the billiard table and the red, red walls.

A less welcoming café than the one van Gogh portrays in this painting is difficult to imagine. The garish colors and harsh light make everyone look sick and 30 sad. Who other than the drunks and depressives depicted would sit in this awful room? In a letter, van Gogh described the café as "a place where one can ruin one's self, run mad or commit a crime." After the pleasant, sunny landscapes he painted in the summer of 1888, *The Night Café* clearly indicates the gloomy outlook that had begun to affect van Gogh's mind and art. 35

5. The author's primary purpose in the passage is to

a. analyze van Gogh's painting *The Night Café* and relate it to his emotional state.

b. instruct the reader in art appreciation and its importance.

c. contrast van Gogh's painting *The Night Café* with his other work.

d. discuss van Gogh's success as an artist.

The Coriolis force, named for the nineteenth-century French mathematician Gaspard de Coriolis, refers to the way Earth's rotation influences moving objects. Coriolis first described the force to explain why prevailing winds on Earth move in curved rather than straight lines. The Coriolis force also explains why hurricanes above the equator rotate counterclockwise and those below the equator 5 move clockwise. Because it works only on a large scale, however, the Coriolis force has almost no effect on one phenomenon with which it is often incorrectly linked: the direction water circles before flowing down a drain.

Here's the myth: in the Northern Hemisphere, water always circles counterclockwise before draining out of the bathtub, sink, or toilet and water in the 10 Southern Hemisphere moves clockwise. The same myth claims that water does not circle at all when the toilet, tub, or sink is directly over the equator. (To make matters even more confusing, some of these false claims even get the direction of the Coriolis force wrong, stating that the tub or toilet in the Northern Hemisphere is the clockwise one.) The physical facts are not nearly as intriguing or as 15 simple as this false "fun fact," which makes it difficult for scientists to convince the public that the toilet-water story has been definitively known to be false for several decades.

In any case, here's the truth: the size of the Coriolis force is so negligible in a sink, toilet, or bathtub that other forces have much more power to influence the 20 direction of water going down the drain. The direction of water flowing out of a relatively small container is affected most by the direction the water was traveling as it entered. If water flows in clockwise, it is likely to retain the clockwise motion as it swirls out—and vice versa. The direction can also be influenced by the movement of pulling out the plug and by the shape of the container. 25

Since the general public has no monopoly on wondering why water swirls out of toilets in a certain direction, scientists have, not surprisingly, studied the Coriolis force in small containers. However, in a 1962 experiment at the Massachusetts Institute of Technology, researcher Ascher Shapiro filled a six-foot circular tank six inches deep with the water entering clockwise. He covered the tank 30 to prevent disturbances from outside, kept the temperature constant, and waited. When he pulled the plug after two hours, the water drained out clockwise, presumably because it retained some of the motion from the clockwise filling. However, after twenty-four hours the water swirled completely counterclockwise as

Shapiro drained it, in keeping with the direction of the Coriolis force in the 35
Northern Hemisphere.

Shapiro's experiment more than forty years ago and people's general observations of the drains they encounter daily have not yet laid to rest the myth that water always drains counterclockwise in the Northern Hemisphere and clockwise in the Southern Hemisphere. The Coriolis force is real, but it shows up most 40 readily in hurricanes, not in toilets.

6. The author's primary purpose in the passage is to

a. define the Coriolis force.

b. explain the misconceptions about the Coriolis force.

c. compare the Coriolis force to Ascher Shapiro's theory.

d. analyze the influence of the Coriolis force on scientific theory.

What kind of driver are you? If you're like most Americans, you think you're a pretty good driver—better than average. Unfortunately, it's statistically impossible for a majority of people to be better than average at anything, so some "better-than-average" drivers are kidding themselves. Maybe you're one of the following types of better-than-average drivers; if so, you might want to try to 5 change your ways behind the wheel.

If you're a better-than-average-but-angry driver, you tailgate to let other drivers know that they're moving too slowly. You honk your horn a fraction of a second after the light turns green to let other drivers know that it's time to move. You swerve ostentatiously around slower traffic, making dangerous lane 10 changes, because the other cars are in your way.

If you're a better-than-average-but-distracted driver, you're changing the CD, cheering the home run, and talking on the cell phone while you're supposed to be watching the road. You're thinking about what to cook for dinner or deciding just to pick up some pizza instead of focusing on the traffic. When the angry 15 driver tailgates you as you speed up and slow down, apparently at random, you don't notice. You almost hit him because you're drifting into the next lane as he passes, but you don't notice that, either.

If you're a better-than-average-but-tired driver, you're the one dozing off at the traffic light. You have slow reaction times when the distracted driver in front 20 slams on the brakes in response to something a deejay has said. You may have a terrific excuse—you were up late changing the newborn's diapers, or you had to get up early to study for the midterm—but you are dangerous to yourself and others on the road.

Which one are you? At different times, you've probably been all of the 25 above—and so has every other driver. Everyone gets angry; after all, most of

(continued)

those other drivers are so much worse than average! Everyone gets distracted. Everyone gets tired. The trick is to notice these states. If another driver makes you angry, take a deep breath and let it go. If you are often distracted, force yourself to concentrate on the task at hand: driving. If you're tired, get more rest, and in the meantime, take public transportation where you can safely close your eyes. Maybe the thing genuinely better-than-average drivers know is that nobody can always be better than average—and they try to drive safely even when they aren't at their best.

7. The author's primary purpose in the passage is to

    a.   entertain the reader with amusing anecdotes about drivers.

    b.   describe different styles of driving.

    c.   persuade drivers to drive more carefully.

    d.   illustrate dangers involved with driving.

My grandmother is one of the most gifted and well-rounded people I have ever met. I feel lucky to know her, and I don't expect to meet her match very often as I get older. She seems to know how to do everything—and she still finds time to spend with me.

Grandma Anna knows how to catch a fish. She also knows how to make a fishing pole, find bait, clean the fish, and cook it so that it tastes better than anything else I can imagine. Her fishing ability saved the whole family one hard autumn when her daddy was laid up with influenza. She says he taught her everything, and her skills with a line and pole kept her and her younger brothers fed.

She didn't have much formal education—she says nobody expected her to need it. But when the next town got a library, my grandmother walked there once a week and took home all the books she could carry. She read aloud to her brothers, and she tells me that she just happens to have a really good memory. To this day, she can quote whole Shakespeare plays and reams of poems by authors from the Middle Ages to the Harlem Renaissance. When I was little, she used to act out plays that she had learned by heart, reciting the lines and playing all the roles, while I helped her in her garden.

But the best thing of all about Grandma Anna is the pottery she makes in her woodshed. Nobody taught her how to do it—she just learned by trial and error. The pots she makes see a lot of hard use in the house and garden, but they aren't just utensils. They are works of art that are even more beautiful because they are functional. Someday, she says she'll teach me how she does it. She says I just might have the right hands to make a good clay pot. I hope she's right; I would be very pleased to have even a fraction of her talent.

Grandma Anna has been helping my mother take care of me since I was a baby. I feel lucky every day that I've gotten a chance to spend so much time with her and to learn a few of the many things she knows. I may not have Shakespeare memorized, but I plan to follow in Grandma Anna's footsteps as far as I am able.

8. The main purpose of the passage is

    a.   to praise the author's grandmother.

    b.   to describe Grandma Anna's hobbies.

    c.   to compare Grandma Anna with more typical grandmothers.

    d.   to contrast the hobbies of fishing, reading, and pottery.

Cave art fascinates historians, art historians, and the general public. So many people express interest in these early artworks that the most popular caves often restrict visitors in order to protect the sites from too many eager viewers. But hordes of tourists are not likely to descend on a recently discovered Australian cave that contains aboriginal drawings from about four thousand to about two hundred years ago. Specialists are particularly thrilled with the find—which only one expert had seen as of 2003—because the cave's inaccessibility may protect the beauty and historical value of the contents.

The works in the cave have been protected from sunlight by the cave's north-facing opening. Some drawings depict local animals, such as wallabies and wombats, and others depict half-human, half-animal forms that feature in aboriginal creation stories. Handprints, outlined by pigments blown through a hollow tube, also line the walls. In all, the cave contains some two hundred well-preserved figures.

The newest drawings found at the site date from the eighteenth century, when white settlers first began to arrive in Australia. The cave's location just sixty miles west of Sydney, Australia's largest city and one of its first ports, meant that it was closer to the new residents than many aboriginal people wanted to come. For two hundred years, the cave was apparently disturbed only by small animals. Hikers found it by accident in 1995.

The wilderness of the region makes access difficult, even for those who are eager to see the art firsthand. An anthropologist from the Australian Museum, Paul Tacon, was the only specialist to have traveled to the cave as of 2003. He and five aboriginal colleagues flew as close to the cave as they could by helicopter and then made an arduous trek through the desert landscape to their destination. The group left the site after spending a single night when water began to run out.

Tacon persuaded Australian government officials to restrict access to the cave and not to disclose its location. These measures please anthropologists and

(continued)

art experts, but the restrictions are probably just a precaution. Visiting a site that 30 the first expert could not reach for eight years is probably beyond the abilities of all but the hardiest tourists. Isolation has protected the cave's artworks for centuries, and everyone concerned about the preservation of the drawings believes that continued isolation is the best hope for their future.

9. The primary purpose of the passage is to

    a.   analyze cave art dating from aboriginal cave art to modern cave art.

    b.   discuss a recent cave art finding.

    c.   list the elements of cave art.

    d.   argue for the Australian government to increase accessibility to the newly discovered cave.

Coal fires require little oxygen to smolder, and those that ignite veins of ore in underground mines are notoriously difficult to put out. Underground coal fires may burn for years and do extensive damage. The fires are surprisingly common in coal-mining parts of the United States; thirty-six are currently burning in Pennsylvania. The worst of these fires is under the town—or former town—of 5 Centralia.

Centralia had about eleven hundred residents in 1962, many of whom worked in the coal mines nearby. When the town burned its garbage at the local dump that May, the fire surprised everyone by burning for a month. Then, workers clearing away the debris discovered that the trash fire had ignited a coal vein 10 near the surface. An underground coal fire was under way.

According to Centralia's current mayor, Lamar Mervine, no one did anything about the fire for several months. Later, locals used material on hand—fly ash from burned coal—to try to smother the fire. It didn't work. Coal fires are hard to smother because mines usually have many airways and tunnels, and coal 15 needs only about a tenth as much oxygen as is found in air in order to keep burning. Coal fires in mines also tend to burn hottest in the ceilings of the tunnels, meaning that the entire tunnel needs to be filled to the brim to smother the fire.

The arrangement of Centralia's coal veins, which veer down from the surface at angles as steep as sixty degrees, also worked against the firefighters. Digging a hole deep enough to get underneath the fire was simply not possible after it had been burning for some time. Locals eventually dug a trench to try to contain the fire, but it had spread faster and farther than anyone realized and had already moved beyond the trench.

The blaze continued unhindered for twenty-one years. Then, in 1983, part 25 of Route 61—a major roadway south of Centralia—collapsed from the effects of the fire under it. The cracked and smoldering section of road was permanently closed. On investigation, the U.S. Office of Surface Mining determined that putting out the fire would cost 663 million dollars. The government chose the cheaper alternative: it paid the people of Centralia to leave the area. Only about 30 twenty citizens remain in town today.

The biggest thing in Centralia now is the coal fire. It covers about 1.8 square kilometers, above which the ground is hot to the touch. Some geologists estimate that the coal near the fire takes up another twelve square kilometers. With that much fuel, the fire is expected to burn for another 100 to 250 years. 35

10. The primary purpose of the passage is to

a. illustrate the incredible damage that coal fires can cause.

b. argue that the government should take serious actions to prevent coal fires from damaging towns in the future.

c. list the problems that the town of Centralia suffered as a result of its coal fire.

d. persuade readers to avoid living in coal-mining towns for their own safety.

2.2A IDENTIFYING PATTERNS OF ORGANIZATION

What Are Patterns of Organization?

Writers organize paragraphs and essays following logical **patterns**. A written passage can use more than one pattern; for example, one paragraph may appear in time order while the overall pattern of the essay is comparison and contrast. The following tables identify the major patterns of organization.

PATTERNS FOR ORDERING IDEAS

Type of Order	Use	Ways to Order Ideas
Spatial	To describe a physical place, object, or person	Top to bottom/bottom to top, near to far/far to near, left to right/right to left, back to front/front to back
Time	To explain when events happened	First to last/last to first, most recent to least recent/least recent to most recent
Importance	To arrange ideas according to importance, interest, or surprise value	Most important to least important/least important to most important

PATTERNS FOR DEVELOPING IDEAS

Strategy	Use	Type/Pattern of Support
Illustration or example	To show, explain, or prove a point	Includes main point and detailed examples
Process analysis	To explain how to do something or how something works	Includes detailed steps in a process
Classification	To organize or sort items or people into categories	Includes categories and examples of items in each category
Listing	To list subjects to prove a point	Includes at least one list
Definition	To explain meaning of a term or concept	Includes basic definition and examples to clarify meaning
Comparison and contrast	To show similarities and/or differences between two or among more subjects	Includes several points of similarity or difference and compares/contrasts point by point or whole to whole
Cause and effect	To show what made an event happen (cause) or what happened or will happen as a result (effect)	Includes explanation of causes and/or effects of an event
Statement and clarification (inductive argument)	To give specific observations or details to draw a general conclusion	Moves from specific examples to a general conclusion or claim
Generalization and example (deductive argument)	To give a general principle and specific examples to draw a conclusion or make an argument	Moves from a generally accepted statement and one or more specific examples to a claim

How Do You Identify Patterns of Organization?

To determine how a passage is organized, ask the following questions:

- How are the ideas in the passage arranged?

  — *Spatial* order describes a physical arrangement.

  — *Time*, or *temporal*, order describes the sequence of events.

  — Order of *importance* either starts with the most important idea or leads from the least important to the most important.

- How is the passage developed?

  — An *illustration*, or illustrative passage, explains its main point using specific examples.

  — A *process analysis* goes through the steps of a process to show readers how to do it or to explain to them how it works.

  — A *classification* begins with subjects—people, things, concepts—and arranges them into groups according to guidelines that the passage sets out.

  — A *listing* begins with categories and then lists members of each category. Note that a listing differs from space order, time order, and order of importance, which describe features or steps according to space, time, and importance.

  — A *definition* defines a subject and provides examples to clarify the definition.

  — A *comparison* looks at similarities between two or among more subjects that have something in common; a *contrast* looks at differences. A *comparison and contrast* can examine both similarities and differences.

  — A *cause-and-effect* passage explains why something happened (the cause of an effect) or what did or will happen as a result of something (the effect of a cause).

  — A *statement and clarification*, or *inductive argument*, looks at specific details and draws a general conclusion.

  — A *generalization and examples*, or *deductive argument*, looks at general principles and draws conclusions based on specific examples from the generalization.

Practice Identifying Patterns of Organization

Read the following passages and try to identify the logical patterns of organization in them. Then answer the questions about them. Answers and explanations appear on pp. 246–47.

> The question of who owns intellectual property such as literature, symbols, images, and ideas frequently ends up being answered in court. Does Pepperidge Farm own the idea of fish-shaped, cheese-flavored crackers? Does the yoga master who invented a method of teaching yoga in a very hot room own the technique? These and other questions have been the subject of recent legal discussion. 5
> As a result of intellectual property disputes, certain ideas and symbols become unavailable for public use—a trend that ultimately punishes all Americans.

(continued)

The cases of the cracker company and the yoga teacher share a theme: the originator—or at least popularizer—of an idea, image, or symbol wants to limit or prevent others' use of it. Pepperidge Farm wants to restrict competitors from selling a similar product, and the yoga master wants to prevent rivals from benefiting from his idea. The benefits to Pepperidge Farm and the yoga teacher are clear if courts rule in their favor, but it is equally clear that consumers will gain nothing from allowing corporations and individuals to copyright such intellectual property.

Limiting competition among rivals limits the choices available to consumers. If only one fish-shaped cheese cracker is allowed on the market, the price may be higher than it would be if the cracker had a close competitor, and consumers are denied the decision of which cracker is more appealing. If one yoga master controls the use of a technique, consumers may have to pay more for classes under instructors who have paid for a license from the original master; in addition, yoga teachers might be prevented from introducing changes to the technique that would appeal to some customers.

This last effect is, in fact, the worst problem with granting ownership of ideas and images to one company or individual: if one party owns them, others are prevented from building on them or using them in innovative ways. The result may be a limit on creativity. The point of competition, after all, is to ensure that the best ideas win. If only one corporation or person is allowed to compete in a given area, there is no way for the best idea to succeed and no incentive to improve an idea.

For the good of American consumers, artists, entrepreneurs, and others, ideas should remain free. If ideas and symbols are owned by anyone with enough money and legal clout to copyright them and order others not to use them, everyone suffers.

1. For this passage, the author uses an overall organizational pattern that
   a. lists examples of literature, symbols, images, and ideas that are common in American culture.
   b. contrasts ideas and symbols.
   c. shows how limiting freedom of ideas results in negative effects for American consumers.
   d. defines intellectual property and gives examples.

Most Americans are familiar with spaghetti and macaroni, the most popular pasta shapes in the United States, and children may have eaten pasta shaped like favorite cartoon characters. But traditional Italian pasta comes in almost as many shapes as cartoons do. In all its variety, pasta can offer a feast for the imagination.

Indeed, imaginative names and shapes are plentiful in pastas available in 5
neighborhoods in Italy. Traditional pastas include shapes named for almost anything; some popular categories include household articles, creatures, and body
parts. Pastas are named for thimbles (*ditali*), ribbons (*fetucce*), and radiators (*radiatore*). They resemble little worms (*vermicelli*), conch shells (*conchiglie*), melon
seeds (*semi de melone*), or butterflies (*farfalle*). Some even take the shape of ears 10
(*orecchiette*) and moustaches (*mostaccioli*).

Pasta lovers who want to try new things can avail themselves of four basic
types of pasta. These four include long pastas such as *linguine* (which means "little tongues") that are often tossed with sauces; hollow pasta tubes like *ziti*
(which means "bridegrooms") that can be baked; tiny pastas such as *acini di* 15
peppe (which means "peppercorns") intended for soups; and specialty pastas like
manicotti (which means "little muffs") that are often stuffed with cheese or other
fillings. Cooks in Italy use these different types to ensure variety in the pasta
courses of their meals, and more and more Americans are also enjoying the discovery of pasta novelty. 20

While spaghetti and meatballs or macaroni and cheese may continue to be
the leading pasta choices in U.S. homes, spaghetti and macaroni are no longer
the only shapes of pasta available in grocery stores in this country. American diners, always fond of their pasta, now have access to an abundance of exotic pasta
shapes and sizes. 25

2. For this passage, the author uses an overall organizational pattern that
   a. lists various shapes of pasta.
   b. classifies pasta into different categories.
   c. compares pasta to other nutritious food groups.
   d. illustrates how pasta is an important part of everyday meals.

Many Americans spend their healthiest and most vigorous years working very
hard toward a time in the future when they will be able to relax and enjoy life.
All too often, however, people in this situation discover that the imagined leisure
time never arrives. Trying to get a higher-paying job, many workers feel that they
must put in longer hours; once the good job arrives, people feel trapped into try- 5
ing to pay for ever-larger houses and cars or increasingly elaborate vacations. Instead of looking for ways to make more money, many people would be happier if
they tried to make more time for things that really satisfy them.

The first step in avoiding the cycle of earning more and spending more is for
families and individuals to think about what would really bring them happiness. 10
Is the ultimate goal of life to devote more time to a hobby? to spend more time
with family or friends? to have children? to travel? Some may think at first that

(continued)

the goal is simply to make as much money as possible—but these people should ask themselves what the money is for.

After identifying goals, each person needs to figure out how to reach them. Most overworked Americans find that more free time is the luxury item they most covet. These people should try to find a way to cut down on hours at work. In most cases, deciding to work less means accepting less money; wages drop when someone works fewer hours, and chances for advancement dwindle for an employee who does not seem to make the job a high priority.

15

20

3. For this passage, the author uses an overall organizational pattern that

    a.   describes why Americans usually seek out the highest-paying jobs.

    b.   explains a process that Americans can employ to achieve greater happiness.

    c.   contrasts the quality of life for rich and poor Americans.

    d.   analyzes the positive and negative features of the American workplace.

Gardeners refer to any plant that they dislike, or that is simply in the wrong place, as a weed. But in biological terms, *weed* has a specific meaning. Weeds are plants—and animals, or even microbes—that reproduce quickly, take advantage of new surroundings, and thrive in a variety of habitats. Once they have been transplanted to new locations, they are very hard to get rid of. Weedy species often compete with less hardy varieties of living things for limited resources; the result is that weeds severely pressure or kill more fragile plants and animals in the region. In biological terms, fast-growing vines like kudzu are weeds; so are rats, cockroaches, crows, certain viruses—and humans.

5

4. This paragraph is organized by

    a.   defining and giving examples of weeds.

    b.   illustrating the damaging effect of weeds.

    c.   contrasting animals and plants, which can both be weeds.

    d.   listing examples of weeds.

The Night Café depicts a harshly lit room and the unhappy-looking people who gather there. The viewer's eye first falls on the central object, a large green billiard table casting a shadow over the pale yellow floor. To the right of the table is a standing man in pale clothing. His hair, reflecting the ceiling, appears green. He is the only one of the several people present who is definitely awake. Farther to the right, the blood-red wall of the café slants sharply toward the foreground. The table at the far right of the painting is occupied by two seated men. One has his back to the viewer and his head covered with a large yellow hat while his companion, facing front, props his head drunkenly on one hand. Behind the

5

second man is a long table on which an empty bottle and glass sit abandoned by 10
an earlier solitary drinker.

Moving counterclockwise, toward the red rear wall of the café, the eye comes to the top of the painting, where a bile-green ceiling clashes sharply with the dominant yellows and reds of the room. Hanging lamps that resemble squinting eyes radiate yellowish light, painted in the thick, wavy lines typical of van 15 Gogh's brushwork. Farther left, a half-open curtain reveals the café's back room, also lit with a yellow glare. The other patrons appear along the left side of the painting: a man and woman hunch dejectedly side by side in the rear left corner of the room, while the table in front of theirs is occupied by a man alone who is either asleep or dejected, with his head resting on his folded arms. Two more ta- 20 bles on the lower left are littered with debris from departed guests. At the bottom of the painting is an empty expanse of pale yellow floorboards leading back to the billiard table and the red, red walls.

5. For this passage, the author uses an overall organizational pattern that

    a.   compares the people and the background in the painting.

    b.   contrasts the colors used by van Gogh in *The Night Café*.

    c.   describes the spatial relationships among the different parts of the painting.

    d.   lists the different people and objects included in the painting.

Many medical tests are very effective at assisting doctors in diagnosing ailments and diseases early, when they can still be treated effectively. Some of these tests are recommended for most adults at certain stages of life—tests for certain cancers, for example. One new type of test, the full-body scan, has been heavily promoted as a way for patients to discover problems in any part of the body before 5 symptoms arise. But experts argue that full-body scans may do more harm than good.

In a full-body scan, radiation provides detailed images of the body's interior organs and systems. The procedure is painless and noninvasive. Many people who are concerned about their health are eager to undergo full-body scans to set 10 their minds at ease, and the procedure is becoming increasingly common. Patients often seek out scans without being referred by a doctor; in this case, they pay for the scans, which are rarely covered by insurance.

Patients obviously want the results of the scan to be negative. If the scan does discover some problem, they want to find out all that they can about the 15 problem so that it can be resolved. However, the results of full-body scans are often false positives—indications of health problems that turn out to be nothing. Before the frightened patient learns that she doesn't have a tumor, she has to suffer the trauma of believing that she may be about to die; then she must undergo

(continued)

uncomfortable, possibly dangerous procedures to discover that there is no tumor. 20
Unnecessary surgery, like necessary surgery, always carries the risk of serious
complications including death. In addition, it is expensive. For people covered by
insurance, the out-of-pocket expenses may not be high, but the insurance companies pass the higher costs on to other customers in the form of increased rates.

Medical professionals also point out that high doses of radiation are in- 25
volved in any scan. A full-body scan, which affects much more tissue than a typical CAT scan, exposes a body to considerably higher amounts of radiation than a
standard X-ray does. Thus, a man who undergoes an annual scan may actually
increase his risk of developing a tumor. Even though the full-body scan procedure may not cause problems for patients, health experts urge all people to limit 30
their voluntary exposure to radiation.

Patients should take responsibility for keeping an eye on their health, most
doctors agree. But according to many physicians, undergoing a full-body scan
merely gives people the impression that they are taking charge of their lives. A
better, and cheaper, alternative is to follow the recommendations of a doctor the 35
patient knows and trusts.

6. For this passage, the author uses an overall organizational pattern that
    a.   states the possible harmfulness of full-body scans and then clarifies that statement
        with explanations.
    b.   describes different types of body scan.
    c.   contrasts full-body scans with partial body scans.
    d.   argues in favor of better medical care.

The Coriolis force, named for the nineteenth-century French mathematician Gaspard de Coriolis, refers to the way Earth's rotation influences moving objects.
Coriolis first described the force to explain why prevailing winds on Earth move
in curved rather than straight lines. The Coriolis force also explains why hurricanes above the equator rotate counterclockwise and those below the equator 5
move clockwise. Because it works only on a large scale, however, the Coriolis
force has almost no effect on one phenomenon with which it is often incorrectly
linked: the direction water circles before flowing down a drain.

Here's the myth: in the Northern Hemisphere, water always circles counterclockwise before draining out of the bathtub, sink, or toilet, and water in the 10
Southern Hemisphere moves clockwise. The same myth claims that water does
not circle at all when the toilet, tub, or sink is directly over the equator. (To make
matters even more confusing, some of these false claims even get the direction of
the Coriolis force wrong, stating that the tub or toilet in the Northern Hemisphere is the clockwise one.) The physical facts are not nearly as intriguing or as 15

simple as this false "fun fact," which makes it difficult for scientists to convince the public that the toilet-water story has been definitively known to be false for several decades.

In any case, here's the truth: the size of the Coriolis force is so negligible in a sink, toilet, or bathtub that other forces have much more power to influence the direction of water going down the drain. The direction of water flowing out of a relatively small container is affected most by the direction the water was traveling as it entered. If water flows in clockwise, it is likely to retain the clockwise motion as it swirls out, and vice versa. The direction can also be influenced by the movement of pulling out the plug and by the shape of the container. 25

Since the general public has no monopoly on wondering why water swirls out of toilets in a certain direction, scientists have, not surprisingly, studied the Coriolis force in small containers. However, in a 1962 experiment at the Massachusetts Institute of Technology, researcher Ascher Shapiro filled a six-foot circular tank six inches deep with the water entering clockwise. He covered the tank 30 to prevent disturbances from outside, kept the temperature constant, and waited. When he pulled the plug after two hours, the water drained out clockwise, presumably because it retained some of the motion from the clockwise filling. However, after twenty-four hours the water swirled completely counterclockwise as Shapiro drained it, in keeping with the direction of the Coriolis force in the 35 Northern Hemisphere.

7. Paragraphs 2 and 3 are organized by

    a.   listing the elements of the Coriolis force.

    b.   defining the impact of the Coriolis force.

    c.   contrasting the myth about the Coriolis force with facts about it.

    d.   comparing the significance of the Coriolis force with other scientific theories.

Since the general public has no monopoly on wondering why water swirls out of toilets in a certain direction, scientists have, not surprisingly, studied the Coriolis force in small containers. However, in a 1962 experiment at the Massachusetts Institute of Technology, researcher Ascher Shapiro filled a six-foot circular tank six inches deep with the water entering clockwise. He covered the tank to prevent disturbances from outside, kept the temperature constant, and waited. When he pulled the plug after two hours, the water drained out clockwise, presumably because it retained some of the motion from the clockwise filling. However, after twenty-four hours the water swirled completely counterclockwise as Shapiro drained it, in keeping with the direction of the Coriolis force in the 10 Northern Hemisphere.

8. This paragraph is organized by

    a.   describing the sequence of Ascher Shapiro's experiment.

    b.   defining the Coriolis force and giving examples.

    c.   summarizing the myths about the Coriolis force.

    d.   classifying Shapiro's experiment as an important scientific discovery.

Democracy depends on having a population of people who are informed about and interested in the political process and who care enough to vote. As the past few decades in the United States have demonstrated, fewer and fewer eligible citizens are going to the polls in this country, even for the elections when much seems to be at stake. Why don't more Americans vote? 5

One reason many people give for failing to cast a ballot is that they don't have enough time. While Americans obviously lead busy lives, this excuse is simply that—an excuse. People would find time to vote if they cared strongly about it, especially when the polls are open from six a.m. to nine p.m. and the process takes only a few minutes. 10

A more important reason many citizens supply for not voting is that they don't know what the candidates stand for. Discovering a candidate's real views on a subject has indeed become more difficult in the past twenty years or so. Aware that news coverage of their campaign will be limited to fifteen-second sound bites on television, most candidates limit their remarks to dull platitudes 15 that no one could possibly find offensive. For example, every candidate will claim to support education and economic growth (whatever that means). But although finding out what candidates really plan to do in office may not be easy, it is not impossible; reputable newspapers almost always print in-depth looks at the candidates. The problem, once again, is getting the voting public to care enough 20 to find out.

The most important problem, then, is that voters don't seem to care enough about their right to vote. They can't be bothered to take the minimal trouble necessary to choose, and cast a vote for, a candidate. According to some experts, the reason for this apathy may be that most people don't feel that their vote makes 25 much difference. When major corporations, special interest groups, and professional lobbyists appear to gain access to politicians on the basis of enormous campaign contributions, Americans who don't have the resources to buy time with their representatives can easily become convinced that their views—and their votes—don't matter. This isn't so much a problem of indifference to policy 30 as of a (possibly correct) perception that little people have little influence on policy. If this perception is widespread, the fact that ordinary Americans stay home in greater numbers with each election is an understandable response.

Until something happens to make American adults believe that their choice of candidates can make a real difference in their lives, voter indifference will 35 continue. Leaving the polls open for twenty-four hours and interviewing every candidate at length won't bring people to voting booths unless they are convinced that the act can have a positive effect on their lives.

9. Paragraphs 2 and 3 are organized by

   a.   listing reasons why citizens are apathetic about voting.

   b.   defining voter apathy.

   c.   contrasting the types of media coverage of political campaigns.

   d.   explaining the order of importance of reasons that many citizens don't vote.

Twice in the 1970s, a female athlete competed one-on-one against a male athlete in a heavily promoted sports match. For many people, both events symbolized the era's battle over women's rights. Thousands of ticket holders and millions of television viewers wanted to know whether female champions could hold their own, or even triumph, against male competitors. However, while observers of the   5
first event—a tennis match—enjoyed a comedy that permanently raised the status of women players, observers of the second—a horse race—witnessed a tragedy that offered no solace to any supporters of the sport.

   In September 1973, the first competition, a tennis match between aging Wimbledon champion Bobby Riggs and rising star Billie Jean King left everyone   10
except Riggs laughing. Riggs had boasted loudly that "any half-decent male player" could beat any female tennis champion. After challenging and defeating a top-seeded woman, Riggs took on Billie Jean King. He tried to intimidate her by sending flowers and making insulting pronouncements, but King maintained a sense of humor about the event. Riggs arrived at the Houston Astrodome   15
flanked by women in bikinis. Not to be outdone, King arranged to be carried in on a sedan chair borne by musclemen. Unable to win a psychological victory, Riggs, who was fifty-five, was trounced in straight sets by the female champion as millions who had never before cared about tennis watched. Analysts believe that this huge publicity stunt set women's tennis on the course to its present pop-   20
ularity.

   The second contest involved two athletes in their prime: a pair of three-year-old racehorses. Like the Riggs-King match, the Foolish Pleasure–Ruffian race in July 1975 pitted an able female champion who had competed only with other females against a male competitor. Ruffian had not only triumphed in the Filly   25
Triple Crown but had won each of her ten races with obvious ease. She had never even been passed by another horse on a racetrack, and she had broken track records set by such great horses as Man O'War and Secretariat. Foolish Pleasure, her opponent, was the 1975 Kentucky Derby champion. At the start of the race, Foolish Pleasure nosed ahead for a few seconds, and then Ruffian began   30

(continued)

to pull in front of him. The two horses had run less than a mile when Ruffian's anklebone suddenly snapped. Foolish Pleasure finished the race alone, and Ruffian had to be euthanized later that day when surgery failed to save her. The unexpected catastrophe left some stunned viewers—many of whom had been drawn to the match as a symbolic battle of the sexes—unwilling to watch another thoroughbred race. 35

The contests between Billie Jean King and Bobby Riggs and between Ruffian and Foolish Pleasure both symbolized the battle of the sexes in the 1970s. King's triumph over Riggs provided comic relief and a boost to one women's sport. The tragic outcome of the horse race, however, left few with the heart for any additional symbolic matches. 40

10. For this passage, the author uses an overall organizational pattern of

a. comparing and contrasting the two battles and their outcomes.

b. analyzing the effect of the King-Riggs match on the popularity of women's tennis.

c. listing the gender battles that have taken place in recent history.

d. arguing the importance of contests between the sexes.

When is communication not really communication? This may sound like a joke, but the answer—"when it tries to conceal rather than to convey information"—isn't very funny. Communication that is really a cover-up aims to confuse or even intimidate an audience. If you can recognize communication cover-ups, you will be less likely to be taken in by incomprehensible or misleading language. 5

One type of misleading communication is bad academic writing. In fact, academic jargon probably sets the gold standard for the most incomprehensible writing anywhere. If you ask a roomful of English teachers to explain the meaning of a sentence in another English professor's article and no one can define either the point of the sentence or the meaning of words in it without a dictionary, 10 then the sentence in question isn't brilliantly analyzing literature—it's just plain bad. The purpose of this kind of cover-up is simple: to disguise mundane ideas as innovative and to prevent readers from recognizing what is really being said.

Another type of confusing communication is business language, which slips into mindless jargon far too often and at other times is used to cover up bad 15 business practices and greed. Whether or not you've ever worked for a corporation, you have probably encountered clichés like "on the same page" and "vision statement." This kind of bloated, self-important jargon serves no purpose other than making insiders feel like insiders (and outsiders feel like outsiders). Even worse are new creations such as "rightsizing" (another word for "downsizing"), 20 which gloss over the fact that employees are losing their jobs while implying that the jobs were unnecessary in the first place. When businesses use language to hide things, let the listener beware.

The final, and most important, type of misleading communication is political and military jargon. Political leaders manipulate buzzwords designed to make the policies of their political party look good and those of the other party look foolish or evil. When you develop the critical ear to recognize these attempts to use emotional language to confuse and mislead, you take the first step toward being able to resist and think for yourself. More disgusting is the deliberate use of bland or meaningless phrases to describe horrors, as when officials report "collateral damage" to disguise the deaths of innocent civilians. Whether the language is hiding terrible things with boring phrases or whipping up emotions to confuse listeners, the best defense is recognizing the cover-up for what it is.

English is a complex language that offers speakers and writers many ways to say something. Some people choose to communicate clearly, and some deliberately choose not to. If you become aware of the common types of misleading communication, you will be less likely to fall for mindless and confusing constructions—and less likely to mangle the language by using them yourself.

11. For this passage, the author uses an overall organizational pattern that

    a.   lists models of effective communication.

    b.   generalizes about communication cover-ups and gives examples.

    c.   contrasts jargon and buzzwords.

    d.   compares good communication practices with poor communication practices.

What kind of driver are you? If you're like most Americans, you think you're a pretty good driver—better than average. Unfortunately, it's statistically impossible for a majority of people to be better than average at anything, so some "better-than-average" drivers are kidding themselves. Maybe you're one of the following types of better-than-average drivers; if so, you might want to try to change your ways behind the wheel.

If you're a better-than-average-but-angry driver, you tailgate to let other drivers know that they're moving too slowly. You honk your horn a fraction of a second after the light turns green to let other drivers know that it's time to move. You swerve ostentatiously around slower traffic, making dangerous lane changes, because the other cars are in your way.

If you're a better-than-average-but-distracted driver, you're changing the CD, cheering the home run, and talking on the cell phone while you're supposed to be watching the road. You're thinking about what to cook for dinner or deciding just to pick up some pizza instead of focusing on the traffic. When the angry driver tailgates you as you speed up and slow down, apparently at random, you don't notice. You almost hit him because you're drifting into the next lane as he passes, but you don't notice that, either.

(continued)

If you're a better-than-average-but-tired driver, you're the one dozing off at the traffic light. You have slow reaction times when the distracted driver in front slams on the brakes in response to something a deejay has said. You may have a terrific excuse—you were up late changing the newborn's diapers, or you had to get up early to study for the midterm—but you are dangerous to yourself and others on the road.

Which one are you? At different times, you've probably been all of the above—and so has every other driver. Everyone gets angry; after all, most of those other drivers are so much worse than average! Everyone gets distracted. Everyone gets tired. The trick is to notice these states. If another driver makes you angry, take a deep breath and let it go. If you are often distracted, force yourself to concentrate on the task at hand: driving. If you're tired, get more rest, and in the meantime, take public transportation where you can safely close your eyes. Maybe the thing genuinely better-than-average drivers know is that nobody can always be better than average—and they try to drive safely even when they aren't at their best.

12. For this passage, the author uses an overall organizational pattern that
   a. compares good and bad driving styles.
   b. summarizes the history of the average driver.
   c. defines the characteristics of a good driver and gives examples.
   d. classifies different styles of bad drivers.

(2.2B) IDENTIFYING RELATIONSHIPS WITHIN AND BETWEEN SENTENCES

What Are Transitional Devices?

Transitional words and phrases indicate the relationships within and between sentences. They indicate the connections and signal the reader about what to expect. Common transitions include words such as *next* and *however* and phrases such as *for example* and *as a result*. In the following example, the transitions are underlined.

   EXAMPLE

   What should small children be taught about fire safety? First, they should understand what matches are and what the consequences of playing with them can be. In addition, they should be taught that matches are not toys and that they can cause great damage. Children should also be taught how to avoid contact burns from stove burners, hot liquids, and electrical appliances. (Timothy E. Miles, "Fighting Fire with Fire Safety Education")

How Do Transitional Devices Indicate Relationships?

Understanding the meaning of each transition clarifies the relationship the author sees between the sentences or between parts of a sentence. Different transitions have different meanings, as the following table indicates.

COMMON TRANSITIONAL WORDS AND PHRASES CATEGORIZED BY MEANING			
Space			
above	below	near	to the right
across	beside	next to	to the side
at the bottoms	beyond	opposite	under
at the bottom	farther/further	over	where
at the top	inside	to the left	
Time			
after	eventually	meanwhile	soon
as	finally	next	then
at last	first	now	when
before	last	second	while
during	later	since	
Importance			
above all	in fact	more important	most
best	in particular	most important	worst
especially			
Example			
for example	for instance	for one thing	one reason
Addition			
additionally	and	as well as	in addition
also	another	furthermore	moreover
Contrast			
although	in contrast	nevertheless	still
but	instead	on the other hand	yet
however			
Effect/Result			
as a result	finally	so	therefore
because	thus		

In the following passage, underlined transitions indicate relationships *within* a sentence; double-underlined transitions indicate relationships *between* sentences.

EXAMPLE

Many people mistakenly believe that Pete Rose went to prison for betting on baseball and that, for this reason, he should be kept out of the Baseball Hall of Fame. The fact is, however, that Rose went to prison for tax-law violations. He

(continued)

failed to pay income tax on his gambling winnings and on the money he made at baseball-card shows. <u>Even so</u>, when has the Hall of Fame ever been reserved for perfect people? Babe Ruth was an adulterer and a serious drinker, but he still holds a place in the Hall. Mickey Mantle and Willie Mays were barred from baseball for being employees of an Atlantic City casino (an obvious gambling connection), <u>but</u> even this decision was eventually overturned. (John Fleeger, "Why Isn't Pete Rose in the Hall of Fame?") 5

10

How Do Transitional Devices Indicate Organization?

Certain transitions can help readers recognize the pattern a writer is using to organize and develop ideas. (Main idea statements can also indicate the pattern of organization.) The following table links organizational patterns with common transitional words and phrases. Notice that some transitional words and phrases appear in more than one category. You must look at the transition's context to discover what the writer wants it to indicate.

COMMON TRANSITIONAL WORDS AND PHRASES CATEGORIZED BY FUNCTION	
Indicate importance	above all, best of all, especially, in fact, in particular, more important, most important, remember, the last point to consider, worst of all
Indicate position and spatial relationship	above, across, at the bottom, at the top, behind, below, beside, beyond, farther/further, inside, near, next to, opposite, over, to the left, to the right, to the side, under, where
Indicate time	after, as, at last, before, during, eventually, finally, first, last, later, meanwhile, next, now, second, since, soon, then, when, while
Illustrate	also, another, finally, for example, for instance, for one thing, in addition
Classify	another, the final, the first kind, the first type, the first group, the second kind, the second type, the second group, the third kind, the third type, the third group, these sorts/forms/categories/classes
Compare	one similarity, another similarity, similarly, like, both
Contrast	one difference, another difference, in contrast, now/then, unlike, while
Indicate cause and effect	one cause/reason/effect/result, a second cause/reason/effect/result, also, another, as a result, because, since
Move from one point to another	also, another fact to consider, another reason, another thing, consider that, for example, in addition, in the first place

In the following passage, the underlined transitions indicate that the passage is organized by time order.

EXAMPLE

When they get lost driving, women and men have very different ways to find the right route. <u>As soon as</u> a woman thinks she might be lost, she will pull into a store or gas station and ask for directions. As she continues on, if she's still not sure of the directions, she will stop <u>again</u> and ask someone else for help. <u>Until</u> they know they are on the right track, women will continue to ask for directions. In contrast, men would rather turn around and go home than stop and ask for 5 directions. First, a man doesn't readily admit he is lost. When it is clear that he is, he will pull over and consult a map. If he still finds himself lost, he will again pull out that map. Either the map will finally put the man on the right route, or as a last resort he will reluctantly stop at a store or gas station and let his wife go in and ask for directions. Many battles of the sexes have raged over what to do when lost in the car. 10

Practice Identifying Relationships within and between Sentences

Try to identify the relationships within and between the following sentences. Answers and explanations appear on pp. 247–49.

CONNECTIONS WITHIN SENTENCES

1. What is the relationship between the parts of the following sentence?

   "If one yoga master controls the use of the technique, consumers may have to pay more for classes under instructors who have paid for a license from the original master."

   a. addition
   b. spatial relationship
   c. comparison
   d. cause and effect

2. What is the relationship between the parts of the following sentence?

   "Weed animals often either eat other local creatures—coyotes are one such species spreading rapidly across the United States—or consume much of the food available, starving out less hardy species."

   a. comparison
   b. time order
   c. example
   d. cause and effect

3. What is the relationship between the parts of the following sentence?

   "After identifying goals, each person needs to figure out how to reach them."

   a. time order
   b. contrast
   c. example
   d. addition

4. What is the relationship between the parts of the following sentence?

"Farther to the right, the blood-red wall of the café slants sharply toward the foreground."

a. time order

b. contrast

c. spatial relationship

d. example

5. What is the relationship between the parts of the following sentence?

"When major corporations, special interest groups, and professional lobbyists appear to gain access to politicians on the basis of enormous campaign contributions, Americans who don't have the resources to buy time with their representatives can easily become convinced that their views—and their votes—don't matter."

a. time order

b. cause and effect

c. comparison

d. example

6. What is the relationship between the parts of the following sentence?

"These workers are not candidates for a typical bank loan—they lack collateral and credit, and the amount of money they need to borrow is simply too small for most banks to lend."

a. contrast

b. time order

c. clarification

d. cause and effect

7. What is the relationship between the parts of the following sentence?

"While spaghetti and meatballs or macaroni and cheese may continue to be the leading pasta choices in U.S. homes, spaghetti and macaroni are no longer the only shapes of pasta available in grocery stores in this country."

a. contrast

b. spatial relationship

c. time order

d. example

8. What is the relationship between the parts of the following sentence?

"The other patrons appear along the left side of the painting: a man and woman hunch dejectedly side by side in the rear left corner of the room, while the table in front of theirs is occupied by a man alone who is either asleep or dejected, with his head resting on his folded arms."

    a.   comparison

    b.   spatial relationship

    c.   example

    d.   cause and effect

9. What is the relationship between the parts of the following sentence?

"Like the Riggs-King match, the Foolish Pleasure–Ruffian race in July 1975 pitted an able female champion who had competed only with females against a male competitor."

    a.   contrast

    b.   comparison

    c.   time order

    d.   cause and effect

10. What is the relationship between the parts of the following sentence?

"The people at CSPI have tested popular types of foods in the past few years, including Chinese, Italian, and Mexican items and such perennial favorites as ice cream."

    a.   comparison

    b.   time order

    c.   addition

    d.   example

CONNECTIONS BETWEEN SENTENCES

11. What is the relationship between the two following sentences?

"These and other questions have been the subject of recent legal discussion. As a result of intellectual property disputes, certain ideas and symbols become unavailable for public use—a trend that ultimately punishes all Americans."

    a.   time order

    b.   contrast

    c.   example

    d.   cause and effect

12. What is the relationship between the two following sentences?

"Once a borrower is approved, the microlender lends a small amount of money —usually a few hundred dollars or less—for a short period of time. The interest rate is generally just high enough to pay for the cost of making the loan."

    a.   addition

    b.   comparison

    c.   time order

    d.   example

13. What is the relationship between the two following sentences?

"At the start of the race, Foolish Pleasure nosed ahead, and then Ruffian began to pull in front of him. The two horses had run less than a mile when Ruffian's anklebone suddenly snapped."

    a.   example

    b.   spatial relationship

    c.   time order

    d.   contrast

14. What is the relationship between the two following sentences?

"If you're a better-than-average driver, you tailgate to let other drivers know that they're moving too slowly. You honk your horn a fraction of a second after the light turns green to let other drivers know that it's time to move."

    a.   addition

    b.   contrast

    c.   spatial relationship

    d.   time order

15. What is the relationship between the two following sentences?

"Logic apparently has little to do with many fearful reactions. Cars, which injure many more people than snakes do, rarely inspire phobias."

    a.   example

    b.   comparison

    c.   contrast

    d.   cause and effect

16. What is the relationship between the two following sentences?

"When a teenager eats a whole bag of her favorite treat, cinnamon jelly beans, one afternoon and then wakes up the following morning with a nasty stomach virus, she may find that her former favorite now repulses her and that it will be years—or a lifetime—before she can stand to eat cinnamon jelly beans again. Many people have experienced similar taste aversions in association with a single unpleasant instance."

    a.   contrast

    b.   cause and effect

    c.   comparison

    d.   time order

17. What is the relationship between the two following sentences?

"Grandma Anna knows how to catch a fish. She also knows how to make a fishing pole, find bait, clean the fish, and cook it so that it tastes better than anything else I can imagine."

    a.   spatial relationship

    b.   addition

    c.   time order

    d.   contrast

18. What is the relationship between the two following sentences?

"Planets have elliptical, or oval, orbits as they travel around the sun. This means that they are much closer to the sun at some periods in the orbit than in others."

    a.   clarification

    b.   example

    c.   addition

    d.   comparison

19. What is the relationship between the two following sentences?

> "Hanging lamps that resemble squinting eyes radiate yellowish light, painted in the thick, wavy lines typical of van Gogh's brushwork. Farther left, a half-open curtain reveals the café's back room, also lit with a yellow glare."

    a.   example

    b.   comparison

    c.   spatial relationship

    d.   clarification

20. What is the relationship between the two following sentences?

> "The script, co-written by Anderson and his frequent collaborator Owen Wilson, makes the characters and situations quirky enough to be interesting and three-dimensional enough to be believable. The character Max isn't exactly Every Adolescent, but we've probably all met—or been—teenagers who resemble him in some ways."

    a.   comparison

    b.   example

    c.   sequence

    d.   addition

2.3A IDENTIFYING WORD MEANING BASED ON CONTEXTUAL CLUES

What Is Context?

The **context** in which a word appears—the words, sentences, and paragraphs before and after it—provides clues to its meaning. When you read, you can use context to make educated guesses about the meaning of words you don't recognize.

How Do You Use Context to Understand Words?

Five kinds of context clue can help you figure out what unfamiliar words mean.

- **Restatement.** Writers may restate an important term, phrase, or idea using synonyms, a formal dictionary definition, or a general, informal definition.

  EXAMPLE

  Athletes who play many sports usually work on their *aerobic conditioning*. Improving the efficiency of the heart and lungs is important, no matter what the level of play.

- **Examples.** Writers often provide examples to illustrate and clarify the meaning of an unfamiliar word.

  EXAMPLE

  Percussionists, including those who play kettledrums, bass drums, cymbals, and triangles, usually have their own section in an orchestra.

- **Comparisons.** Writers use comparisons to indicate similarities. Knowing the characteristics of one part of a comparison will help you understand the meaning of words in the other part.

  EXAMPLE

  Marco always kept his office clean and organized, and Marla was just as *fastidious*.

- **Contrast.** Writers use contrast to indicate differences. If you understand one part of a contrast, think of opposite meanings to get clues about the other part.

  EXAMPLE

  We expected him to be *compliant*, but instead we found him stubborn and uncooperative.

- **General knowledge.** When you do not see other context clues, you may be able to figure out the meaning of a word from your general knowledge of the context.

EXAMPLE

It seemed incongruous to have the rusted, old-fashioned skeleton key open the door of a high-tech, top-secret laboratory.

Practice Using Contextual Clues

Read the following passages, then answer the questions about contextual clues. Answers and explanations appear on pp. 249–50.

When is communication not really communication? This may sound like a joke, but the answer—"when it tries to conceal rather than to convey information"—isn't very funny. Communication that is really a cover-up aims to confuse or even intimidate an audience. If you can recognize communication cover-ups, you will be less likely to be taken in by incomprehensible or misleading language.   5

One type of misleading communication is bad academic writing. In fact, academic jargon probably sets the gold standard for the most incomprehensible writing anywhere. If you ask a roomful of English teachers to explain the meaning of a sentence in another English professor's article and no one can define either the point of the sentence or the meaning of words in it without a dictionary,   10 then the sentence in question isn't brilliantly analyzing literature—it's just plain bad. The purpose of this kind of cover-up is simple: to disguise mundane ideas as innovative and to prevent readers from recognizing what is really being said.

Another type of confusing communication is business language, which slips into mindless jargon far too often and at other times is used to cover up bad   15 business practices and greed. Whether or not you've ever worked for a corporation, you have probably encountered clichés like "on the same page" and "vision statement." This kind of bloated, self-important jargon serves no purpose other than making insiders feel like insiders (and outsiders feel like outsiders). Even worse are new creations such as "rightsizing" (another word for "downsizing"),   20 which gloss over the fact that employees are losing their jobs while implying that the jobs were unnecessary in the first place. When businesses use language to hide things, let the listener beware.

The final, and most important, type of misleading communication is political and military jargon. Political leaders manipulate buzzwords designed to make   25 the policies of their political party look good and those of the other party look foolish or evil. When you develop the critical ear to recognize these attempts to use emotional language to confuse and mislead, you take the first step toward being able to resist and think for yourself. More disgusting is the deliberate use of bland or meaningless phrases to describe horrors, as when officials report   30 "collateral damage" to disguise the deaths of innocent civilians. Whether the language is hiding terrible things with boring phrases or whipping up emotions to confuse listeners, the best defense is recognizing the cover-up for what it is.

English is a complex language that offers speakers and writers many ways to say something. Some people choose to communicate clearly, and some deliberately choose not to. If you become aware of the common types of misleading communication, you will be less likely to fall for mindless and confusing constructions—and less likely to mangle the language by using them yourself. 35

1. As used in line 12, "mundane" most nearly means
   a. ordinary.
   b. creative.
   c. faulty.
   d. confusing.

2. The word *jargon* as used in line 15 means
   a. nonsense.
   b. character.
   c. language.
   d. employment.

3. The term *gloss over* as used in line 21 most nearly means
   a. dwell on.
   b. ignore.
   c. emphasize.
   d. delay.

Democracy depends on having a population of people who are informed about and interested in the political process and who care enough to vote. As the past few decades in the United States have demonstrated, fewer and fewer eligible citizens are going to the polls in this country, even for the elections when much seems to be at stake. Why don't more Americans vote? 5

One reason many people give for failing to cast a ballot is that they don't have enough time. While Americans obviously lead busy lives, this excuse is simply that—an excuse. People would find time to vote if they cared strongly about it, especially when the polls are open from six a.m. to nine p.m. and the process takes only a few minutes. 10

Another reason many citizens supply for not voting is that they don't know what the candidates stand for. Discovering a candidate's real views on a subject has indeed become more difficult in the past twenty years or so. Aware that news coverage of their campaign will be limited to fifteen-second sound bites on television, most candidates limit their remarks to dull platitudes that no one could 15

(continued)

2

possibly find offensive. For example, every candidate will claim to support education and economic growth (whatever that means). But although finding out what candidates really plan to do in office may not be easy, it is not impossible; reputable newspapers almost always print in-depth looks at the candidates. The problem, once again, is getting the voting public to care enough to find out. 20

The most important problem, then, is that voters don't seem to care enough about their right to vote. They can't be bothered to take the minimal trouble necessary to choose, and cast a vote for, a candidate. According to some experts, the reason for this apathy may be that most people don't feel that their vote makes much difference. When major corporations, special interest groups, and profes- 25 sional lobbyists appear to gain access to politicians on the basis of enormous campaign contributions, Americans who don't have the resources to buy time with their representatives can easily become convinced that their views—and their votes—don't matter. This isn't so much a problem of indifference to policy as of a (possibly correct) perception that little people have little influence on pol- 30 icy. If this perception is widespread, the fact that ordinary Americans stay home in greater numbers with each election is an understandable response.

Until something happens to make American adults believe that their choice of candidates can make a real difference in their lives, voter indifference will continue. Leaving the polls open for twenty-four hours and interviewing every candi- 35 date at length won't bring people to voting booths unless they are convinced that the act can have a positive effect on their lives.

4. The word *offensive* as used in line 16 means

   a.   timely.

   b.   distasteful.

   c.   appealing.

   d.   beneficial.

5. The word *reputable* as used in line 19 most nearly means

   a.   highly regarded.

   b.   weekly.

   c.   questionable.

   d.   daily.

6. The word *apathy* as used in line 24 means

   a.   sensitivity.

   b.   knowledge.

   c.   choice of vote.

   d.   lack of interest.

Cave art fascinates historians, art historians, and the general public. So many people express interest in these early artworks that the most popular caves often restrict visitors in order to protect the sites from too many eager viewers. But hordes of tourists are not likely to descend on a recently discovered Australian cave that contains aboriginal drawings from about four thousand to about two hundred years ago. Specialists are particularly thrilled with the find—which only one expert had seen as of 2003—because the cave's inaccessibility may protect the beauty and historical value of the contents.

The works in the cave have been protected from sunlight by the cave's north-facing opening. Some drawings depict local animals, such as wallabies and wombats, and others depict half-human, half-animal forms that feature in aboriginal creation stories. Handprints, outlined by pigments blown through a hollow tube, also line the walls. In all, the cave contains some two hundred well-preserved figures.

The newest drawings found at the site date from the eighteenth century, when white settlers first began to arrive in Australia. The cave's location just sixty miles west of Sydney, Australia's largest city and one of its first ports, meant that it was closer to the new residents than many aboriginal people wanted to come. For two hundred years, the cave was apparently disturbed only by small animals. Hikers found it by accident in 1995.

The wilderness of the region makes access difficult, even for those who are eager to see the art firsthand. An anthropologist from the Australian Museum, Paul Tacon, was the only specialist to have traveled to the cave as of 2003. He and five aboriginal colleagues flew as close to the cave as they could by helicopter and then made an arduous trek through the desert landscape to their destination. The group left the site after spending a single night when water began to run out.

Tacon persuaded Australian government officials to restrict access to the cave and not to disclose its location. These measures please anthropologists and art experts, but the restrictions are probably just a precaution. Visiting a site that the first expert could not reach for eight years is probably beyond the abilities of all but the hardiest tourists. Isolation has protected the cave's artworks for centuries, and everyone concerned about the preservation of the drawings believes that continued isolation is the best hope for their future.

5

10

15

20

25

30

7. The word *hordes* as used in line 4 most nearly means

   a. reputations.

   b. complaints.

   c. masses.

   d. small groups.

8. The word *aboriginal* as used in line 5 most nearly means

    a.   creative.

    b.   native.

    c.   ink.

    d.   modern.

9. The word *arduous* as used in line 25 most nearly means

    a.   tough.

    b.   senseless.

    c.   coordinated.

    d.   repeat.

10. The word *precaution* as used in line 30 most nearly means

    a.   necessity.

    b.   surprise.

    c.   mistake.

    d.   safeguard.

2.3B IDENTIFYING BIASED LANGUAGE

What Is Biased Language?

Language that reflects the writer's inclination to favor one side of an issue or topic or to prefer one group of people over another is **biased**. Biased language implies a strong positive or negative view of issues or people. In some cases, biased language simply clarifies a strong point of view. In other cases, bias is a matter of ignorance of or indifference to the feelings of other groups of people.

> **EXAMPLES**
>
> There was no reason for such a disgustingly emotional outburst.
>
> There was good cause for such a passionate, committed plea.
>
> Chris Fox is the lady mayor of Port London, Maine.

How Do You Identify Bias?

To determine if writing is biased, ask the following questions:

- Does the writing include potentially offensive references to a person's age, race, ethnicity, physical condition, or sexual orientation?
- Does the writing make assumptions about the gender of people in certain occupations?
- Does the writing mention a nonwhite person's race but not a white person's?
- Does the writing mention information about a woman (such as marital status or appearance) that would not be noted about a man?

- Would a reasonable person of the same sex, race, age, physical condition, and/or sexual orientation as the person being described be likely to object to the description?

- Does the writing use "loaded words" to give a positive or negative impression?

- Would someone with an opposing point of view disagree with the way the information is presented?

If the answer to any of these questions is *yes*, the writing is probably biased.

Note that bias can be expressed rather subtly. It does not always appear in specific statements; rather, a writer's examples, assertions, and other information may build to give you the sense that he or she is favoring a particular side of an issue. Also, biased language does not always concern age, race, gender, physical condition, and the like. A writer may show a bias in favor of, say, creating better after-school programs or against, for instance, the construction of a new mall in town.

Some of the following exercises will give you practice in identifying subtler forms of bias.

Practice Identifying Bias

Read the following passages and answer the questions about identifying bias. Answers and explanations appear on pp. 250–51.

The question of who owns intellectual property such as literature, symbols, images, and ideas frequently ends up being answered in court. Does Pepperidge Farm own the idea of fish-shaped, cheese-flavored crackers? Does the yoga master who invented a method of teaching yoga in a very hot room own the technique? These and other questions have been the subject of recent legal discussion. 5 As a result of intellectual property disputes, certain ideas and symbols become unavailable for public use—a trend that ultimately punishes all Americans.

The cases of the cracker company and the yoga teacher share a theme: the originator—or at least popularizer—of an idea, image, or symbol wants to limit or prevent others' use of it. Pepperidge Farm wants to restrict competitors from 10 selling a similar product, and the yoga master wants to prevent rivals from benefiting from his idea. The benefits to Pepperidge Farm and the yoga teacher are clear if courts rule in their favor, but it is equally clear that consumers will gain nothing from allowing corporations and individuals to copyright such intellectual property. 15

Limiting competition among rivals limits the choices available to consumers. If only one fish-shaped cheese cracker is allowed on the market, the price may be higher than it would be if the cracker had a close competitor, and consumers are denied the decision of which cracker is more appealing. If one yoga master controls the use of a technique, consumers may have to pay more for classes under 20 instructors who have paid for a license from the original master; in addition, yoga teachers might be prevented from introducing changes to the technique that would appeal to some customers. *(continued)*

This last effect is, in fact, the worst problem with granting ownership of ideas and images to one company or individual: if one party owns them, others are prevented from building on them or using them in innovative ways. The result may be a limit on creativity. The point of competition, after all, is to ensure that the best ideas win. If only one corporation or person is allowed to compete in a given area, there is no way for the best idea to succeed and no incentive to improve an idea.

For the good of American consumers, artists, entrepreneurs, and others, ideas should remain free. If ideas and symbols are owned by anyone with enough money and legal clout to copyright them and order others not to use them, everyone suffers.

1. In this passage, the author is biased in favor of

    a.   corporate ownership of intellectual property.

    b.   intellectual property remaining available to everyone.

    c.   individual ownership of intellectual property.

    d.   the use of the court system to establish legal ownership of intellectual property.

2. In this passage, the author expresses a bias against

    a.   limiting competition in the business world.

    b.   free choice for consumers.

    c.   encouraging competition in the business world.

    d.   encouraging creativity.

Many Americans spend their healthiest and most vigorous years working very hard toward a time in the future when they will be able to relax and enjoy life. All too often, however, people in this situation discover that the imagined leisure time never arrives. Trying to get a higher-paying job, many workers feel that they must put in longer hours; once the good job arrives, people feel trapped into trying to pay for ever-larger houses and cars or increasingly elaborate vacations. Instead of looking for ways to make more money, many people would be happier if they tried to make more time for things that really satisfy them.

The first step in avoiding the cycle of earning more and spending more is for families and individuals to think about what would really bring them happiness. Is the ultimate goal of life to devote more time to a hobby? to spend more time with family or friends? to have children? to travel? Some may think at first that the goal is simply to make as much money as possible—but these people should ask themselves what the money is for.

After identifying goals, each person needs figure out how to reach them. Most overworked Americans find that more free time is the luxury item they most covet. These people should try to find a way to cut down on hours at work.

In most cases, deciding to work less means accepting less money; wages drop when someone works fewer hours, and chances for advancement dwindle for an employee who does not seem to make the job a high priority.   20

Working less and earning less need not mean a lower quality of life, however. The next step for the person determined to keep off the earning-and-spending treadmill is to figure out how to be satisfied with less money. Simplification is often the key. How big does a house have to be? Which expenses are essential and which are not? Can simpler items substitute for more luxurious ones—a   25 smaller car instead of an SUV, for example? Simplifying life can also mean learning to enjoy less expensive pleasures, such as taking a walk or visiting a park instead of relying on technology for entertainment. Using creativity—and spending time interacting with people instead of a computer—might be a novel and immensely satisfying experience for many Americans.   30

Those who stop trying to earn as much as possible often become much more pleased with their lives. Many people find working long hours unsatisfying. Perhaps they shouldn't try so hard to be on top. Instead, they might want to stop, think, accept less money, and see if they will be content with more time.

3. In this passage, the author expresses a bias in favor of

   a.   earning as much money as possible.

   b.   seeking promotions in the workplace.

   c.   simplifying one's life.

   d.   working hard to earn money for retirement.

4. The author shows a bias against

   a.   spending time enjoying hobbies.

   b.   spending time to travel.

   c.   spending time with family.

   d.   spending time enjoying technology-created entertainment.

Many medical tests are very effective at assisting doctors in diagnosing ailments and diseases early, when they can still be treated effectively. Some of these tests are recommended for most adults at certain stages of life—tests for certain cancers, for example. One new type of test, the full-body scan, has been heavily promoted as a way for patients to discover problems in any part of the body before   5 symptoms arise. But experts argue that full-body scans may do more harm than good.

In a full-body scan, radiation provides detailed images of the body's interior organs and systems. The procedure is painless and noninvasive. Many people who are concerned about their health are eager to undergo full-body scans to set   10

(continued)

their minds at ease, and the procedure is becoming increasingly common. Patients often seek out scans without being referred by a doctor; in this case, they pay for the scans, which are rarely covered by insurance.

Patients obviously want the results of the scan to be negative. If the scan does discover some problem, they want to find out all that they can about the problem so that it can be resolved. However, the results of full-body scans are often false positives—indications of health problems that turn out to be nothing. Before the frightened patient learns that she doesn't have a tumor, she has to suffer the trauma of believing that she may be about to die; then she must undergo uncomfortable, possibly dangerous procedures to discover that there is no tumor. Unnecessary surgery, like necessary surgery, always carries the risk of serious complications including death. In addition, it is expensive. For people covered by insurance, the out-of-pocket expenses may not be high, but the insurance companies pass the higher costs on to other customers in the form of increased rates.

Medical professionals also point out that high doses of radiation are involved in any scan. A full-body scan, which affects much more tissue than a typical CAT scan, exposes a body to considerably higher amounts of radiation than a standard X-ray does. Thus, a man who undergoes an annual scan may actually increase his risk of developing a tumor. Even though the full-body scan procedure may not cause problems for patients, health experts urge all people to limit their voluntary exposure to radiation.

Patients should take responsibility for keeping an eye on their health, most doctors agree. But according to many physicians, undergoing a full-body scan merely gives people the impression that they are taking charge of their lives. A better, and cheaper, alternative is to follow the recommendations of a doctor the patient knows and trusts.

5. In this passage, the author expresses a bias against
   a. full-body scans.
   b. surgery.
   c. doctors.
   d. health insurance.

6. In this passage, the author shows a bias in favor of
   a. exposure to radiation.
   b. patients undergoing every available health test.
   c. patients undergoing an annual full-body scan.
   d. faith in a competent physician.

The Center for Science in the Public Interest (CSPI) is a nonprofit research group that looks closely at what Americans eat and recommends changes for a healthier diet. The group urges people to eat smaller portions, fewer calories, and less saturated fat—all commonsense ideas for people who want to maintain a healthy weight. Yet journalists seem to announce every new release of data from CSPI with irritation, and the public responds the same way. Why does CSPI bother so many Americans? The probable answer is that nobody wants to hear what the organization has to say.

In the past few years, the people at CSPI have tested popular types of food, including Chinese, Italian, and Mexican items and such perennial favorites as ice cream. The results have not been pretty. Lab results for popular items like egg rolls, fettuccine alfredo, enchiladas, and ice cream sundaes show that diners who consume all that is put in front of them are absorbing an astonishing number of calories and a huge amount of saturated fat. But why should anyone be surprised by this? Egg rolls are deep-fried, fettuccine alfredo comes with a sauce made chiefly of cream and butter, enchiladas are dipped in oil and topped with cheese, and sundaes are mainly ice cream. People are not consuming these foods in the belief that such items are good for them.

Why, then, are people consuming them, and why do they continue to do so after the CSPI reports? The answer is that people are trying to fool themselves (their expanding waistlines notwithstanding) either about what's on their plates or about how regularly they allow themselves such "treats." CSPI has never argued that people should always forgo goodies, just that everyone should be aware of how fatty the goodies are and how special the occasion should be for such an indulgence. The problem for consumers lies in CSPI's painful honesty, which makes obvious the true costs of consuming premium ice cream or a burrito platter with refried beans. Customers seem to be asking CSPI, "How do you expect us to enjoy these things when you keep telling us the truth?"

The Center for Science in the Public Interest isn't going to fade quietly away, as many increasingly large Americans might prefer. Instead, the group is likely to continue pointing out the huge gap between what people know they should be eating and what they actually consume. CSPI offers data that Americans need but do not want to hear. Only those who are already determined to avoid excess calories and fats can possibly welcome the facts it insists on providing.

7. In this passage, the author shows a bias in favor of

a. nonprofit research groups.

b. the Center for Science in the Public Interest.

c. food testing.

d. dieting.

8. The author shows a bias against

   a.   excess calories and fats.

   b.   CSPI's release of data.

   c.   popular international foods.

   d.   diets.

The ice cream social, once an American summer ritual, has now gone the way of the black-and-white television screen. A few people still make ice cream at home, it's true, but most modern Americans who buy ice cream freezers choose a kind with an electric motor. What could they be thinking? Making ice cream ought to be a social event, and to ensure that it is one, people should invest in old- 5 fashioned hand-cranked ice cream freezers to do the job right.

Making ice cream by hand requires planning and sweat. Ice cream makers must procure good cream and cook it gently with sugar and vanilla beans (and, if they must, other flavorings like ripe peaches or even chocolate). Then they have to lay their hands on rock salt and plenty of ice. When the cream has been chilled, it's 10 time to gather strong-armed and strong-willed volunteers for the cranking, and then additional cranking, followed by more cranking. (This part of the process is best done out of doors because the melting ice trickles salty water down the sides of the machine.) After an eternity, when even the strongest muscles have been defeated by the task of turning the handle, the ice cream is finished—and, fittingly, 15 the hard work comes with a just reward: the best-tasting dessert on the planet.

In contrast, an ice cream freezer with a motor is child's play. One person alone can pour the ice cream mixture into the freezer. Then this lonely gourmet probably watches television in air-conditioned comfort while the infernal machine whirs away unattended on the kitchen counter. Where is the fun in that? 20 "It tastes the same," some deluded food critics have been known to declare, but they are wrong. Everyone knows that a prize that is earned is always more appealing than a prize that comes after little or no effort.

So let Americans everywhere pull the plugs on their sad electric ice cream freezers. Instead, they should be encouraged to get the real thing and gather 25 friends to celebrate one of the best warm-weather rituals there is. If they don't have enough friends to crank an ice cream freezer, they've probably been spending too much time alone—but anyone who invests in a hand-cranked ice cream freezer will assuredly attract a few more friends.

9. In this passage, the author shows a bias in favor of

   a.   isolation.

   b.   time-saving kitchen appliances.

   c.   socialization.

   d.   modernization.

10. The author shows a bias against

    a.   hard work.

    b.   black-and-white television.

    c.   some food critics.

    d.   child's play.

2.3C IDENTIFYING TONE

What Is Tone?

Tone is the way the writer's voice sounds in the reader's mind. Writers convey their attitude toward a subject with the words, details, and examples they choose. A writer's tone may be enthusiastic, humorous, sarcastic, ironic, angry, joyful, serious, playful, admiring, pessimistic, or neutral, or it may express some other feeling or attitude.

How Do You Identify the Author's Tone?

The key to understanding tone is to look closely at and listen closely to a writer's sentences and language. What emotions, if any, does he or she seem to express? What feeling do you get from the writing? Choose the description that best seems to match what the writer is expressing.

    In the following example, the underlined words indicate an angry tone.

> **EXAMPLE**
>
> In the United States, one of four children is born into poverty. The United States is the world's wealthiest nation, but much of that wealth is concentrated in the hands of a few. The combined wealth of the top 1 percent of American families is nearly equal to that of the entire bottom 95 percent. Such <u>obscene inequality</u> is <u>totally inappropriate</u> for a democratic country. (Adapted from Holly Sklar, 5 *Chaos or Community*)

Practice Identifying the Author's Tone

Read the following passages and answer the questions about identifying tone. Answers and explanations appear on pp. 251–52.

> Gardeners refer to any plant that they dislike, or that is simply in the wrong place, as a weed. But in biological terms, *weed* has a specific meaning. Weeds are plants—and animals, or even microbes—that reproduce quickly, take advantage of new surroundings, and thrive in a variety of habitats. Once they have been transplanted to new locations, they are very hard to get rid of. Weedy species 5 often compete with less hardy varieties of living things for limited resources; the result is that weeds severely pressure or kill more fragile plants and animals in the region. In biological terms, fast-growing vines like kudzu are weeds; so are rats, cockroaches, crows, certain viruses—and humans. *(continued)*

Many plants and animals cause no problems in their original habitats; they become weeds only when they disperse to new areas, where other species lack defenses against them and allow them to take over. In modern times, human mobility has allowed many organisms to turn into weeds now that global travel and commerce ensure that plants, animals, and viruses move around the world along with humans. Sometimes people disperse a species intentionally, as when gardeners import nonnative plants. Sometimes humans simply act as unwitting transportation.

However weed organisms arrive in their new homes, they all adapt quickly and aggressively to new surroundings. Most weed plants grow quickly, spread seeds easily, and return year after year; dandelions are just one example of an aggressive, fast-spreading weed that was once cultivated as an ornamental flower. Weed animals often either eat other local creatures—coyotes are one such species spreading rapidly across the United States—or consume much of the food available, thereby starving out less hardy species. Weed microbes adapt easily to new hosts, perhaps crossing species or leaping from birds or small mammals to humans.

In many cases, weed organisms actually change the ecosystem as they drive out former competitors and increase their own numbers. The mark of a truly successful weed species is its ability to continue to adapt as its environment changes. By this definition, no other weed can compare to humans, the most innovative users of the environment—and the ones most likely to change their habitats and kill much of the varied but fragile life found there.

Established weeds are notoriously difficult, but not always impossible, to eradicate. Like dandelions and coyotes, humans are survivors whose population continues to grow, and people seem to be in no danger of losing their ability to exert at least some control over most habitats and living things. But human beings should remember one important fact about weeds: no one knows when the next aggressive and highly adaptive species will take advantage of a lucky chance.

1. What is the overall tone of this passage?
   a. argumentative
   b. informative
   c. compassionate
   d. bitter

Millions of impoverished people around the world make their livings by selling vegetables or homemade food or clothing. Unfortunately, bad weather, bad health, and other unpredictable calamities can sometimes push even the costs of necessities such as seeds, cooking fuel, and fabric out of reach of some of these

workers. These workers are not candidates for a typical bank loan—they lack 5
collateral and credit, and the amount of money they need to borrow is simply
too small for most banks to lend. But microlending, a new strategy in which
lenders make small loans to needy self-employed workers, provides a way to end
the cycle of struggle for some poor families.

Microlending institutions seek people who have a business plan in place and 10
a real need for a small loan. In some areas, loan officers go out into the community and talk to small-scale sellers. Many of these vendors require only a little new
equipment or some raw materials to increase the amount of goods they can sell.

Next, microlenders examine the likelihood that a small loan will be repaid.
Most of their borrowers do not have traditional collateral—savings, homes, 15
cars, and other goods—so they would be a poor risk for a traditional loan. But
microlenders take many other factors into consideration. After observing the entrepreneur at work, loan officers also talk to customers and neighbors. Institutions sometimes even offer a loan without collateral if the loan officers' instincts
tell them that the entrepreneur is a good risk. 20

Once a borrower is approved, the microlender lends a small amount of
money—usually a few hundred dollars or less—for a short time. The interest
rate is generally just high enough to pay for the cost of making the loan. The borrower buys the equipment or goods needed and then, if all goes well, uses his or
her higher profits to pay the loan and continue to produce at an increased rate. 25

After paying back the loan, the borrower is eligible for more, larger loans,
and is soon well on the way to establishing a good credit rating. Because borrowers from microlenders are actually less likely than traditional borrowers to de-
fault on their loans, microlending institutions tend to turn a profit, and many
investors are eager to assist them. As a result, more money is available to other 30
poverty-stricken entrepreneurs.

Microlending makes little news in the world of finance because the loans are
small and the stakes for making them are comparatively low. For the borrower,
however, a microloan makes an enormous difference. It often shows a willing,
hardworking person the way out of poverty. 35

2. What is the overall tone of this passage?
   a.   neutral
   b.   ambivalent
   c.   optimistic
   d.   sarcastic

I have never won a prize in my life, so I don't see why I should get one at this
year's bake-off at the Madison Fair. Sure, I've worked hard on my entry—triple
chocolate fudge cookies. For three years, I have been perfecting the recipe, and I

(continued)

think it's about as good as it's going to get. Nonetheless, I'm not getting my hopes up. I'm sure David Lupo will win this year, just as he wins almost every year. Last year, he inspired "oohs" and "ahhs" with his "peanut butter fantasy cake." How can my chocolate cookies stand up to whatever grand creation he's cooking up now?

3. The tone of this passage can best be described as

a.   pessimistic.

b.   excited.

c.   flattering.

d.   confident.

Many Americans spend their healthiest and most vigorous years working very hard toward a time in the future when they will be able to relax and enjoy life. All too often, however, people in this situation discover that the imagined leisure time never arrives. Trying to get a higher-paying job, many workers feel that they must put in longer hours; once the good job arrives, people feel trapped into trying to pay for ever-larger houses and cars or increasingly elaborate vacations. Instead of looking for ways to make more money, many people would be happier if they tried to make more time for things that really satisfy them.

   The first step in avoiding the cycle of earning more and spending more is for families and individuals to think about what would really bring them happiness. Is the ultimate goal of life to devote more time to a hobby? to spend more time with family or friends? to have children? to travel? Some may think at first that the goal is simply to make as much money as possible—but these people should ask themselves what the money is for.

   After identifying goals, each person needs figure out how to reach them. Most overworked Americans find that more free time is the luxury item they most covet. These people should try to find a way to cut down on hours at work. In most cases, deciding to work less means accepting less money; wages drop when someone works fewer hours, and chances for advancement dwindle for an employee who does not seem to make the job a high priority.

   Working less and earning less need not mean a lower quality of life, however. The next step for the person determined to keep off the earning-and-spending treadmill is to figure out how to be satisfied with less money. Simplification is often the key. How big does a house have to be? Which expenses are essential and which are not? Can simpler items substitute for more luxurious ones—a smaller car instead of an SUV, for example? Simplifying life can also mean learning to enjoy less expensive pleasures, such as taking a walk or visiting a park instead of relying on technology for entertainment. Using creativity—and spending time interacting with people instead of a computer—might be a novel and immensely satisfying experience for many Americans. 30

Those who stop trying to earn as much as possible often become much more pleased with their lives. Many people find working long hours unsatisfying. Perhaps they shouldn't try so hard to be on top. Instead, they might want to stop, think, accept less money, and see if they will be content with more time.

4. The tone of this passage can best be described as

   a. optimistic.

   b. cautionary.

   c. sentimental.

   d. self-pitying.

Twice in the 1970s, a female athlete competed one-on-one against a male athlete in a heavily promoted sports match. For many people, both events symbolized the era's battle over women's rights. Thousands of ticket holders and millions of television viewers wanted to know whether female champions could hold their own, or even triumph, against male competitors. However, while observers of the 5 first event—a tennis match—enjoyed a comedy that permanently raised the status of women players, observers of the second—a horse race—witnessed a tragedy that offered no solace to any supporters of the sport.

In September 1973, the first competition, a tennis match between aging Wimbledon champion Bobby Riggs and rising star Billie Jean King, left everyone 10 except Riggs laughing. Riggs had boasted loudly that "any half-decent male player" could beat any female tennis champion. After challenging and defeating a top-seeded woman, Riggs took on Billie Jean King. He tried to intimidate her by sending flowers and making insulting pronouncements, but King maintained a sense of humor about the event. Riggs arrived at the Houston Astrodome 15 flanked by women in bikinis. Not to be outdone, King arranged to be carried in on a sedan chair borne by musclemen. Unable to win a psychological victory, Riggs, who was fifty-five, was trounced in straight sets by the female champion as millions who had never before cared about tennis watched. Analysts believe that this huge publicity stunt set women's tennis on the course to its present pop- 20 ularity.

The second contest involved two athletes who were both in their prime: a pair of three-year-old racehorses. Like the Riggs-King match, the Foolish Pleasure–Ruffian race in July 1975 pitted an able female champion who had competed only with other females against a male competitor. Ruffian had not only 25 triumphed in the Filly Triple Crown but had won each of her ten races with obvious ease. She had never even been passed by another horse on a racetrack, and

(continued)

she had broken track records set by such great horses as Man O'War and Secretariat. Foolish Pleasure, her opponent, was the 1975 Kentucky Derby champion. At the start of the race, Foolish Pleasure nosed ahead for a few seconds, and then Ruffian began to pull in front of him. The two horses had run less than a mile when Ruffian's anklebone suddenly snapped. Foolish Pleasure finished the race alone, and Ruffian had to be euthanized later that day when surgery failed to save her. The unexpected catastrophe left some stunned viewers—many of whom had been drawn to the match as a symbolic battle of the sexes—unwilling to watch another thoroughbred race.

The contests between Billie Jean King and Bobby Riggs and between Ruffian and Foolish Pleasure both symbolized the battle of the sexes in the 1970s. King's triumph over Riggs provided comic relief and a boost to one women's sport. The tragic outcome of the horse race, however, left few with the heart to wish for any additional symbolic matches.

5. What is the overall tone of this passage?

   a. regretful

   b. humorous

   c. subjective

   d. objective

I was tremendously grateful to get a letter telling me that I'd been turned down for financial aid from the college I had planned to attend in the fall. What a lucky break for me! Now I get to pay for everything myself. The school expects my parents to pay my tuition and expenses. I guess the administrators missed the part of my application where I explained that my father was laid off from work two years ago and that he hasn't found steady employment since. Maybe they also failed to notice that my mother is working two part-time jobs to pay the rent, and that my little brother and I have been working for whoever would hire us every summer and on weekends. Boy, will the whole family be delighted to learn that we have plenty of money for my tuition and books!

With this stroke of good fortune, I might even be able to take a year off from school, just like those kids I've heard about who spend a few months backpacking around Europe before they start college. Backpacking doesn't really appeal to me, but that's okay—I'm not a strong enough swimmer to get to Europe anyway. Maybe I'll spend this leisure time doing something really rewarding, like helping others. Yes, that's it. I'll help others super-size their orders, and I'll be sure to ask if they want fries on the side.

6. The tone of this passage can best be described as

    a.   solemn.

    b.   straightforward.

    c.   sarcastic.

    d.   impartial.

> Last year I took a better-paying job, sure that it would improve my life in every way. I like the new work, and I get along with everyone, but the hours are very long and the commute is twice the distance of my old one. Also, I've had to buy an expensive new wardrobe because the atmosphere is more formal than in my last job. Over time, I've determined that the increase in pay is being offset by the 5 cost of the longer commute and the expense of the fancier clothes. Considering also the longer hours I'm working, I'm coming to believe that the older job was actually a better deal for me, not just financially but personally. It's funny how something you think will make your life better doesn't always do so. The good news is that my old employer wants to know if I'll come back. 10

7. The tone of this paragraph can best be described as

    a.   ironic.

    b.   forgiving.

    c.   tolerant.

    d.   ambivalent.

> The ice cream social, once an American summer ritual, has now gone the way of the black-and-white television screen. A few people still make ice cream at home, it's true, but most modern Americans who buy ice cream freezers choose a kind with an electric motor. What could they be thinking? Making ice cream ought to be a social event, and to ensure that it is one, people should invest in old- 5 fashioned hand-cranked ice cream freezers and do the job right.

8. The tone of this paragraph can best be described as

    a.   objective.

    b.   hesitant.

    c.   humorous.

    d.   nostalgic.

> One of the best films I've ever seen is Wes Anderson's *Rushmore*. The unlikely main character—a prep-school kid with ambitious dreams and almost nothing to back them up—doesn't win audiences over immediately; but by the end of the

(continued)

film, it's impossible not to root for him to succeed. Although Max's grand ambitions to be the most important pupil at Rushmore Academy and to have a future 5 with the beautiful widowed first-grade teacher come to nothing, the scaling back of his hopes to something a bit more realistic is not at all a downer. Max comes through with flying colors, and so does filmmaker and co-screenwriter Anderson.

Every detail of Anderson's involvement pays off. The excellent and surprising music choices—from Donovan's "Jersey Thursday" to the Who's "A Quick 10 One"—are just unfamiliar enough to make us really sit up and listen, and better still, they add something to what is happening onscreen. The cast is astonishingly good, from newcomer Jason Schwartzman as the geeky, overbearing, and completely unafraid Max to Bill Murray, who gives one of the best and most nuanced comic-tragic performances ever seen in film. The script, co-written by Anderson 15 and his frequent collaborator Owen Wilson, makes the characters and situations quirky enough to be interesting and three-dimensional enough to be believable. The character Max isn't exactly Every Adolescent, but we've probably all met— or been—teenagers who resemble him in some ways.

Rushmore wasn't a big box-office hit, but the reasons had nothing to do 20 with the quality of this extremely funny and winning film. I urge anyone who's interested in good movies to rush out to the video store and rent a copy now. Better yet, buy one—this film stands up to repeated viewings, and you'll want to show it to your friends.

9. What is the overall tone of this passage?

   a. enthusiastic

   b. objective

   c. tolerant

   d. mocking

My grandmother is one of the most gifted and well-rounded people I have ever met. I feel lucky to know her and I don't expect to meet her match very often as I get older. She seems to know how to do everything—and she still finds time to spend with me.

Grandma Anna knows how to catch a fish. She also knows how to make a 5 fishing pole, find bait, clean the fish, and cook it so that it tastes better than anything else I can imagine. Her fishing ability saved the whole family one hard autumn when her daddy was laid up with influenza. She says he taught her everything, and her skills with a line and pole kept her and her younger brothers fed.

She didn't have much formal education—she says nobody expected her to 10 need it. But when the next town got a library, my grandmother walked there once a week and took home all the books she could carry. She read aloud to her brothers, and she tells me that she just happens to have a really good memory. To this day, she can quote whole Shakespeare plays and reams of poems by authors from the Middle Ages to the Harlem Renaissance. When I was little, she used to 15 act out plays that she had learned by heart, reciting the lines and playing all the roles, while I helped her in her garden.

But the best thing of all about Grandma Anna is the pottery she makes in her woodshed. Nobody taught her how to do it—she just learned by trial and error. The pots she makes see a lot of hard use in the house and garden, but they 20 aren't just utensils. They are works of art that are even more beautiful because they are functional. Someday, she says she'll teach me how she does it. She says I just might have the right hands to make a good clay pot. I hope she's right; I would be very pleased to have even a fraction of her talent.

Grandma Anna has been helping my mother take care of me since I was a 25 baby. I feel lucky every day that I've gotten a chance to spend so much time with her and to learn a few of the many things she knows. I may not have Shakespeare memorized, but I plan to follow in Grandma Anna's footsteps as far as I am able.

10. The overall tone of this passage is

    a.   forgiving.

    b.   authoritative.

    c.   admiring.

    d.   impartial.

2.4A   DISTINGUISHING FACT FROM OPINION

What Is Fact and What Is Opinion?

Facts are based on observations, measurements, or research, and they can be verified or proved. **Opinions** express an attitude or a point of view about an idea, a situation, a person, a thing, or even a fact or set of facts; they cannot be completely proved or completely disproved the way a statement of fact can.

How Do You Distinguish Fact from Opinion?

Critical readers distinguish between facts, which can be used as evidence to support ideas, and opinions, which writers should support with facts or other evidence. Facts can be true or false. Opinions can be reasonable or unreasonable—but what is reasonable to one person may not be to another.

    The following chart will help you distinguish fact from opinion.

DISTINGUISHING BETWEEN FACT AND OPINION

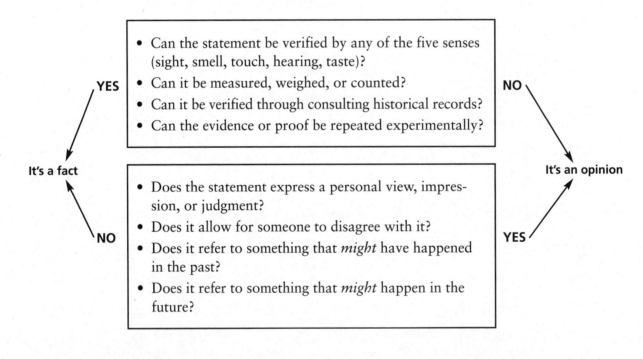

EXAMPLES

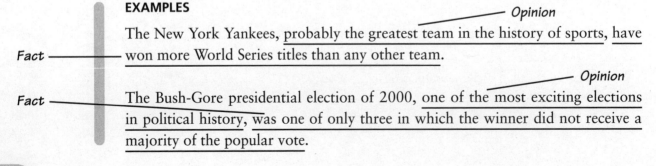

                                                            — *Opinion*

The New York Yankees, probably the greatest team in the history of sports, have

Fact — won more World Series titles than any other team.

                                                             — *Opinion*

Fact — The Bush-Gore presidential election of 2000, one of the most exciting elections in political history, was one of only three in which the winner did not receive a majority of the popular vote.

Note that opinions are often signaled by qualitative or judgment words (such as *bad*, *good*, *better*, *best*, *least*, *most*, and *worst*) or perception words (such as *feel* and *believe*).

Practice Distinguishing Fact from Opinion

Read the following essay and answer the questions about distinguishing fact from opinion. Answers and explanations appear on pp. 252–53.

The ice cream social, once an American summer ritual, has now gone the way of the black-and-white television screen. A few people still make ice cream at home, it's true, but most modern Americans who buy ice cream freezers choose a kind with an electric motor. What could they be thinking? Making ice cream ought to be a social event, and to ensure that it is one, people should invest in old-fashioned hand-cranked ice cream freezers to do the job right. [5]

Making ice cream by hand requires planning and sweat. Ice cream makers must procure good cream and cook it gently with sugar and vanilla beans (and, if they must, other flavorings like ripe peaches or even chocolate). Then they have to lay their hands on rock salt and plenty of ice. When the cream has been chilled, it's [10] time to gather strong-armed and strong-willed volunteers for the cranking, and then additional cranking, followed by more cranking. (This part of the process is best done out of doors because the melting ice trickles salty water down the sides of the machine.) After an eternity, when even the strongest muscles have been defeated by the task of turning the handle, the ice cream is finished—and, fittingly, [15] the hard work comes with a just reward: the best-tasting dessert on the planet.

In contrast, an ice cream freezer with a motor is child's play. One person alone can pour the ice cream mixture into the freezer. Then this lonely gourmet probably watches television in air-conditioned comfort while the infernal machine whirs away unattended on the kitchen counter. Where is the fun in that? [20] "It tastes the same," some deluded food critics have been known to declare, but they are wrong. Everyone knows that a prize that is earned is always more appealing than a prize that comes after little or no effort.

So let Americans everywhere pull the plugs on their sad electric ice cream freezers. Instead, they should be encouraged to get the real thing and gather [25] friends to celebrate one of the best warm-weather rituals there is. If they don't have enough friends to crank an ice cream freezer, they've probably been spending too much time alone—but anyone who invests in a hand-cranked ice cream freezer will assuredly attract a few more friends.

1. "'It tastes the same,' some deluded food critics have been known to declare, but they are wrong."
   This is a statement of

   a. fact.

   b. opinion.

2. "Everyone knows that a prize that is earned is always more appealing than a prize that comes after little or no effort."

This is a statement of

a. fact.

b. opinion.

3. "More disgusting is the deliberate use of bland or meaningless phrases to describe horrors, as when officials report 'collateral damage' to disguise the deaths of innocent civilians."

This is a statement of

a. fact.

b. opinion.

4. "If you ask a roomful of English teachers to explain the meaning of a sentence in another English professor's article and no one can define either the point of the sentence or the meaning of words in it without a dictionary, then the sentence isn't brilliantly analyzing literature—it's just plain bad."

This is a statement of

a. fact.

b. opinion.

5. Which sentence is a statement of opinion?

a. "Psychologists have induced experimental subjects to form similar taste aversions to food."

b. "To test the idea that some fears may be ingrained, psychologists have tried to condition certain volunteers to fear harmless objects."

c. "Taste aversion, then, may be an ancient biological safety mechanism."

d. "Nevertheless, most psychologists believe that human genes do program even modern people toward developing age-old aversions and phobias."

6. "Experimental subjects saw pictures of flowers and then experienced a mild electric shock."

This is a statement of

a. fact.

b. opinion.

7. "A less welcoming café than the one van Gogh portrays in this painting is difficult to imagine."

This is a statement of

a. fact.

b. opinion.

8. "At the bottom of the painting is an empty expanse of pale yellow floorboards leading back to the billiard table and the red, red walls."
    This is a statement of

a.   fact.

b.   opinion.

9. "People would find time for voting if they cared strongly about it, especially when the polls are open from six a.m. to nine p.m. and the process takes only a few minutes."
    This is a statement of

a.   fact.

b.   opinion.

10. "As the past few decades in the United States have demonstrated, fewer and fewer eligible citizens are going to the polls in this country."
    This is a statement of

a.   fact.

b.   opinion.

2.4B   DRAWING INFERENCES AND CONCLUSIONS

What Are Inferences and Conclusions?

An **inference** is an educated guess about the meaning and significance of details and connections, based on observation and knowledge—"reading between the lines." When readers make connections among inferences, they form a **conclusion**—an overall impression of what a particular reading means.

EXAMPLE

Inference

Boston has Heartbreak at mile 21. Bloomsday has Cemetery and Doomsday. The San Blas Half-Marathon has The Strangler. Apparently, just plain running isn't tough enough. So race directors, in their infinite wisdom, have decided we need hills. Big ones. And if they have sadistic-sounding names, so much the better.

The first paragraph begins with examples, but the writer does not say of what. What can you infer that Heartbreak, Cemetery, Doomsday, and The Strangler are?

They are hills. The end of the passage refers to hills with sadistic-sounding names. Heartbreak, Cemetery, Doomsday, and The Strangler are all sadistic-sounding names, so we can infer that they apply to hills.

EXAMPLE

Conclusion

Every society trades goods with its neighbors, often as symbols of mutual good will. Civilizations, however, typically conduct large-scale trading operations at great distances.

From these sentences, is it reasonable to conclude that the authors use the terms *society* and *civilizations* to mean the same thing? Why or why not?

> No. The author attributes different levels of one behavior, trading, to them, so we can infer that the actors differ. Also, the use of "however" indicates a contrast to some or all of the preceding statement.

How Do You Draw Inferences and Conclusions from Readings?

1. Read carefully. Pay special attention to the language. What impressions does it seem to be trying to make on the reader?

2. Make a mental leap from what you know, based on your reading or other sources or on your own experiences, to what you do not know absolutely—what the text appears to be saying to readers. This leap is an inference.

3. Collect inferences from a reading selection and see where they lead you.

4. Modify inferences or conclusions if the reading does not seem to support the inferences or conclusions you first developed.

EXAMPLE

Inference: Snakes, spiders, heights, and small enclosed places usually aren't very dangerous.

Conclusion: Fears aren't very rational.

Psychologist Martin Seligman noticed that phobias seem to be quite selective. Extreme, irrational fears of snakes, spiders, heights, and small enclosed places . . . are relatively common. But very few people are phobic of stairs, ladders, electrical outlets or appliances, or sharp objects, even though these things are far more likely to be associated with traumatic experiences or accidents. 5

Practice Drawing Inferences and Conclusions from Readings

Read the following passages and answer the questions about inferences and conclusions. Answers and explanations appear on pp. 253–55.

Most Americans are familiar with spaghetti and macaroni, the most popular pasta shapes in the United States, and children may have eaten pasta shape like favorite cartoon characters. But traditional Italian pasta comes in almost as many shapes as cartoons do. In all its variety, pasta can offer a feast for the imagination.

Indeed, imaginative names and shapes are plentiful in pastas available in 5 neighborhoods in Italy. Traditional pastas include shapes named for almost anything; some popular categories include household articles, creatures, and body parts. Pastas are named for thimbles (*ditali*), ribbons (*fetucce*), and radiators (*radiatore*). They resemble little worms (*vermicelli*), conch shells (*conchiglie*), melon seeds (*semi de melone*) or butterflies (*farfalle*). Some even take the shape of ears 10 (*orecchiette*) and moustaches (*mostaccioli*).

Pasta lovers who want to try new things can avail themselves of four basic types of pasta. These four include long pastas such as *linguine* (which means "little tongues") that are often tossed with sauces; hollow pasta tubes like *ziti* (which means "bridegrooms") that can be baked; tiny pastas such as *acini di peppe* 15 (which means "peppercorns") intended for soups; and specialty pastas like *mani-*

cotti (which means "little muffs") that are often stuffed with cheese or other fillings. Cooks in Italy use these different types to ensure variety in the pasta courses of their meals, and more and more Americans are also enjoying the discovery of pasta novelty. 20

While spaghetti and meatballs or macaroni and cheese may continue to be the leading pasta choices in U.S. homes, spaghetti and macaroni are no longer the only shapes of pasta available in grocery stores in this country. American diners, always fond of their pasta, now have access to an abundance of exotic pasta shapes and sizes. 25

1. A conclusion that can be drawn from this passage is that

   a. many Americans are unaware of the different varieties of pasta.

   b. Italian pasta is falling out of favor with consumers.

   c. pasta is by far the most popular American food.

   d. pasta shapes are most often named after creatures and body parts.

2. A conclusion that can be drawn from this passage is that

   a. macaroni and cheese is a poor choice for dinner.

   b. a great variety of shapes of pasta has not always been available in U.S. markets.

   c. Americans who choose macaroni or spaghetti for pasta are not creative people.

   d. Americans should eat more pasta.

3. What does the following sentence suggest about English teachers?

   "If you ask a roomful of English teachers to explain the meaning of a sentence in another English professor's article and no one can define either the point of the sentence or the meaning of words in it without a dictionary, then the sentence in question isn't brilliantly analyzing literature—it's just plain bad."

   a. English teachers are more intelligent than science teachers.

   b. English teachers generally enjoy judging each other's writing.

   c. English teachers, by virtue of their background, are good judges of writing.

   d. English teachers often write incomprehensibly despite their training.

The final, and most important, type of misleading communication is political and military jargon. Political leaders manipulate buzzwords designed to make the policies of their political party look good and those of the other party look foolish or evil. When you develop the critical ear to recognize these attempts to use emotional language to confuse and mislead, you take the first step toward being able to resist and think for yourself. More disgusting is the deliberate use of 5

(continued)

bland or meaningless phrases to describe horrors, as when officials report "collateral damage" to disguise the deaths of innocent civilians. Whether the language is hiding terrible things with boring phrases or whipping up emotions to confuse listeners, the best defense is recognizing the cover-up for what it is.   10

4. A conclusion that can be drawn from this paragraph is that
   a. no politicians can be trusted.
   b. politicians sometimes use "dirty tactics" and misrepresent the truth.
   c. politicians use misleading communication more often than military leaders.
   d. cover-ups are most often used by the military.

The ice cream social, once an American summer ritual, has now gone the way of the black-and-white television screen. A few people still make ice cream at home, it's true, but most modern Americans who buy ice cream freezers choose a kind with an electric motor. What could they be thinking? Making ice cream ought to be a social event, and to ensure that it is one, people should invest in old-   5 fashioned hand-cranked ice cream freezers and do the job right.

5. A conclusion that can be drawn from this paragraph is that
   a. modern methods are inferior to old-fashioned methods.
   b. it is always better to socialize rather than do things alone.
   c. a hand-cranked ice cream freezer requires group effort.
   d. black-and-white televisions should be more popular.

6. What does the following sentence suggest about ice cream flavors?

   "The ice cream makers must procure good cream and cook it gently with sugar and vanilla beans (and, if they must, other flavorings like ripe peaches or even chocolate)."

   a. Vanilla ice cream is the best.
   b. Peach ice cream is the best flavor but only when made with ripe peaches.
   c. Vanilla, peach, and chocolate ice cream are all equally good.
   d. The author has no strong preference when it comes to choosing ice cream flavors.

Coal fires require little oxygen to smolder, and those that ignite veins of ore in underground mines are notoriously difficult to put out. Underground coal fires may burn for years and do extensive damage. The fires are surprisingly common in coal-mining parts of the United States; thirty-six are currently burning in Pennsylvania. The worst of these fires is under the town—or former town—of   5 Centralia.

Centralia had about eleven hundred residents in 1962, many of whom worked in the coal mines nearby. When the town burned its garbage at the local dump that May, the fire surprised everyone by burning for a month. Then, workers clearing away the debris discovered that the trash fire had ignited a coal vein 10 near the surface. An underground coal fire was underway.

According to Centralia's current mayor, Lamar Mervine, no one did anything about the fire for several months. Later, locals used material on hand—fly ash from burned coal—to try to smother the fire. It didn't work. Coal fires are hard to smother because mines usually have many airways and tunnels, and coal 15 needs only about a tenth as much oxygen as is found in air in order to keep burning. Coal fires in mines also tend to burn hottest in the ceilings of the tunnels, meaning that the entire tunnel needs to be filled to the brim to smother the fire.

The arrangement of Centralia's coal veins, which veer down from the surface at angles as steep as sixty degrees, also worked against the firefighters. Dig- 20 ging a hole deep enough to get underneath the fire was simply not possible after it had been burning for some time. Locals eventually dug a trench to try to contain the fire, but it had spread faster and farther than anyone realized and had already moved beyond the trench.

The blaze continued unhindered for twenty-one years. Then, in 1983, part 25 of Route 61—a major roadway south of Centralia—collapsed from the effects of the fire under it. The cracked and smoldering section of road was permanently closed. On investigation, the U.S. Office of Surface Mining determined that putting out the fire would cost 663 million dollars. The government chose the cheaper alternative: it paid the people of Centralia to leave the area. Only about 30 twenty citizens remain in town today.

The biggest thing in Centralia now is the coal fire. It covers about 1.8 square kilometers, above which the ground is hot to the touch. Some geologists estimate that the coal near the fire takes up another twelve square kilometers. With that much fuel, the fire is expected to burn for another 100 to 250 years. 35

7. A conclusion that can be drawn from paragraph 5 is that

   a. there was major above-ground damage during the first twenty-one years of the Centralia coal fire.

   b. the twenty people who remain in Centralia are choosing to risk loss of life or livelihood.

   c. the U.S. government wanted to restore the town of Centralia regardless of the expense.

   d. Route 61 will never be rebuilt.

8. A conclusion that can be drawn from this passage is that

  a. the citizens of Centralia initially did nothing about the fire for several months because they didn't care.

  b. the citizens of Centralia were initially unaware of the seriousness of the situation.

  c. the citizens of Centralia were thrilled with the government's offer to pay them to relocate.

  d. the citizens of Centralia were devastated to have to leave.

I was tremendously grateful to get a letter telling me that I'd been turned down for financial aid from the college I had planned to attend in the fall. What a lucky break for me! Now I get to pay for everything myself. The school expects my parents to pay my tuition and expenses. I guess the administrators missed the part of my application where I explained that my father was laid off from work   5
two years ago and that he hasn't found steady employment since. Maybe they also failed to notice that my mother is working two part-time jobs to pay the rent, and that my little brother and I have been working for whoever would hire us every summer and on weekends. Boy, will the whole family be delighted to learn that we have plenty of money for my tuition and books!   10

   With this stroke of good fortune, I might even be able to take a year off from school, just like those kids I've heard about who spend a few months back-packing around Europe before they start college. Backpacking doesn't really ap-peal to me, but that's okay—I'm not a strong enough swimmer to get to Europe anyway. Maybe I'll spend this leisure time doing something really rewarding, like   15
helping others. Yes, that's it. I'll help others super-size their orders, and I'll be sure to ask if they want fries on the side.

9. What does the first sentence of the passage suggest about the speaker's real feelings about his application for financial aid?

  a. The student is genuinely happy to find out he wouldn't be receiving financial aid.

  b. The student would rather go backpacking than attend school.

  c. The student had supplied a false financial statement trying to qualify for financial aid.

  d. The student is being sarcastic and is disappointed about not getting financial aid.

10. A conclusion that can be drawn from this passage is that

  a. the family is struggling to make ends meet.

  b. the father has not seriously been looking for employment.

  c. the mother is unable to find a full-time job.

  d. the children work after school as well as on weekends.

2.4C ASSESSING SUPPORT FOR REASONING

What Is Support?

Support includes facts, reasons, examples, and details that show, explain, or prove the writer's main point. Effective support turns a statement of opinion into a convincing argument.

EXAMPLE

Topic sentence

Support for "amazing evolution of computers"

Support for "amazing evolution in music"

The amazing evolution of computers over the last twenty years has allowed for an equally amazing evolution in music. Today electronic music can be produced on a home computer, using sequencer software to record, edit, and reproduce digital sounds in patterns and sequences at will. Advanced synthesizers now produce their stuff in real time (as the simpler synthesizers of popular music have been doing for years). They can interact via computer with live musicians as they perform, to produce today's cutting-edge interactive computer music. (Joseph Kerman and Gary Tomlinson, with Vivian Kerman, *Listen*)

How Do You Assess Support?

Support is evidence; it is more specific than the general idea being developed. Supporting details, both major and minor, include whatever evidence the writer introduces to back up the main point. Major support usually introduces an example, an idea, or a reason that relates directly to the topic sentence of a paragraph or the thesis statement of an essay. Minor support explains and clarifies the major support.

Good support has the following features:

- It relates to the main point the writer is making.
- It considers the readers that it aims to convince.
- It is detailed and specific enough to be easy to understand.

Such support is said to be **adequate**. The following example illustrates adequate support.

EXAMPLE

Topic sentence

Support for topic sentence

Drama languished in Europe after the fall of Rome during the fifth and sixth centuries. From about 400 CE to 900 CE almost no record of dramatic productions exists except for those of minstrels and other entertainers, such as acrobats and jugglers, who traveled through the countryside. The Catholic church was instrumental in suppressing drama because the theater—represented by the excesses of Roman productions—was seen as subversive. No state-sponsored festivals brought people together in huge theaters the way they had in Greek and Roman times. (Michael Meyer, *The Bedford Introduction to Literature*)

The second sentence relates to the topic sentence by showing how drama languished. It addresses readers interested in hearing about the decline of drama after the fall of Rome and offers details—"minstrels and other entertainers, such as acrobats and jugglers."

Now consider this next passage.

> **EXAMPLE**
>
> Last year's employee training program succeeded for three reasons: all of the managers supported it, all of them provided adequate training to their staff members, and managers followed up with employees later to make sure they really understood the tasks. Managers were able to provide sufficient training and follow-up because they were given the funds to do so. The result was big savings for 5 the company.

The writer begins by stating that the training program succeeded for three reasons, and she goes on to provide **adequate support** for that statement by specifying the reasons and providing details about them. But take a look at the last sentence. What proof is there that the program provided "big savings"? This statement is **inadequately supported**, and it needs to be backed by evidence like the underlined sentence in the next example.

> **EXAMPLE**
>
> Last year's employee training program succeeded for three reasons: all of the managers supported it, all of them provided adequate training to their staff members, and managers followed up with employees later to make sure they really understood the tasks. Managers were able to provide sufficient training and follow-up because they were given the funds to do so. The result was big savings for 5 the company. <u>Though training costs increased, worker productivity and efficiency improved, saving the company an estimated $100,000 last year.</u>

Practice Assessing Support

Read the following essay and answer the questions about assessing support. Answers and explanations appear on p. 255.

> The question of who owns intellectual property such as literature, symbols, images, and ideas frequently ends up being answered in court. Does Pepperidge Farm own the idea of fish-shaped, cheese-flavored crackers? Does the yoga master who invented a method of teaching yoga in a very hot room own the technique? These and other questions have been the subject of recent legal discussion. 5 As a result of intellectual property disputes, certain ideas and symbols become unavailable for public use—a trend that ultimately punishes all Americans.
>
>   The cases of the cracker company and the yoga teacher share a theme: the originator—or at least popularizer—of an idea, image, or symbol wants to limit or prevent others' use of it. Pepperidge Farm wants to restrict competitors from 10 selling a similar product, and the yoga master wants to prevent rivals from bene-

fiting from his idea. The benefits to Pepperidge Farm and the yoga teacher are clear if courts rule in their favor, but it is equally clear that consumers will gain nothing from allowing corporations and individuals to copyright such intellectual property.   15

Limiting competition among rivals limits the choices available to consumers. If only one fish-shaped cheese cracker is allowed on the market, the price may be higher than it would be if the cracker had a close competitor, and consumers are denied the decision of which cracker is more appealing. If one yoga master controls the use of a technique, consumers may have to pay more for classes under   20 instructors who have paid for a license from the original master; in addition, yoga teachers might be prevented from introducing changes to the technique that would appeal to some customers.

This last effect is, in fact, the worst problem with granting ownership of ideas and images to one company or individual: if one party owns them, others   25 are prevented from building on them or using them in innovative ways. The result may be a limit on creativity. The point of competition, after all, is to ensure that the best ideas win. If only one corporation or person is allowed to compete in a given area, there is no way for the best idea to succeed and no incentive to improve an idea.   30

For the good of American consumers, artists, entrepreneurs, and others, ideas should remain free. If ideas and symbols are owned by anyone with enough money and legal clout to copyright them and order others not to use them, everyone suffers.

1. The author's claim that "Limiting competition among rivals limits the choices available to consumers" is

   a.   adequately supported by personal experience and strongly held opinion.

   b.   inadequately supported by the lack of factual evidence.

2. Which statement offers the best support for the author's claim that "As a result of intellectual property disputes, certain ideas and symbols become unavailable for public use—a trend that ultimately punishes all Americans"?

   a.   Pepperidge Farm wants to control the cracker market by restricting competitors from selling products that resemble its own.

   b.   Ideas and symbols can be owned by those who are able to copyright them.

   c.   Yoga can be a very expensive hobby.

   d.   Creativity and consumer choices can be limited when ownership of intellectual property is permitted.

When is communication not really communication? This may sound like a joke, but the answer—"when it tries to conceal rather than to convey information"—isn't very funny. Communication that is really a cover-up aims to confuse or even intimidate an audience. If you can recognize communication cover-ups, you will be less likely to be taken in by incomprehensible or misleading language. 5

One type of misleading communication is bad academic writing. In fact, academic jargon probably sets the gold standard for the most incomprehensible writing anywhere. If you ask a roomful of English teachers to explain the meaning of a sentence in another English professor's article and no one can define either the point of the sentence or the meaning of words in it without a dictionary, 10 then the sentence in question isn't brilliantly analyzing literature—it's just plain bad. The purpose of this kind of cover-up is simple: to disguise mundane ideas as innovative and to prevent readers from recognizing what is really being said.

Another type of confusing communication is business language, which slips into mindless jargon far too often and at other times is used to cover up bad 15 business practices and greed. Whether or not you've ever worked for a corporation, you have probably encountered clichés like "on the same page" and "vision statement." This kind of bloated, self-important jargon serves no purpose other than making insiders feel like insiders (and outsiders feel like outsiders). Even worse are new creations such as "rightsizing" (another word for "downsizing"), 20 which gloss over the fact that employees are losing their jobs while implying that the jobs were unnecessary in the first place. When businesses use language to hide things, let the listener beware.

The final, and most important, type of misleading communication is political and military jargon. Political leaders manipulate buzzwords designed to make 25 the policies of their political party look good and those of the other party look foolish or evil. When you develop the critical ear to recognize these attempts to use emotional language to confuse and mislead, you take the first step toward being able to resist and think for yourself. More disgusting is the deliberate use of bland or meaningless phrases to describe horrors, as when officials report 30 "collateral damage" to disguise the deaths of innocent civilians. Whether the language is hiding terrible things with boring phrases or whipping up emotions to confuse listeners, the best defense is recognizing the cover-up for what it is.

English is a complex language that offers speakers and writers many different ways to say something. Some people choose to communicate clearly, and 35 some deliberately choose not to. If you become aware of the common types of misleading communication, you will be less likely to fall for mindless and confusing constructions—and less likely to mangle the language by using them yourself.

3. The author's claim, in lines 3 and 4, that "Communication that is really a cover-up aims to confuse or even intimidate an audience" is

   a. adequately supported with relevant details and examples.

   b. inadequately supported based on strong personal opinion.

4. The author's claim, in lines 29–31, that "More disgusting is the deliberate use of bland or meaningless phrases to describe the horrors, as when officials report 'collateral damage' to disguise the deaths of innocent civilians" is

   a. adequately supported by factual details.

   b. inadequately supported based on strong personal opinion.

Many medical tests are very effective at assisting doctors in diagnosing ailments and diseases early, when they can still be treated effectively. Some of these tests are recommended for most adults at certain stages of life—tests for certain cancers, for example. One new type of test, the full-body scan, has been heavily promoted as a way for patients to discover problems in any part of the body before   5 symptoms arise. But experts argue that full-body scans may do more harm than good.

In a full-body scan, radiation provides detailed images of the body's interior organs and systems. The procedure is painless and noninvasive. Many people who are concerned about their health are eager to undergo full-body scans to set   10 their minds at ease, and the procedure is becoming increasingly common. Patients often seek out scans without being referred by a doctor; in this case, they pay for the scans, which are rarely covered by insurance.

Patients obviously want the results of the scan to be negative. If the scan does discover some problem, they want to find out all that they can about the   15 problem so that it can be resolved. However, the results of full-body scans are often false positives—indications of health problems that turn out to be nothing. Before the frightened patient learns that she doesn't have a tumor, she has to suffer the trauma of believing that she may be about to die; then she must undergo uncomfortable, possibly dangerous procedures to discover that there is no tumor.   20 Unnecessary surgery, like necessary surgery, always carries the risk of serious complications including death. In addition, it is expensive. For people covered by insurance, the out-of-pocket expenses may not be high, but the insurance companies pass the higher costs on to other customers in the form of increased rates.

Medical professionals also point out that high doses of radiation are in-   25 volved in any scan. A full-body scan, which affects much more tissue than a typical CAT scan, exposes a body to considerably higher amounts of radiation than a standard X-ray does. Thus, a man who undergoes an annual scan may actually increase his risk of developing a tumor. Even though the full-body scan procedure may not cause problems for patients, health experts urge all people to limit   30 their voluntary exposure to radiation.   *(continued)*

Patients should take responsibility for keeping an eye on their health, most doctors agree. But according to many physicians, undergoing a full-body scan merely gives people the impression that they are taking charge of their lives. A better, and cheaper, alternative is to follow the recommendations of a doctor the patient knows and trusts.   35

5. Which statement offers the best support for the author's claim, in lines 14–16, that "If the scan does discover some problem, they want to find out all that they can about the problem so that it can be resolved."

   a.   Patients tend to ignore symptoms that could indicate serious health problems.

   b.   Patients sometimes undergo unnecessary surgery to follow up on test results.

   c.   Patients do not always have full confidence in their doctors and, as a result, like to take matters into their own hands.

   d.   Full-body scans, when perfected, may replace examinations by physicians.

6. The author's claim that "Experts argue that full-body scans may do more harm than good" is

   a.   adequately supported with relevant details.

   b.   inadequately supported lacking evidence and explanation.

The Coriolis force, named for the nineteenth-century French mathematician Gaspard de Coriolis, refers to the way Earth's rotation influences moving objects. Coriolis first described the force to explain why prevailing winds on Earth move in curved rather than straight lines. The Coriolis force also explains why hurricanes above the equator rotate counterclockwise and those below the equator   5
move clockwise. Because it works only on a large scale, however, the Coriolis force has almost no effect on one phenomenon with which it is often incorrectly linked: the direction water circles before flowing down a drain.

Here's the myth: in the Northern Hemisphere, water always circles counterclockwise before draining out of the bathtub, sink, or toilet and water in the   10
Southern Hemisphere moves clockwise. The same myth claims that water does not circle at all when the toilet, tub, or sink is directly over the equator. (To make matters even more confusing, some of these false claims even get the direction of the Coriolis force wrong, stating that the tub or toilet in the Northern Hemisphere is the clockwise one.) The physical facts are not nearly as intriguing or as   15
simple as this false "fun fact," which makes it difficult for scientists to convince the public that the toilet-water story has been definitively known to be false for several decades.

In any case, here's the truth: the size of the Coriolis force is so negligible in a sink, toilet, or bathtub that other forces have much more power to influence the   20 direction of water going down the drain. The direction of water flowing out of a relatively small container is affected most by the direction the water was traveling as it entered. If water flows in clockwise, it is likely to retain the clockwise motion as it swirls out, and vice versa. The direction can also be influenced by the movement of pulling out the plug and by the shape of the container. 25

Since the general public has no monopoly on wondering why water swirls out of toilets in a certain direction, scientists have, not surprisingly, studied the Coriolis force in small containers. However, in a 1962 experiment at the Massachusetts Institute of Technology, researcher Ascher Shapiro filled a six-foot circular tank six inches deep with the water entering clockwise. He covered the tank 30 to prevent disturbances from outside, kept the temperature constant, and waited. When he pulled the plug after two hours, the water drained out clockwise, presumably because it retained some of the motion from the clockwise filling. However, after twenty-four hours the water swirled completely counterclockwise as Shapiro drained it, in keeping with the direction of the Coriolis force in the 35 Northern Hemisphere.

Shapiro's experiment of more than forty years ago and people's general observations of the drains they encounter daily have not yet laid to rest the myth that water always drains counterclockwise in the Northern Hemisphere and clockwise in the Southern Hemisphere. The Coriolis force is real, but it shows up 40 most readily in hurricanes, not in toilets.

7. The author's claim that "Since the general public has no monopoly on wondering why water swirls out of toilets in a certain direction, scientists have, not surprisingly, studied the Coriolis force in small containers" is

    a.   adequately supported with factual evidence.

    b.   inadequately supported based on personal experience and strongly held opinion.

8. Which statement offers the best support for the author's claim that "Because it works only on a large scale, however, the Coriolis force has almost no effect on one phenomenon with which it is often incorrectly linked: the direction water circles before flowing down a drain."?

    a.   The general public has difficulty understanding complex scientific theories.

    b.   The Coriolis force does not apply to bathtubs, sinks, and toilets because they are all in the Northern Hemisphere.

    c.   Results of scientific experiments such as Ascher Shapiro's gave evidence as to the forces at work in larger containers.

    d.   The Coriolis force was significant in the nineteenth century but is no longer in effect.

Are humans biologically inclined to develop certain kinds of fears and aversions? Evolution may well have prepared human beings to learn very quickly to avoid foods that seem to cause illness and to fear objects and situations that would have threatened people in prehistoric times.

Taste aversions provide an interesting example of possible biological hard-wiring. When a teenager eats a whole bag of her favorite treat, cinnamon jelly beans, one afternoon and then wakes up the following morning with a nasty stomach virus, she may find that her former favorite now repulses her and that it will be years—maybe even a lifetime—before she can stand to eat cinnamon jelly beans again. Even knowing that a stomach flu was going around and that the jelly beans didn't make her sick probably won't enable that teen to enjoy the candy again. Many people have similar taste aversions as a result of a single unpleasant instance.

Psychologists have induced experimental subjects to form similar taste aversions to foods. Taste aversion, then, may be an ancient biological safety mechanism. Prehistoric humans learned what not to eat by experiment. Those who were sickened by a meal and then refused to eat the food again were more likely to pass along genetically useful information: nausea is a warning to avoid that food in the future. Modern humans' minds may accept that the food didn't cause the problem, but their bodies—acting on information passed down for millennia—don't believe it.

Fears also appear to have a biological component. Many people don't need to be taught to fear snakes, for instance. A small child who finds a snake is more likely to run away than to snatch up the reptile. In the United States, at least, the chances are good that the snake is harmless, but even a child who knows that the creature is a common garter snake instead of a poisonous rattler may resist moving toward it. Logic apparently has little to do with many fearful reactions. Cars, which injure many more people than snakes do, rarely inspire phobias.

To test the idea that some fears may be ingrained, psychologists have tried to condition volunteers to fear harmless objects. Experimental subjects saw pictures of flowers and then experienced a mild electric shock. No one was eventually trained to fear daffodils in this experiment; but a similar experiment, in which the subjects saw photographs of spiders instead of flowers, did result in the subjects' increased fear of the eight-legged creatures. Clearly, humans are programmed to be more afraid of some things than of others. Creatures and situations that might have frightened prehistoric people are more likely to cause irrational phobias than are items like cars that ancient humans did not encounter.

Biological information, over which people have no control, does not determine everything about what humans avoid and fear. Obviously, humans today are more than just updated cave dwellers. Nevertheless, most psychologists believe that human genes do program even modern people toward developing age-old aversions and phobias.

9. Which statement offers the best support for the author's claim, in line 22, that "Fears also appear to have a biological component."?

    a. Psychologists conducted experiments using flowers and electric shock.

    b. Food aversions are primarily based on trial-and-error experimentation.

    c. Human beings are generally not fearful of automobiles.

    d. A small child who finds a snake is more likely to run away than to snatch up the reptile.

10. The author's claim, in lines 2–4, that "Evolution may well have prepared human beings to learn very quickly to avoid foods that seem to cause illness and to fear objects and situations that would have threatened people in prehistoric times" is

    a. adequately supported with factual evidence and examples.

    b. inadequately supported based on strong personal opinion.

3 Mastering the Writing Test

3.1 Main Idea, Support, and Structure

3.1A IDENTIFYING THESIS STATEMENTS AND TOPIC SENTENCES

What Are Thesis Statements and Topic Sentences?

The **main idea** of a paragraph or essay is the most important point the author is trying to get across, and often it summarizes key points of a piece of writing. You can also think of the main idea as the most general idea the author is presenting about a topic.

The main idea of an essay occurs in the **thesis statement,** which is the foundation on which the paragraphs that support the thesis are built. The thesis statement can be expressed in a single sentence, but sometimes a writer uses two or more sentences to convey the overall point. A thesis statement is sometimes implied instead of stated directly.

The main idea of a paragraph is usually in a **topic sentence** to which all the other sentences in the paragraph relate. The topic sentence is usually the most general sentence in the paragraph.

EXAMPLE

Thesis statement —— More and more smokers today are aware of the serious risks smoking poses for themselves and for the nonsmokers around them. Many of them would like to quit but just do not think they can. However, several strategies can help smokers achieve this goal.

Topic sentence —— The first and easiest strategy is to substitute something for the cigarette that they have become used to holding. Some people use a pencil, a straw, or a coin. I have a friend who started using a Japanese fan. There are even special products available to keep people's hands busy, such as worry beads and small rubber balls. Almost any small object can work.

Topic sentence —— Next, people who quit smoking need to substitute something for the stimulation they get from cigarettes. They might chew a strongly flavored sugarless gum, for example, or take fast, short breaths. Other people splash their faces with ice cold water or do some light exercise. Some even claim that standing on their heads has helped. The point is to find something that gives a physical jolt to the system.

(continued)

Topic sentence — A third strategy is to change habits associated with smoking. For example, people who associate cigarettes with drinking coffee might temporarily switch to tea or another beverage with caffeine, and people who generally smoke while talking on the telephone might try sending e-mail instead. Unfortunately, some smoking-associated activities are difficult to eliminate. People who associate smoking with being in their cars obviously cannot give up driving. The point, though, is to alter as many habits as possible to eliminate situations in which one would normally reach for a cigarette.

Topic sentence — Finally, most people who successfully quit smoking prepare themselves to resist temptation in moments of stress or discomfort. Rather than reaching for a cigarette, they have another sort of treat ready for themselves. Some people, understandably, choose candy or sweets of some kind, but these are not the best alternatives, for obvious reasons. A better idea is to use the money saved by not buying cigarettes to purchase something to pamper oneself with, such as expensive cologne or a personal CD player.

No one would say that it is easy to quit smoking, but this fact should not keep people from recognizing that they can kick the habit. These four antismoking strategies have worked for many ex-smokers, who recommend them highly.

How Do You Identify Effective Thesis Statements and Topic Sentences?

A good thesis statement or topic sentence is general enough to be supported with specific examples, but not so general that it is vague; it does not simply announce the topic, but says something interesting about the topic; and it is not a fact or an obvious statement that most or all readers would immediately agree with.

EXAMPLES

General	Working mothers are busy.
Specific	Most working mothers suffer from exhaustion and a lack of time for themselves.
Specific	Many working mothers need to plan every minute of their day.
Forceful	Students are tempted to cheat when they run out of time and become desperate.
Weak	In this paragraph, I will talk about cheating.
Forceful	Eighty percent of high school students admit to having cheated at least once.
Obvious	Many people visit Disney World.
Better	People of all ages have fun at Disney World.

Fact	The state of Florida has no income tax.
Better	Many retired people on fixed incomes move to Florida because it has no income tax.

Clearly, a good thesis statement or topic sentence does not make an assertion that is not supported by the rest of the writing.

If, on the test, you cannot readily identify the best main-idea statement, eliminate statements that are too broad or narrow, that merely state a fact, or that clearly aren't supported by the rest of the passage.

Practice Identifying Effective Thesis Statements and Topic Sentences

Each sentence in the following passages has been given a number. Read the passages carefully and then answer the questions, which refer to sentences by number. Answers and explanations appear on pp. 255–56.

1. The last original-design Volkswagen Beetle was manufactured in Puebla, Mexico, on July 30, 2003. **2.** _____. **3.** Volkswagen started as the "people's car" in Germany in the 1930s, and the low-priced, mass-produced car quickly became popular. **4.** For one thing, mechanically it was simple enough that many drivers could do repairs themselves. **5.** The original Beetle had drawbacks: it was both cramped and noisy, with the engine in the rear compartment drowning out most other sounds inside the car. **6.** _____, as the young VW bug drivers of the 1960s grew older and more prosperous, they left the cars behind. **7.** It was also much smaller and more lightweight than many other vehicles and consequently more dangerous to its occupants in a crash. **8.** The low cost of the car and its very basic engine also appealed to members of the 1960s counterculture; hippies, artists, students, and many others of limited money adopted the "love bug." **9.** However, many retained a nostalgic fondness for the Beetle, in spite—or perhaps because—of its flaws. **10.** Volkswagen stopped making the cars in Europe and the United States in the 1970s. **11.** Because of the car's importance in Mexico, however, the Puebla factory remained open. **12.** The car was called a _vocho_ in Mexico. **13.** At last, however, Volkswagen recognized that the original bug's design, much the same as it had been sixty years earlier, was obsolete. **14.** The final car rolled out of the factory, and the Beetle's era was officially over.

1. Which statement, if inserted into blank 2, would provide the best thesis statement for the entire passage?

   a. The Volkswagen Beetle is a very popular car and loved by many.

   b. The car's long history and its strong cultural associations ensured that many in North America and Europe mourned its disappearance.

   c. Although the VW was popular, it had its drawbacks.

   d. The VW began in Germany.

1. _____. **2.** Bartering is the exchange of goods or services that have approximately the same value. **3.** Individuals sometimes barter, as two of my neighbors did recently. **4.** Jonathan, a fine artist who also paints houses for extra income, agreed to paint Shamila's garage in exchange for her putting up his Web site and scanning images of his artwork. **5.** Jonathan has no expertise with computers, so he could not create the Web site himself. **6.** The barter arrangement suited both of them, each offering special skills to do an expert job for the other. **7.** They agreed that each had spent about the same amount of time on his or her project. **8.** _____, neither of them had had to lay out any cash to have the work done. **9.** Business bartering works much like bartered exchanges between individuals, but on a larger scale. **10.** For any business or individual with skills or goods that are not being fully used, the barter system might be a lifesaver.

2. Which statement, if inserted into blank 1, would provide the best thesis statement for the entire passage?

   a.   The barter system has many negative effects.

   b.   Bartering allows for many benefits, but the drawbacks outweigh them.

   c.   The barter system can be an effective way for individuals and businesses to get what they need from others without using cash or credit.

   d.   Since the beginning of time, bartering has been a system used to gain access to goods.

1. _____. **2.** The origin of this arrangement of massive stones in southern England has intrigued scholars for centuries. **3.** One common misconception, that Stonehenge was designed as a Druid temple, is demonstrably false. **4.** The carbon dating of digging tools found at the oldest part of the site, a circular outer ditch, shows that it was created about five thousand years ago, before 3000 BCE. **5.** Most scholars believe that work on this second phase occurred between 2800 and 2200 BCE. **6.** The final part of the monument, the ring of eighty smaller outer stones, was probably completed about 1100 BCE. **7.** During the second phase of the monument's construction, the largest stones—including the thirty-five-ton "heel stone" and other parts of the central rectangle—were put in place. **8.** Since Druids did not appear in the area until sometime around twenty-five hundred years ago, they could not have planned or built the site. **9.** But if Stonehenge isn't a Druid temple, what is it? **10.** The simple answer is that it appears to be a calendar. **11.** Of course, it did not have pages and numbers. **12.** The site probably also had a religious significance of some kind, although the exact purpose for which it was used remains unclear. **13.** _____, scholars know only that if Stonehenge had not been created for religious reasons, the society responsible for it would not have continued the heavy and exacting work for two thousand years.

3. Which statement, if inserted into blank 1, would provide the best thesis statement for the entire passage?

    a.   Why was Stonehenge constructed?

    b.   Stonehenge is a mystery, but it fascinates all who learn about it.

    c.   Stonehenge was constructed five thousand years ago.

    d.   Stonehenge's construction has puzzled many scholars throughout time.

1. _____. **2.** After winning first prize—a cake—on a local radio station's talent show in 1947, she began to sing for extra money for her schoolbooks, and an encouraging instructor told her that she could succeed financially in the music world. **3.** Cruz never looked back. **4.** Cuban listeners, who resisted her at first when she replaced the popular singer of Cuba's best-loved orchestra, soon made her a star in her native country. **5.** The rise of Fidel Castro led to Cruz's defection from Cuba in 1960, and Castro never allowed her to return. **6.** She and the orchestra played for a time in Mexico. **7.** _____, however, they moved north to try to break into the Latino music market in the United States. **8.** Cruz's traditional style did not immediately attract young listeners, but her long association with Tito Puente and her star turn in the rock opera *Hommy* at Carnegie Hall in 1973 finally helped her win the crowds in New York City, her adopted home. **9.** From then until the end of her life, she performed for multiple generations of Cuban-Americans and other Latinos who revered her as the Queen of Salsa. **10.** In addition to her remarkable voice, the costumes she wore onstage also thrilled audiences. **11.** She was married for over forty years. **12.** Cruz, who had hoped that young women might follow in her footsteps and take up salsa singing, never saw a likely successor. **13.** Her death in 2003 left a noticeable gap in the Latin music world.

4. Which statement, if inserted into blank 1, would provide the best thesis statement for the entire passage?

    a.   Celia Cruz was a salsa singer born in Havana, Cuba.

    b.   Celia Cruz was loved by all who listened to her music.

    c.   Celia Cruz, a Havana-born salsa singer, won the hearts of fans in Cuba, in the United States, and in much of the rest of the world.

    d.   Why was Celia Cruz loved by so many people in the Latin music world?

1. The Aral Sea, once the fourth-largest body of water in the world, has shrunk dramatically in the past thirty years. **2.** _____. **3.** Under the administration of the Soviet Union, irrigation canals diverted water away from the rivers flowing into the Aral Sea because Soviet agricultural authorities had designated Kazakhstan as the country's cotton production center. **4.** _____,

(continued)

cotton requires a great deal of water, and soon far less water was reaching the Aral Sea than it had in the past. **5.** While cotton makes good cloth, it is not edible. **6.** People in the sea's fishing ports began to watch the water recede and the fish die as the remaining water became increasingly salty. **7.** As the level of the Aral Sea has dropped—about fifty feet since the irrigation project began—the large sea has become two small ones. **8.** The smaller of the two may be saved, but the other will probably never again sustain life. **9.** Even the air quality is bad because wind stirs up the polluted dust. **10.** The life expectancy of people in Aral Sea communities is the lowest in the former Soviet Union. **11.** This land cannot be farmed, and the salt and chemicals have poisoned the drinking water. **12.** The land that has been uncovered by the disappearing water is saturated with salt and heavily polluted with the agricultural chemicals in whatever water the rivers still bring. **13.** This human-made tragedy could have been prevented by better planning, but now many of the people who live in the Aral Sea region face a stark choice: they can leave now, or they can die of starvation, disease, or chemical poisoning later.

5. Which statement, if inserted into blank 2, would provide the best thesis statement for the entire passage?

a. People living in Aral Sea communities have the lowest life expectancy in the former Soviet Union.

b. Because of many environmental factors, the Aral Sea disaster has been devastating to the former Soviet Union.

c. No one is quite sure why Aral Sea communities have been negatively affected.

d. Humans have caused the Aral Sea disaster, and the disaster is taking an enormous human toll.

1. Dirt roads may not strike many people as the ideal driving surface. **2.** They are often uneven, pitted, and rocky, and they may deteriorate badly in rainy weather. **3.** _____, they can be difficult to plow in winter. **4.** _____. **5.** Road conditions that make driving slow and difficult, for example, are not always a negative for people who live along the road. **6.** Speeding cars in a residential area can be a danger to pets and small children, and they are often an annoyance to everyone who lives there. **7.** Dirt roads act as natural speed bumps for such vehicles. **8.** Another irritation is drivers who play music so loudly that the whole neighborhood vibrates with the sound. **9.** Furthermore, roads made of gravel or dirt can lend a rural atmosphere to an area.

6. Which statement, if inserted into blank 4, would provide the best thesis statement for the entire passage?

a. Dirt roads are just plain dangerous to cross.

b. Yet while dirt roads do have drawbacks, they also have much to recommend them.

c. There are many positive attributes to having dirt roads.

d. Reckless and inconsiderate drivers find dirt roads pleasant and smooth.

1. _____. **2.** According to linguist Michael Krauss, up to half of the six thousand or so languages still in use are endangered and likely to disappear entirely by the end of this century. **3.** A language begins to die when speakers stop teaching their children the language and stop using it at home. **4.** Most of these dying languages are spoken by only a few people, often the elderly, in a tribe or other close-knit group. **5.** The younger generation's lack of interest in the group's historical language may stem from a view of it as outmoded and useless for social and economic advancement. **6.** In the communities where native speakers of disappearing languages still live, even finding young people willing to learn can be a problem. **7.** The rarity of non-native speakers of tribal languages allowed Navajo soldiers to use their native tongue to communicate top-secret information during World War II. **8.** In the United States, some native speakers of English object to hearing non-English languages, adding to the stigma of speaking a rare tongue. **9.** Linguists point out that regions where multilingualism is uncommon or unpopular are losing endangered languages the fastest. **10.** _____, the death of a native tongue has a chilling effect on tribal or group culture. **11.** Linguists are scrambling to record all they can of disappearing languages, but the rate of loss is so high that many endangered languages are likely to vanish before much serious work can be done to preserve them.

7. Which statement, if inserted into blank 1, would provide the best thesis statement for the entire passage?

a. Preserving dying languages is a major undertaking.

b. Linguists know the reasons some languages last and others do not.

c. Hundreds, perhaps thousands, of languages are quietly vanishing.

d. The Navajo language helped communication during World War II.

1. Two or three hundred young people gather suddenly in an expensive New York shoe store and simultaneously make calls on their cell phones. **2.** A large group takes over a San Francisco crosswalk, blocking traffic and doing calisthenics. **3.** Young men and women in Rome descend on a bookstore and all request the same nonexistent book. **4.** _____ _____. **5.** The global happenings follow a certain pattern.

(continued)

6. The plan circulates, usually anonymously, by e-mail and cell phone. **7.** Smaller groups gather in prearranged locations before the big get-together. **8.** Indisputably, many members join a flash mob for the sheer delight of doing something silly—a mindless escape from daily uncertainties. **9.** _____, flash mobs remind some participants and observers of performance art, a brief and unrecorded show that leaves spectators intrigued or, perhaps, puzzled. **10.** Still other participants see the phenomenon as a rebellion. **11.** Whatever reason people have for joining in a flash mob, the events have spread around the world as fast as the electronic word can travel. **12.** Ironically, the computers and cell phones that make flash mobs possible are themselves increasingly disposable.

8. Which statement, if inserted into blank 4, would provide the best thesis statement for the entire passage?

  a. The phenomenon of "flash mobs"—which are part goofy fun, part art, and part a form of protest—has attracted many technologically up-to-date young people.

  b. The phenomenon of "flash mobs" can be observed worldwide.

  c. The phenomenon of "flash mobs" is an intricate form of rebellion used mostly by young men and women of Rome.

  d. The phenomenon of "flash mobs" does not have a definite origin, yet it serves a purpose.

1. _____. **2.** The manatee, or sea cow, belongs to a family of marine animals called *Sirenia* after the Sirens, the mythical water-dwelling women in old Greek stories who mesmerized sailors with their songs. **3.** In fact, manatees may have inspired ancient sailors' stories about mermaids. **4.** _____ manatees have whiskery faces and elephant-like skin, their paddle-tailed bodies are said to have fooled lonely—and perhaps nearsighted—mariners who thought the animals were beautiful women. **5.** Manatees' curiosity about people, their gentle nature, and their funny, friendly-looking faces make them popular with Florida's residents and visitors alike. **6.** Manatees have been spotted as far north as Virginia. **7.** With no natural enemies, these half-ton plant-eating creatures are threatened only by human actions. **8.** Water pollution has killed some manatees, but the most common cause of death for the adult mammals is collisions with motorboats and other recreational watercraft. **9.** Commonsense measures supported by a majority of boaters would provide more protection to the manatee. **10.** Manatees have a long history with humans, who are both their chief enemy and their best hope for survival.

9. Which statement, if inserted into blank 1, would provide the best thesis statement for the entire passage?

    a.   The Florida manatee or sea cow is a slow creature that lives in Florida waters.

    b.   Drunken boaters kill manatees while speeding through Florida's waterways.

    c.   Many efforts have been put in place to prevent the senseless death of Florida manatees.

    d.   Although the Florida manatee has been popular with humans for many years, people still pose a threat to this large, slow sea creature.

1. _____. **2.** Before 1917, most people considered the hymn "God Save the Tsar" a national song of sorts, but after the Russian Revolution, when the tsar was executed and religion officially banned, the song obviously no longer suited the country. **3.** Instead, the brand-new Soviet Union adopted "Internationale." **4.** The song had been a popular anthem among communists in many European countries during the Russian Revolution era. **5.** "Internationale" survived until the middle of World War II, when Soviet officials changed it because they wanted a specifically Soviet song instead of one expressing international solidarity. **6.** A new number, "Unbreakable Union of Free-Born Republics," became the official anthem of the Soviet Union in 1943. **7.** The lyrics were written by a poet, Sergei Mikhalkov. **8.** But the union did prove breakable in 1989, so the song was quietly retired two years later. **9.** _____, Russia lacked an anthem altogether. **10.** The need to choose a new song became urgent just before the Olympic Games of 1996. **11.** Unfortunately, "Patriotic Song" never captured the Russian imagination. **12.** Few people outside of the government even recognized the tune as a Russian anthem. **13.** The melody of a nineteenth-century number, "Patriotic Song," was chosen, and since no one could agree on what the new words should say, the song had no lyrics. **14.** Finally, in December of 2000, the Russian Parliament approved new words for the only tune most Russians recognized as their anthem—the song formerly known as "Unbreakable Union of Free-Born Republics."

10. Which statement, if inserted into blank 1, would provide the best thesis statement for the entire passage?

    a.   Russians have disliked most of the anthems created for them and continue to do so.

    b.   With the tremendous upheavals in twentieth-century Russia and the Soviet Union, Russia's national anthem has changed repeatedly.

    c.   The Russian Revolution brought about the most popular anthem in Soviet history.

    d.   The national anthem of Russia has evolved but remained the same since its inception.

3.1B IDENTIFYING ADEQUATE AND RELEVANT SUPPORT

What Is Adequate and Relevant Support?

Support includes facts, reasons, examples, and details that show, explain, or prove the writer's main point. Effective support turns a statement of opinion into a convincing argument. To be effective, supporting evidence must be adequate—there must be enough of it. It must also be relevant—readers must be able to see how the evidence relates to the point the writer is making.

EXAMPLE

Topic sentence — Drama languished in Europe after the fall of Rome during the fifth and sixth centuries. From about 400 CE to 900 CE almost no record of dramatic productions exists except for those of minstrels and other entertainers, such as acrobats and jugglers, who traveled through the countryside. The Catholic church was instrumental in suppressing drama because the theater—represented by the excesses of Roman productions—was seen as subversive. No state-sponsored festivals brought people together in huge theaters the way they had in Greek and Roman times. (Michael Meyer, *The Bedford Introduction to Literature*)

Support for topic sentence

In this example, the underlined section provides relevant support for the decline of drama. The lack of records is adequate to convince most readers that the thesis is true.

How Do You Determine if Support Is Adequate and Relevant?

Good support has the following features:

- It relates to the main point the writer is making.
- It considers the readers that it aims to convince.
- It is detailed and specific enough to be easy to understand.

To determine if support is adequate and relevant, ask these questions:

- Is the evidence clearly related to the main point? Does it clearly show what the writer claims it does? If so, the evidence is relevant.
- Is there enough evidence to be convincing? Does the writer provide enough examples? Is the support difficult to argue against? If so, the evidence is adequate.

The underlined evidence in the following passage provides **adequate support** for the assertion that the amount on the customer's bill is incorrect.

EXAMPLE

The amount shown on my bill is incorrect. I ordered the bacon-cheeseburger plate, which is $6.99 on the menu. On the bill, the order is correct, but the amount is $16.99.

Now consider this next passage.

> **EXAMPLE**
>
> Last year's employee training program succeeded for three reasons: all of the managers supported it, all of them provided adequate training to their staff members, and managers followed up with employees to make sure they really understood the tasks. Managers were able to provide sufficient training and follow-up because they were given the funds to do so. The result was big savings for the company.

The writer begins by stating that the training program succeeded for three reasons, and she goes on to provide **adequate support** for that statement by specifying the reasons and providing details about them. But take a look at the last sentence. What proof is there that the program provided "big savings"? This statement is **inadequately supported,** and it needs to be backed by evidence like that underlined in the next example.

> **EXAMPLE**
>
> Last year's employee training program succeeded for three reasons: all of the managers supported it, all of them provided adequate training to their staff members, and managers followed up with employees later to make sure they really understood the tasks. Managers were able to provide sufficient training and follow-up because they were given the funds to do so. The result was big savings for the company. Though training costs increased, worker productivity and efficiency improved, saving the company an estimated $100,000 last year.

On the test, when you are asked to identify adequate support for a sentence, a good place to start is with the sentence (or sentences) that immediately follows, like the underlined sentence in the preceding example. If you can't readily identify the best supporting sentence from the choices provided, eliminate the sentences that clearly are not the best support. You can also use the process of elimination to identify sentences that are least relevant to a passage or those that are not supported by specific detail.

You may also be asked to find sentences that lack adequate supporting details. Look for sentences that (like "The result was big savings for the company") make a substantial assertion but without evidence to back it up. Simple statements of fact—or elements of support for other assertions—may not need supporting details (e.g., "Managers were able to provide sufficient training and follow-up because they were given the funds to do so"). Again, you can use the process of elimination to identify the sentence that is least well supported.

Practice Identifying Adequate and Relevant Support

Each sentence in the following passages has been given a number. Read the passages carefully and then answer the questions, which refer to sentences by number. Answers and explanations appear on p. 257.

1. The last original-design Volkswagen Beetle was manufactured in Puebla, Mexico, on July 30, 2003. **2.** _____
_____. **3.** Volkswagen started as the "people's car" in Germany in the 1930s, and the low-priced, mass-produced car quickly became popular. **4.** For one thing, mechanically it was simple enough that many drivers could do repairs themselves. **5.** The original Beetle had drawbacks: it was both cramped and noisy, with the engine in the rear compartment drowning out most other sounds inside the car. **6.** _____, as the young VW bug drivers of the 1960s grew older and more prosperous, they left the cars behind. **7.** It was also much smaller and more lightweight than many other vehicles and consequently more dangerous to its occupants in a crash. **8.** The low cost of the car and its very basic engine also appealed to members of the 1960s counterculture; hippies, artists, students, and many others of limited money adopted the "love bug." **9.** However, many retained a nostalgic fondness for the Beetle, in spite—or perhaps because—of its flaws. **10.** Volkswagen stopped making the cars in Europe and the United States in the 1970s. **11.** Because of the car's importance in Mexico, however, the Puebla factory remained open. **12.** The car was called a *vocho* in Mexico. **13.** At last, however, Volkswagen recognized that the original bug's design, much the same as it had been sixty years earlier, was obsolete. **14.** The final car rolled out of the factory, and the Beetle's era was officially over.

1. Which of the following numbered sentences provides adequate support for sentence 3?

    a. 2   b. 4   c. 7   d. 1

1. _____.
2. Bartering is the exchange of goods or services that have approximately the same value. **3.** Individuals sometimes barter, as two of my neighbors did recently. **4.** Jonathan, a fine artist who also paints houses for extra income, agreed to paint Shamila's garage in exchange for her putting up his Web site and scanning images of his artwork. **5.** Jonathan has no expertise with computers, so he could not create the Web site himself. **6.** The barter arrangement suited both of them, each offering special skills to do an expert job for the other. **7.** Both agreed that each had spent about the same amount of time on his or her project. **8.** _____, neither of them had had to lay out any cash to have the work done. **9.** Business bartering works much like bartered exchanges between individuals, but on a larger scale. **10.** For any business or individual with skills or goods that are not being fully utilized, the barter system may be a lifesaver.

2. Which of the following numbered sentences provides adequate support for sentence 3?

    a. 5   b. 6   c. 4   d. 1

1. _____. **2.** The origin of this arrangement of massive stones in southern England has intrigued scholars for centuries. **3.** One common misconception, that Stonehenge was designed as a Druid temple, is demonstrably false. **4.** The carbon dating of digging tools found at the oldest part of the site, a circular outer ditch, shows that it was created about five thousand years ago, before 3000 BCE. **5.** Most scholars believe that work on this second phase occurred between 2800 and 2200 BCE. **6.** The final part of the monument, the ring of eighty smaller outer stones, was probably completed about 1100 BCE. **7.** During the second phase of the monument's construction, the largest stones—including the thirty-five-ton "heel stone" and other parts of the central rectangle—were put in place. **8.** Since Druids did not appear in the area until sometime around twenty-five hundred years ago, they could not have planned or built the site. **9.** But if Stonehenge isn't a Druid temple, what is it? **10.** The simple answer is that it appears to be a calendar. **11.** Of course, it did not have pages and numbers. **12.** The site probably also had a religious significance of some kind, although the exact purpose for which it was used remains unclear. **13.** _____, scholars know only that if Stonehenge had not been created for religious reasons, the society responsible for it would not have continued the heavy and exacting work for two thousand years.

3. Which of the following numbered sentences provides adequate support for sentence 3?

    a. 8   b. 9   c. 10   d. 1

1. _____. **2.** After winning first prize—a cake—on a local radio station's talent show in 1947, she began to sing for extra money for her schoolbooks, and an encouraging instructor told her that she could succeed financially in the music world. **3.** Cruz never looked back. **4.** Cuban listeners, who resisted her at first when she replaced the popular singer of Cuba's best-loved orchestra, soon made her a star in her native country. **5.** The rise of Fidel Castro led to Cruz's defection from Cuba in 1960, and Castro never allow her to return. **6.** She and the orchestra played for a time in Mexico. **7.** _____, however, they moved north to try to break into the Latino music market in the United States. **8.** Cruz's traditional style did not immediately attract young listeners, but her long association with Tito Puente and her star turn in the rock opera *Hommy* at Carnegie Hall in 1973 finally helped her win the crowds in New York City, her adopted home. **9.** From then until the end of her life, she performed for multiple generations of Cuban-Americans and other Latinos who revered her as the Queen of Salsa. **10.** In addition to her remarkable voice, the costumes she wore onstage also thrilled audiences. **11.** She was married for over forty years. **12.** Cruz, who had hoped that young women might follow in her footsteps and take up salsa singing, never saw a likely successor. **13.** Her death in 2003 left a noticeable gap in the Latin music world.

4. Which of the following numbered sentences provides adequate support for sentence 8?

    a.   11   b.   9   c.   2   d.   13

1. The Aral Sea, once the fourth-largest body of water in the world, has shrunk dramatically in the past thirty years. **2.** _____ _____. **3.** Under the administration of the Soviet Union, irrigation canals diverted water away from the rivers flowing into the Aral Sea because Soviet agricultural authorities had designated Kazakhstan as the country's cotton production center. **4.** _____, cotton requires a great deal of water, and soon far less water was reaching the Aral Sea than it had in the past. **5.** While cotton makes good cloth, it is not edible. **6.** People in the sea's fishing ports began to watch the water recede and the fish die as the remaining water became increasingly salty. **7.** As the level of the Aral Sea has dropped—about fifty feet since the irrigation project began—the large sea has become two small ones. **8.** The smaller of the two may be saved, but the other will probably never again sustain life. **9.** Even the air quality is bad because wind stirs up the polluted dust. **10.** The life expectancy of people in Aral Sea communities is the lowest in the former Soviet Union. **11.** This land cannot be farmed, and the salt and chemicals have poisoned the drinking water. **12.** The land that has been uncovered by the disappearing water is saturated with salt and heavily polluted with the agricultural chemicals in whatever water the rivers still bring. **13.** This human-made tragedy could have been prevented by better planning, but now many of the people who live in the Aral Sea region face a stark choice: they can leave now, or they can die of starvation, disease, or chemical poisoning later.

5. Which of the following sentences provides adequate support for sentence 3?

    a.   10   b.   13   c.   1   d.   4

1. Dirt roads may not strike many people as the ideal driving surface. **2.** They are often uneven, pitted, and rocky, and they may deteriorate badly in rainy weather. **3.** _____, they can be difficult to plow in winter. **4.** _____ _____. **5.** Road conditions that make driving slow and difficult, for example, are not always a negative for people who live along the road. **6.** Speeding cars in a residential area can be a danger to pets and small children, and they are often an annoyance to everyone who lives there. **7.** Dirt roads act as natural speed bumps for such vehicles. **8.** Another irritation is drivers who play music so loudly that the whole neighborhood vibrates with the sound. **9.** Furthermore, roads made of gravel or dirt can lend a rural atmosphere to an area.

6. Which of the following numbered sentences provides adequate support for sentence 5?

    a.   3   b.   6   c.   8   d.   1

1. _____. **2.** According to linguist Michael Krauss, up to half of the six thousand or so languages still in use are endangered and likely to disappear entirely by the end of this century. **3.** A language begins to die when speakers stop teaching their children the language and stop using it at home. **4.** Most of these dying languages are spoken by only a few people, often the elderly, in a tribe or other close-knit group. **5.** The younger generation's lack of interest in the group's historical language may stem from a view of it as outmoded and useless for social and economic advancement. **6.** In the communities where native speakers of disappearing languages still live, even finding young people willing to learn can be a problem. **7.** The rarity of non-native speakers of tribal languages allowed Navajo soldiers to use their native tongue to communicate top-secret information during World War II. **8.** In the United States, some native speakers of English object to hearing non-English languages, adding to the stigma of speaking a rare tongue. **9.** Linguists point out that regions where multilingualism is uncommon or unpopular are losing endangered languages the fastest. **10.** _____, the death of a native tongue has a chilling effect on tribal or group culture. **11.** Linguists are scrambling to record all they can of disappearing languages, but the rate of loss is so high that many endangered languages are likely to vanish before much serious work can be done to preserve them.

7. Which of the following numbered sentences provides adequate support for sentence 8?

    a. 10   b. 9   c. 1   d. 5

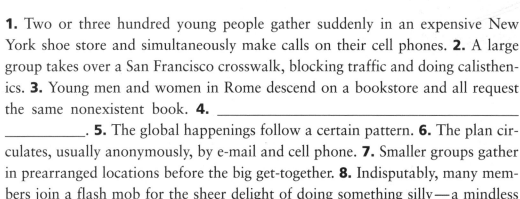

1. Two or three hundred young people gather suddenly in an expensive New York shoe store and simultaneously make calls on their cell phones. **2.** A large group takes over a San Francisco crosswalk, blocking traffic and doing calisthenics. **3.** Young men and women in Rome descend on a bookstore and all request the same nonexistent book. **4.** _____. **5.** The global happenings follow a certain pattern. **6.** The plan circulates, usually anonymously, by e-mail and cell phone. **7.** Smaller groups gather in prearranged locations before the big get-together. **8.** Indisputably, many members join a flash mob for the sheer delight of doing something silly—a mindless escape from daily uncertainties. **9.** _____, flash mobs remind some participants and observers of performance art, a brief and unrecorded show that leaves spectators intrigued or, perhaps, puzzled. **10.** Still other participants see the phenomenon as a rebellion. **11.** Whatever the reason people have for joining a flash mob, the events have spread around the world as fast as the electronic word can travel. **12.** Ironically, the computers and cell phones that make flash mobs possible are themselves increasingly disposable.

3

8. Which of the following numbered sentences provides adequate support for sentence 5?

    a. 4   b. 2   c. 7   d. 9

1. _____. **2.** The manatee, or sea cow, belongs to a family of marine animals called *Sirenia* after the Sirens, the mythical water-dwelling women in old Greek stories who mesmerized sailors with their songs. **3.** In fact, manatees may have inspired ancient sailors' stories about mermaids. **4.** _____ manatees have whiskery faces and elephant-like skin, their paddle-tailed bodies are said to have fooled lonely—and perhaps nearsighted—mariners who thought the animals were beautiful women. **5.** Manatees' curiosity about people, their gentle nature, and their funny, friendly-looking faces make them popular with Florida's residents and visitors alike. **6.** Manatees have been spotted as far north as Virginia. **7.** With no natural enemies, these half-ton plant-eating creatures are threatened only by human actions. **8.** Water pollution has killed some manatees, but the most common cause of death for the adult mammals is collisions with motorboats and other recreational watercraft. **9.** Commonsense measures supported by a majority of boaters would provide more protection to the manatee. **10.** Manatees have a long history with humans, who are both their chief enemy and their best hope for survival.

9. Which of the following numbered sentences provides adequate support for sentence 3?

    a. 4   b. 2   c. 7   d. 9

1. _____. **2.** Before 1917, most people considered the hymn "God Save the Tsar" a national song of sorts; but after the Russian Revolution, when the tsar was executed and religion officially banned, the song obviously no longer suited the country. **3.** Instead, the brand-new Soviet Union adopted "Internationale." **4.** The song had been a popular anthem among communists in many European countries during the Russian Revolution era. **5.** "Internationale" survived until the middle of World War II, when Soviet officials changed it because they wanted a specifically Soviet song instead of one expressing international solidarity. **6.** A new number, "Unbreakable Union of Free-Born Republics," became the official anthem of the Soviet Union in 1943. **7.** The lyrics were written by a poet, Sergei Mikhalkov. **8.** But the union did prove breakable in 1989, so the song was quietly retired two years later. **9.** _____, Russia lacked an anthem altogether. **10.** The need to choose a new song became urgent just before the Olympic Games of 1996. **11.** Unfortunately, "Patriotic Song" never captured the Russian imagination. **12.** Few people outside of the government even recognized the tune as a Russian anthem. **13.** The melody of a nineteenth-century number, "Patriotic Song," was chosen, and since no one could agree on what the new words should say, the song had no lyrics.

14. Finally, in December 2000, the Russian Parliament approved new words for the only tune most Russians recognized as their anthem—the song formerly known as "Unbreakable Union of Free-Born Republics."

10. Which of the following numbered sentences provides adequate support for sentence 3?

   a.   2   b.   4   c.   7   d.   14

Relevant Support/Sufficient Supporting Details

Each sentence in the following passages has been given a number. Read the passages carefully and then answer the questions, which refer to sentences by number. Answers and explanations appear on p. 258.

1. The last original-design Volkswagen Beetle was manufactured in Puebla, Mexico, on July 30, 2003. **2.** _____. **3.** Volkswagen started as the "people's car" in Germany in the 1930s, and the low-priced, mass-produced car quickly became popular. **4.** For one thing, mechanically it was simple enough that many drivers could do repairs themselves. **5.** The original Beetle had drawbacks: it was both cramped and noisy, with the engine in the rear compartment drowning out most other sounds inside the car. **6.** _____, as the young VW bug drivers of the 1960s grew older and more prosperous, they left the cars behind. **7.** It was also much smaller and more lightweight than many other vehicles and consequently more dangerous to its occupants in a crash. **8.** The low cost of the car and its very basic engine also appealed to members of the 1960s counterculture; hippies, artists, students, and many others of limited money adopted the "love bug." **9.** However, many retained a nostalgic fondness for the Beetle, in spite—or perhaps because—of its flaws. **10.** Volkswagen stopped making the cars in Europe and the United States in the 1970s. **11.** Because of the car's importance in Mexico, however, the Puebla factory remained open. **12.** The car was called a *vocho* in Mexico. **13.** At last, however, Volkswagen recognized that the original bug's design, much the same as it had been sixty years earlier, was obsolete. **14.** The final car rolled out of the factory, and the Beetle's era was officially over.

11. Which of the numbered sentences is least relevant to the paragraph?

   a.   10   b.   12   c.   5   d.   2

1. _____. **2.** Bartering is the exchange of goods or services that have approximately the same value. **3.** Individuals sometimes barter, as two of my neighbors did recently. **4.** Jonathan, a fine artist who also paints houses for extra income, agreed to paint Shamila's

(continued)

garage in exchange for her putting up his Web site and scanning images of his artwork. **5.** Jonathan has no expertise with computers, so he could not create the Web site himself. **6.** The barter arrangement suited both of them, each offering special skills to do an expert job for the other. **7.** They agreed that each had spent about the same amount of time on his or her project. **8.** _____, neither of them had had to lay out any cash to have the work done. **9.** Business bartering works much like bartered exchanges between individuals, but on a larger scale. **10.** For any business or individual with skills or goods that are not being fully used, the barter system may be a lifesaver.

12. Which sentence is not supported by specific detail?

    a.   10   b.   9   c.   5   d.   4

1. _____. **2.** The origin of this arrangement of massive stones in southern England has intrigued scholars for centuries. **3.** One common misconception, that Stonehenge was designed as a Druid temple, is demonstrably false. **4.** The carbon dating of digging tools found at the oldest part of the site, a circular outer ditch, shows that it was created about five thousand years ago, before 3000 BCE. **5.** Most scholars believe that work on this second phase occurred between 2800 and 2200 BCE. **6.** The final part of the monument, the ring of eighty smaller outer stones, was probably completed about 1100 BCE. **7.** During the second phase of the monument's construction, the largest stones—including the thirty-five-ton "heel stone" and other parts of the central rectangle—were put in place. **8.** Since Druids did not appear in the area until sometime around twenty-five hundred years ago, they could not have planned or built the site. **9.** But if Stonehenge isn't a Druid temple, what is it? **10.** The simple answer is that it appears to be a calendar. **11.** Of course, it did not have pages and numbers. **12.** The site probably also had a religious significance of some kind, although the exact purpose for which it was used remains unclear. **13.** _____, scholars know only that if Stonehenge had not been created for religious reasons, the society responsible for it would not have continued the heavy and exacting work for two thousand years.

13. Which sentence is not supported by specific detail?

    a.   7   b.   8   c.   10   d.   4

1. _____. **2.** After winning first prize—a cake—on a local radio station's talent show in 1947, she began to sing for extra money for her schoolbooks, and an encouraging instructor told her that she could succeed financially in the music world. **3.** Cruz never looked back. **4.** Cuban listeners, who resisted her at first when she replaced the popular singer of Cuba's best-loved orchestra, soon made her a star in her native country. **5.** The rise of Fidel Castro led to Cruz's defection from Cuba in 1960, and Castro never allowed her to return. **6.** She and the orchestra played for a time in Mexico. **7.** _____, however, they moved north to try to break into the Latino music market in the United States. **8.** Cruz's traditional style did not immediately attract young listeners, but her long association with Tito Puente and her star turn in the rock opera *Hommy* at Carnegie Hall in 1973 finally helped her win the crowds in New York City, her adopted home. **9.** From then until the end of her life, she performed for multiple generations of Cuban-Americans and other Latinos who revered her as the Queen of Salsa. **10.** In addition to her remarkable voice, the costumes she wore onstage also thrilled audiences. **11.** She was married for over forty years. **12.** Cruz, who had hoped that young women might follow in her footsteps and take up salsa singing, never saw a likely successor. **13.** Her death in 2003 left a noticeable gap in the Latin music world.

14. Which sentence is least relevant to the paragraph?

a. 10   b. 8   c. 9   d. 11

1. The Aral Sea, once the fourth-largest body of water in the world, has shrunk dramatically in the past thirty years. **2.** _____. **3.** Under the administration of the Soviet Union, irrigation canals diverted water away from the rivers flowing into the Aral Sea because Soviet agricultural authorities had designated Kazakhstan as the country's cotton production center. **4.** _____, cotton requires a great deal of water, and soon far less water was reaching the Aral Sea than it had in the past. **5.** While cotton makes good cloth, it is not edible. **6.** People in the sea's fishing ports began to watch the water recede and the fish die as the remaining water became increasingly salty. **7.** As the level of the Aral Sea has dropped—about fifty feet since the irrigation project began—the large sea has become two small ones. **8.** The smaller of the two may be saved, but the other will probably never again sustain life. **9.** Even the air quality is bad because wind stirs up the polluted dust. **10.** The life expectancy of people in Aral Sea communities is the lowest in the former Soviet Union. **11.** This land cannot be farmed, and the salt and chemicals have poisoned the drinking water. **12.** The land that has been uncovered by the disappearing water is saturated with salt and heavily polluted with the agricultural chemicals in whatever water the rivers still bring. **13.** This human-made tragedy could have been prevented by better planning, but now many of the people who live in the Aral Sea region face a stark choice: they can leave now, or they can die of starvation, disease, or chemical poisoning later.

15. Which sentence is least relevant to the paragraph?

    a. 5   b. 4   c. 11   d. 9

1. Dirt roads may not strike many people as the ideal driving surface. **2.** They are often uneven, pitted, and rocky, and they may deteriorate badly in rainy weather. **3.** _____, they can be difficult to plow in winter. **4.** _____ _____. **5.** Road conditions that make driving slow and difficult, for example, are not always a negative for people who live along the road. **6.** Speeding cars in a residential area can be a danger to pets and small children, and they are often an annoyance to everyone who lives there. **7.** Dirt roads act as natural speed bumps for such vehicles. **8.** Another irritation is drivers who play music so loudly that the whole neighborhood vibrates with the sound. **9.** Furthermore, roads made of gravel or dirt can lend a rural atmosphere to an area.

16. Which sentence the least relevant to the paragraph?

    a. 9   b. 8   c. 7   d. 4

1. _____. **2.** According to linguist Michael Krauss, up to half of the six thousand or so languages still in use are endangered and likely to disappear entirely by the end of this century. **3.** A language begins to die when speakers stop teaching their children the language and stop using it at home. **4.** Most of these dying languages are spoken by only a few people, often the elderly, in a tribe or other close-knit group. **5.** The younger generation's lack of interest in the group's historical language may stem from a view of it as outmoded and useless for social and economic advancement. **6.** In the communities where native speakers of disappearing languages still live, even finding young people willing to learn can be a problem. **7.** The rarity of non-native speakers of tribal languages allowed Navajo soldiers to use their native tongue to communicate top-secret information during World War II. **8.** In the United States, some native speakers of English object to hearing non-English languages, adding to the stigma of speaking a rare tongue. **9.** Linguists point out that regions where multilingualism is uncommon or unpopular are losing endangered languages the fastest. **10.** _____, the death of a native tongue has a chilling effect on tribal or group culture. **11.** Linguists are scrambling to record all they can of disappearing languages, but the rate of loss is so high that many endangered languages are likely to vanish before much serious work can be done to preserve them.

17. Which sentence is least relevant to the paragraph?

    a. 3   b. 2   c. 7   d. 1

1. Two or three hundred young people gather suddenly in an expensive New York shoe store and simultaneously make calls on their cell phones. **2.** A large group takes over a San Francisco crosswalk, blocking traffic and doing calisthenics. **3.** Young men and women in Rome descend on a bookstore and all request the same nonexistent book. **4.** _____ _____. **5.** The global happenings follow a certain pattern. **6.** The plan circulates, usually anonymously, by e-mail and cell phone. **7.** Smaller groups gather in prearranged locations before the big get-together. **8.** Indisputably, many members join a flash mob for the sheer delight of doing something silly—a mindless escape from daily uncertainties. **9.** _____, flash mobs remind some participants and observers of performance art, a brief and un-recorded show that leaves spectators intrigued or, perhaps, puzzled. **10.** Still other participants see the phenomenon as a rebellion. **11.** Whatever the reason people have for joining in a flash mob, the events have spread around the world as fast as the electronic word can travel. **12.** Ironically, the computers and cell phones that make flash mobs possible are themselves increasingly disposable.

18. Which of the following sentences lacks adequate supporting detail?

    a. 8   b. 9   c. 10   d. 5

1. _____. **2.** The manatee, or sea cow, belongs to a family of marine animals called *Sirenia* after the Sirens, the mythical water-dwelling women in old Greek stories who mesmerized sailors with their songs. **3.** In fact, manatees may have inspired ancient sailors' stories about mermaids. **4.** _____ manatees have whiskery faces and elephant-like skin, their paddle-tailed bodies are said to have fooled lonely—and perhaps nearsighted—mariners who thought the animals were beautiful women. **5.** Man-atees' curiosity about people, their gentle nature, and their funny, friendly-look-ing faces make them popular with Florida's residents and visitors alike. **6.** Manatees have been spotted as far north as Virginia. **7.** With no natural ene-mies, these half-ton plant-eating creatures are threatened only by human actions. **8.** Water pollution has killed some manatees, but the most common cause of death for the adult mammals is collisions with motorboats and other recreational watercraft. **9.** Commonsense measures supported by a majority of boaters would provide more protection to the manatee. **10.** Manatees have a long history with humans, who are both their chief enemy and their best hope for survival.

19. Which of the following sentences lacks adequate supporting detail?

a. 9   b. 8   c. 4   d. 3

1. _____. **2.** Before 1917, most people considered the hymn "God Save the Tsar" a national song of sorts, but after the Russian Revolution, when the tsar was executed and religion officially banned, the song obviously no longer suited the country. **3.** Instead, the brand-new Soviet Union adopted "Internationale." **4.** The song had been a popular anthem among communists in many European countries during the Russian Revolution era. **5.** "Internationale" survived until the middle of World War II, when Soviet officials changed it because they wanted a specifically Soviet song instead of one expressing international solidarity. **6.** A new number, "Unbreakable Union of Free-Born Republics," became the official anthem of the Soviet Union in 1943. **7.** The lyrics were written by a poet, Sergei Mikhalkov. **8.** But the union did prove breakable in 1989, so the song was quietly retired two years later. **9.** _____, Russia lacked an anthem altogether. **10.** The need to choose a new song became urgent just before the Olympic Games of 1996. **11.** Unfortunately, "Patriotic Song" never captured the Russian imagination. **12.** Few people outside of the government even recognized the tune as a Russian anthem. **13.** The melody of a nineteenth-century number, "Patriotic Song," was chosen, and since no one could agree on what the new words should say, the song had no lyrics. **14.** Finally, in December of 2000, the Russian Parliament approved new words for the only tune most Russians recognized as their anthem—the song formerly known as "Unbreakable Union of Free-Born Republics."

20. Which of the following sentences lacks adequate supporting detail?

a. 4   b. 7   c. 8   d. 10

3.1C   ARRANGING IDEAS IN A LOGICAL PATTERN

What Is a Logical Pattern of Organization?

To make writing easy to follow, experienced writers typically organize paragraphs and essays according to logical **patterns**. There is no single right way to organize a piece of writing; rather, the organization depends on a writer's purpose and audience.

Also, a given passage may use more than one pattern. For example, a paragraph can appear in time order while the overall pattern of the essay is comparison and contrast. The following tables identify the major patterns of organization.

PATTERNS FOR ORDERING IDEAS

Type of Order	Use	Ways to Order Ideas
Spatial	Describes a physical place, object, or person	Top to bottom/bottom to top, near to far/far to near, left to right/right to left, back to front/front to back
Time (temporal)	Explains when events happened	First to last/last to first, most recent to least recent/least recent to most recent
Importance	Arranges ideas according to importance, interest, or surprise value	Most important to least important/least important to most important

On the test, you will be asked to choose the best order of sentences for passages in which the sentences have been scrambled. Keeping in mind the patterns described here—and looking for violations of them—can help. You will also be asked to choose a sentence that, if inserted into a paragraph, would make the passage clearer. In both cases, using the process of elimination to rule out clearly incorrect answers will help.

PATTERNS FOR DEVELOPING IDEAS

Strategy	Use	Type/Pattern of Support
Spatial	Describes a physical place, object, or person	Top to bottom/bottom to top, near to far/far to near, left to right/right to left, back to front/front to back
Illustration or example	Shows, explains, or proves a point	Main point and detailed examples
Process analysis	Explains how to do something or how something works	Detailed steps in a process or descriptions of a technique or method
Classification	Organizes or sorts items or people into categories	Categories and examples of items in each category
Listing	Lists subjects to prove a point	List(s)
Definition	Explains meaning of a term or concept	Basic definition and examples to clarify meaning
Comparison and contrast	Shows similarities and/or differences between two or among more subjects	Several points of similarity or difference that are compared or contrasted point by point or whole to whole
Cause and effect	Shows what made an event happen (cause) or what happened or will happen as a result (effect)	Explanation of causes and/or effects of an event
Statement and clarification (inductive argument)	Specific observations or details to draw a general conclusion	Progression from specific examples to a general conclusion or claim
Generalization and example (deductive argument)	A general principle and specific examples to draw a conclusion or make an argument	Progression from a generally accepted statement and one or more specific examples to a claim

Practice Arranging Ideas in a Logical Pattern

Each sentence in the following passages has been given a number. Read the passages carefully and then answer the questions, which refer to sentences by number. Answers and explanations appear on pp. 258–59.

1. The last original-design Volkswagen Beetle was manufactured in Puebla, Mexico, on July 30, 2003. **2.** _____.
3. Volkswagen started as the "people's car" in Germany in the 1930s, and the low-priced, mass-produced car quickly became popular. **4.** For one thing, mechanically it was simple enough that many drivers could do repairs themselves. **5.** The original Beetle had drawbacks: it was both cramped and noisy, with the engine in the rear compartment drowning out most other sounds inside the car. **6.** _____
_____, as the young VW bug drivers of the 1960s grew older and more prosperous, they left the cars behind. **7.** It was also much smaller and more lightweight than many other vehicles and consequently more dangerous to its occupants in a crash. **8.** The low cost of the car and its very basic engine also appealed to members of the 1960s counterculture; hippies, artists, students, and many others of limited money adopted the "love bug." **9.** However, many retained a nostalgic fondness for the Beetle, in spite—or perhaps because—of its flaws. **10.** Volkswagen stopped making the cars in Europe and the United States in the 1970s. **11.** Because of the car's importance in Mexico, however, the Puebla factory remained open. **12.** The car was called a *vocho* in Mexico. **13.** At last, however, Volkswagen recognized that the original bug's design, much the same as it had been sixty years earlier, was obsolete. **14.** The final car rolled out of the factory, and the Beetle's era was officially over.

1. Choose the most logical organization and sequence of sentences 4, 5, 6, 7, and 8.

a. For one thing, mechanically it was simple enough that many drivers could do repairs themselves. The original Beetle had drawbacks: it was both cramped and noisy, with the engine in the rear compartment drowning out most other sounds inside the car. Not surprisingly, as the young VW bug drivers of the 1960s grew older and more prosperous, they left the cars behind. It was also much smaller and more lightweight than many other vehicles and consequently more dangerous to its occupants in a crash. The low cost of the car and its very basic engine also appealed to members of the 1960s counterculture; hippies, artists, students, and many others of limited money adopted the "love bug."

b. It was also much smaller and more lightweight than many other vehicles and consequently more dangerous to its occupants in a crash. The low cost of the car and its very basic engine also appealed to members of the 1960s counterculture: hippies, artists, students, and many others of limited money adopted the "love bug." For one thing, mechanically it was simple enough that many drivers could do repairs themselves. The original Beetle had drawbacks: it was both cramped and noisy, with the engine in the rear compartment, drowning out most other sounds inside the car. Not surprisingly, as the young VW bug drivers of the 1960s grew older and more prosperous, they left the cars behind.

c. For one thing, mechanically it was simple enough that many drivers could do repairs themselves. The low cost of the car and its very basic engine also appealed to members of the 1960s counterculture; hippies, artists, students, and many others of limited money adopted the "love bug." The original Beetle had drawbacks: it was both cramped and noisy, with the engine in the rear compartment drowning out most other sounds inside the car. It was also much smaller and more lightweight than many other vehicles and consequently more dangerous to its occupants in a crash. Not surprisingly, as the young VW bug drivers of the 1960s grew older and more prosperous, they left the cars behind.

d. Not surprisingly as the young VW bug drivers of the 1960s grew older and more prosperous, they left the cars behind. It was also much smaller and more lightweight than many other vehicles and consequently more dangerous to its occupants in a crash. For one thing, mechanically it was simple enough that many drivers could do repairs themselves. The original Beetle had drawbacks: it was both cramped and noisy, with the engine in the rear compartment drowning out the sounds inside the car. The low cost of the car and its very basic engine also appealed to members of the 1960s counterculture; hippies, artists, students, and many others of limited money adopted the "love bug."

1._____. 2. Bartering is the exchange of goods or services that have approximately the same value. 3. Individuals sometimes barter, as two of my neighbors did recently. 4. Jonathan, a fine artist who also paints houses for extra income, agreed to paint Shamila's garage in exchange for her putting up his Web site and scanning images of his artwork. 5. Jonathan has no expertise with computers, so he could not create the Web site himself. 6. The barter arrangement suited both of them, each offering special skills to do an expert job for the other. 7. They agreed that each had spent about the same amount of time on his or her project. 8. _____, neither of them had had to lay out any cash to have the work done. 9. Business bartering works much like bartered exchanges between individuals, but on a larger scale. 10. For any business or individual with skills or goods that are not being fully utilized, the barter system may be a lifesaver.

2. Which is the most logical placement for this sentence to make the paragraph clearer?

Shamila, on the other hand, has been able to find only part-time work as a computer consultant in the past six months and had no extra money to hire someone to give her garage a badly needed paint job.

a. immediately after 3

b. immediately after 5

c. immediately after 4

d. immediately after 1

1. _____. **2.** The origin of this arrangement of massive stones in southern England has intrigued scholars for centuries. **3.** One common misconception, that Stonehenge was designed as a Druid temple, is demonstrably false. **4.** The carbon dating of digging tools found at the oldest part of the site, a circular outer ditch, shows that it was created about five thousand years ago, before 3000 BCE. **5.** Most scholars believe that work on this second phase occurred between 2800 and 2200 BCE. **6.** The final part of the monument, the ring of eighty smaller outer stones, was probably completed about 1100 BCE. **7.** During the second phase of the monument's construction, the largest stones—including the thirty-five-ton "heel stone" and other parts of the central rectangle—were put in place. **8.** Since Druids did not appear in the area until sometime around twenty-five hundred years ago, they could not have planned or built the site. **9.** But if Stonehenge isn't a Druid temple, what is it? **10.** The simple answer is that it appears to be a calendar. **11.** Of course, it did not have pages and numbers. **12.** The site probably also had a religious significance of some kind, although the exact purpose for which it was used remains unclear. **13.** _____, scholars know only that if Stonehenge had not been created for religious reasons, the society responsible for it would not have continued the heavy and exacting work for two thousand years.

3. Choose the most logical organization and sequence of sentences 4, 5, 6, and 7.

a. The carbon dating of digging tools found at the oldest part of the site, a circular outer ditch, shows that it was created about five thousand years ago, before 3000 BCE. Most scholars believe that work on this second phase occurred between 2800 and 2200 BCE. The final part of the monument, the ring of eighty smaller outer stones, was probably completed about 1100 BCE. During the second phase of the monument's construction, the largest stones—including the thirty-five-ton "heel stone" and other parts of the central rectangle—were put in place.

b. The carbon dating of digging tools found at the oldest part of the site, a circular outer ditch, shows that it was created about five thousand years ago, before 3000 BCE. During the second phase of the monument's construction, the largest stones—including the thirty five-ton "heel stone" and other parts of the central rectangle—were put in place. Most scholars believe that work on this second phase occurred between 2800 and 2200 BCE. The final part of the monument, the ring of eighty smaller outer stones, was probably completed about 1100 BCE.

c. During the second phase of the monument's construction, the largest stones—including the thirty-five ton "heel stone" and other parts of the central rectangle—were put in place. Most scholars believe that the work on this second phase occurred between 2800 and 2200 BCE. The carbon dating of digging tools found at the oldest part of the site, a circular ditch, shows that it was created about five thousand years ago, before 3000 BCE. The final part of the monument, the ring of eighty smaller outer stones, was probably completed about 1100 BCE.

d. The final part of the monument, the ring of eighty smaller outer stones, was probably completed about 1100 BCE. The carbon dating of digging tools found at the oldest part of the site, a circular ditch, shows that it was created about five thousand years ago, before 3000 BCE. Most scholars believe that the work on this second phase occurred between 2800 and 2200 BCE. During the second phase of the monument's construction, the largest stones—including the thirty-five-ton "heel stone" and other parts of the central rectangle—were put in place.

1. _____. **2.** After winning first prize—a cake—on a local radio station's talent show in 1947, she began to sing for extra money for her schoolbooks, and an encouraging instructor told her that she could succeed financially in the music world. **3.** Cruz never looked back. **4.** Cuban listeners, who resisted her at first when she replaced the popular singer of Cuba's best-loved orchestra, soon made her a star in her native country. **5.** The rise of Fidel Castro led to Cruz's defection from Cuba in 1960, and Castro never allowed her to return. **6.** She and the orchestra played for a time in Mexico. **7.** _____, however, they moved north to try to break into the Latino music market in the United States. **8.** Cruz's traditional style did not immediately attract young listeners, but her long association with Tito Puente and her star turn in the rock opera *Hommy* at Carnegie Hall in 1973 finally helped her win the crowds in New York City, her adopted home. **9.** From then until the end of her life, she performed for multiple generations of Cuban-Americans and other Latinos who revered her as the Queen of Salsa. **10.** In addition to her remarkable voice, the costumes she wore onstage also thrilled audiences. **11.** She was married for over forty years. **12.** Cruz, who had hoped that young women might follow in her footsteps and take up salsa singing, never saw a likely successor. **13.** Her death in 2003 left a noticeable gap in the Latin music world.

4. Which is the most logical placement for this sentence to make the paragraph clearer?

Cruz originally trained to teach literature.

a.   immediately after 1

b.   immediately after 3

c.   immediately after 5

d.   immediately after 7

1. The Aral Sea, once the fourth-largest body of water in the world, has shrunk dramatically in the past thirty years. **2.** _____. **3.** Under the administration of the Soviet Union, irrigation canals diverted water away from the rivers flowing into the Aral Sea because Soviet agricultural authorities had designated Kazakhstan as the country's cotton production center. **4.** _____, cotton requires a great deal of water, and soon far less water was reaching the Aral Sea than it had in the past. **5.** While cotton

(continued)

makes good cloth, it is not edible. **6.** People in the sea's fishing ports began to watch the water recede and the fish die as the remaining water became increasingly salty. **7.** As the level of the Aral Sea has dropped—about fifty feet since the irrigation project began—the large sea has become two small ones. **8.** The smaller of the two may be saved, but the other will probably never again sustain life. **9.** Even the air quality is bad because wind stirs up the polluted dust. **10.** The life expectancy of people in Aral Sea communities is the lowest in the former Soviet Union. **11.** This land cannot be farmed, and the salt and chemicals have poisoned the drinking water. **12.** The land that has been uncovered by the disappearing water is saturated with salt and heavily polluted with the agricultural chemicals in whatever water the rivers still bring. **13.** This human-made tragedy could have been prevented by better planning, but now many of the people who live in the Aral Sea region face a stark choice: they can leave now, or they can die of starvation, disease, or chemical poisoning later.

5. Choose the most logical organization and sequence of sentences 9, 10, 11, and 12.

    a. Even the air quality is bad because wind stirs up the polluted dust. The life expectancy of people in Aral Sea communities is the lowest in the former Soviet Union. This land cannot be farmed, and the salt and chemicals have poisoned the drinking water. The land that has been uncovered by the disappearing water is saturated with salt and heavily polluted with the agricultural chemicals in whatever water the rivers still bring.

    b. The land that has been uncovered by the disappearing water is saturated with salt and heavily polluted with the agricultural chemicals in whatever water the rivers still bring. Even the air quality is bad because wind stirs up the polluted dust. This land cannot be farmed, and the salt and chemicals have poisoned the drinking water. The life expectancy of people in Aral Sea communities is the lowest in the former Soviet Union.

    c. The life expectancy of people in Aral Sea communities is the lowest in the former Soviet Union. Even the air quality is bad because the wind stirs up the polluted dust. The land that has been uncovered by the disappearing water is saturated with salt and heavily polluted with the agricultural chemicals in whatever water the rivers still bring. This land cannot be farmed, and the salt and chemicals have poisoned the drinking water.

    d. The land that has been uncovered by the disappearing water is saturated with salt and heavily polluted with the agricultural chemicals in whatever water the rivers still bring. This land cannot be farmed, and the salt and chemicals have poisoned the drinking water. Even the air quality is bad because the wind stirs up the polluted dust. The life expectancy of people in Aral Sea communities is the lowest in the former Soviet Union.

1. Dirt roads may not strike many people as the ideal driving surface. **2.** They are often uneven, pitted, and rocky, and they may deteriorate badly in rainy weather. **3.** _____, they can be difficult to plow in winter. **4.** _____ _____. **5.** Road conditions that make driving slow and difficult, for example, are not always a negative for people who live along the road. **6.** Speeding cars in a residential area can be a danger to pets and small children, and they are often an annoyance to everyone who lives there. **7.** Dirt roads act as natural speed bumps for such vehicles. **8.** Another irritation is drivers who play music so loudly that the whole neighborhood vibrates with the sound. **9.** Furthermore, roads made of gravel or dirt can lend a rural atmosphere to an area.

6. Which is the most logical placement for the sentence below to make the paragraph clearer?

In fact, many who reside near unpaved roads want to maintain that atmosphere, and they find their rougher roads worth all of the trouble.

a.	immediately before 6	b.	immediately after 9
c.	immediately before 9	d.	immediately after 3

1. _____. **2.** According to linguist Michael Krauss, up to half of the six thousand or so languages still in use are endangered and likely to disappear entirely by the end of this century. **3.** A language begins to die when speakers stop teaching their children the language and stop using it at home. **4.** Most of these dying languages are spoken by only a few people, often the elderly, in a tribe or other close-knit group. **5.** The younger generation's lack of interest in the group's historical language may stem from a view of it as outmoded and useless for social and economic advancement. **6.** In the communities where native speakers of disappearing languages still live, even finding young people willing to learn can be a problem. **7.** The rarity of non-native speakers of tribal languages allowed Navajo soldiers to use their native tongue to communicate top-secret information during World War II. **8.** In the United States, some native speakers of English object to hearing non-English languages, adding to the stigma of speaking a rare tongue. **9.** Linguists point out that regions where multilingualism is uncommon or unpopular are losing endangered languages the fastest. **10.** _____, the death of a native tongue has a chilling effect on tribal or group culture. **11.** Linguists are scrambling to record all they can of disappearing languages, but the rate of loss is so high that many endangered languages are likely to vanish before much serious work can be done to preserve them.

7. Choose the most logical organization and sequence of sentences 3, 4, 5, and 6.

a. A language begins to die when speakers stop teaching their children the language and stop using it at home. Most of these dying languages are spoken by only a few people, often the elderly, in a tribe or other close-knit group. The younger generation's lack of interest in the group's historical language may stem from a view of it as outmoded and useless for social and economic advancement. In the communities where native speakers of disappearing languages still live, even finding young people willing to learn can be a problem.

b. A language begins to die when speakers stop teaching their children the language and stop using it at home. In the communities where native speakers of disappearing languages still live, even finding young people willing to learn can be a problem. The younger generation's lack of interest in the group's historical language may stem from a view of it as outmoded and useless for social and economic advancement. Most of these dying languages are spoken by only a few people, often the elderly, in a tribe or other close-knit group.

c. Most of these dying languages are spoken by only a few people, often the elderly, in a tribe or other close-knit group. A language begins to die when speakers stop teaching their children the language and stop using it at home. In the communities where native speakers of disappearing languages still live, even finding young people willing to learn can be a problem. The younger generation's lack of interest in the group's historical language may stem from a view of it as outmoded and useless for social and economic advancement.

d. In the communities where native speakers of disappearing languages still live, even finding young people willing to learn can be a problem. The younger generation's lack of interest in the group's historical language may stem from a view of it as outmoded and useless for social and economic advancement. A language begins to die when speakers stop teaching their children the language and stop using it at home. Most of these dying languages are spoken by only a few people, often the elderly, in a tribe or other close-knit group.

1. Two or three hundred young people gather suddenly in an expensive New York shoe store and simultaneously make calls on their cell phones. **2.** A large group takes over a San Francisco crosswalk, blocking traffic and doing calisthenics. **3.** Young men and women in Rome descend on a bookstore and all request the same nonexistent book. **4.** _____ _____. **5.** The global happenings follow a certain pattern. **6.** The plan circulates, usually anonymously, by e-mail and cell phone. **7.** Smaller groups gather in prearranged locations before the big get-together. **8.** Indisputably, many members join a flash mob for the sheer delight of doing something silly—a mindless escape from daily uncertainties. **9.** _____, flash mobs remind some participants and observers of performance art, a brief and unrecorded show that leaves spectators intrigued or, perhaps, puzzled. **10.** Still other participants see the phenomenon as a rebellion. **11.** Whatever the reason people have for joining in a flash mob, the events have spread around the world as fast as the electronic word can travel. **12.** Ironically, the computers and cell phones that make flash mobs possible are themselves increasingly disposable.

8. Which is the most logical placement for this sentence to make the paragraph clearer?

Suddenly, the small groups form a large one, and after two or three minutes of some planned but often pointless activity, the crowd melts away again.

a. immediately after 7
b. immediately before 8
c. immediately after 9
d. immediately before 6

1. _____. **2.** The manatee, or sea cow, belongs to a family of marine animals called *Sirenia* after the Sirens, the mythical water-dwelling women in old Greek stories who mesmerized sailors with their songs. **3.** In fact, manatees may have inspired ancient sailors' stories about mermaids. **4.** _____ manatees have whiskery faces and elephant-like skin, their paddle-tailed bodies are said to have fooled lonely—and perhaps nearsighted—mariners who thought the animals were beautiful women. **5.** Manatees' curiosity about people, their gentle nature, and their funny, friendly-looking faces make them popular with Florida's residents and visitors alike. **6.** Manatees have been spotted as far north as Virginia. **7.** With no natural enemies, these half-ton plant-eating creatures are threatened only by human actions. **8.** Water pollution has killed some manatees, but the most common cause of death for the adult mammals is collisions with motorboats and other recreational watercraft. **9.** Commonsense measures supported by a majority of boaters would provide more protection to the manatee. **10.** Manatees have a long history with humans, who are both their chief enemy and their best hope for survival.

9. Which is the most logical placement for this sentence to make the paragraph clearer?

Certainly, manatees have been known to offer bristly "kisses" to human divers.

a. immediately before 7
b. immediately after 4
c. immediately after 10
d. immediately after 8

3

1. _____. **2.** Before 1917, most people considered the hymn "God Save the Tsar" a national song of sorts, but after the Russian Revolution, when the tsar was executed and religion officially banned, the song obviously no longer suited the country. **3.** Instead, the brand-new Soviet Union adopted "Internationale." **4.** The song had been a popular anthem among communists in many European countries during the Russian Revolution era. **5.** "Internationale" survived until the middle of World War II, when Soviet officials changed it because they wanted a specifically Soviet song instead of one expressing international solidarity. **6.** A new number, "Unbreakable Union of Free-Born Republics," became the official anthem of the Soviet Union in 1943. **7.** The lyrics were written by a poet, Sergei Mikhalkov. **8.** But the union did prove breakable in 1989, so the song was quietly retired two years later. **9.** _____, Russia lacked an anthem altogether. **10.** The need to choose a new song became urgent just before the Olympic Games of 1996. **11.** Unfortunately, "Patriotic Song" never captured the Russian imagination. **12.** Few people outside of the government even recognized the tune as a Russian anthem. **13.** The melody of a nineteenth-century number, "Patriotic Song," was chosen, and since no one could agree on what the new words should say, the song had no lyrics. **14.** Finally, in December of 2000, the Russian Parliament approved new words for the only tune most Russians recognized as their anthem—the song formerly known as "Unbreakable Union of Free-Born Republics."

10. Choose the most logical organization and sequence of sentences 11, 12, 13, and 14.

a. Unfortunately, "Patriotic Song" never captured the Russian imagination. Few people outside of the government even recognized the tune as a Russian anthem. The melody of a nineteenth-century number, "Patriotic Song," was chosen, and since no one could agree on what the new words should say, the song had no lyrics. Finally, in December of 2000, the Russian Parliament approved new words for the only tune most Russians recognized as their anthem—the song formerly known as "Unbreakable Union of Free-Born Republics."

b. Finally, in December of 2000, the Russian Parliament approved new words for the only tune most Russians recognized as their anthem—the song formerly known as "Unbreakable Union of Free-Born Republics." The melody of a nineteenth-century number, "Patriotic Song," was chosen, and since no one could agree on what the new words should say, the song had no lyrics. Few people outside of the government even recognized the tune as a Russian anthem. Unfortunately, "Patriot Song" never captured the Russian imagination.

c. The melody of a nineteenth-century number, "Patriotic Song," was chosen, and since no one could agree on what the new words should say, the song had no lyrics. Finally, in December of 2000, the Russian Parliament approved new words for the only tune most Russians recognized as their anthem—the song formerly known as "Unbreakable Union of Free-Born Republics." Few people outside of the government even recognized the tune as a Russian anthem. Unfortunately, "Patriotic Song" never captured the Russian imagination.

d. The melody of a nineteenth-century number, "Patriotic Song," was chosen, and since no one could agree on what the new words should say, the song had no lyrics. Unfortunately, "Patriotic Song" never captured the Russian imagination. Few people outside of the government even recognized the tune as a Russian anthem. Finally, in December of 2000, the Russian Parliament approved new words for the only tune most Russians recognized as their anthem—the song formerly known as "Unbreakable Union of Free-Born Republics."

3.1D USING EFFECTIVE TRANSITIONAL DEVICES

What Are Connections and Transitional Devices?

Connections, or **transitional words and phrases,** indicate the relationships within and between sentences. They send signals that tell the reader what to expect. Common transitions include words such as *next* and *however* and phrases such as *for example* and *as a result*. In the following passage transitions are underlined.

> **EXAMPLE**
>
> <u>Another</u> essential part of fire safety education for children is learning how to extinguish fires when their own clothing ignites. Many children are burned by their own clothing. The chance of injury can be prevented if they are taught how to "Stop, Drop, and Roll." <u>One way</u> of teaching this is for the adult to cut out a "flame" from paper and tape it lightly to the child. <u>When</u> the child actually stops, drops, and rolls on the ground, the "flame" will fall off, thereby "extinguishing" the "fire." (Timothy E. Miles, "Fighting Fire with Fire Safety Education")

How Do You Choose Transitional Devices?

Different transitions have different meanings, as the following table indicates. Experienced writers choose transitions that make sense and serve the purpose of a sentence, paragraph, or essay.

COMMON TRANSITIONAL WORDS AND PHRASES

Space

above	below	near	to the right
across	beside	next to	to the side
at the bottom	beyond	opposite	under
at the top	farther/further	over	where
behind	inside	to the left	

Time

after	eventually	meanwhile	soon
as	finally	next	then
at last	first	now	when
before	last	second	while
during	later	since	

Importance

above all	in fact	more important	most
best	in particular	most important	worst
especially			

Example

for example	for instance	for one thing	one reason

Addition

additionally	and	as well as	in addition
also	another	furthermore	moreover

Contrast

although	in contrast	nevertheless	still
but	instead	on the other hand	yet
however			

Consequence

as a result	finally	so	therefore
because			

Again, note the use of the transitions that are underlined in the following paragraph.

EXAMPLE

Of course, educating children is not enough in itself to ensure fire safety; parents and other adults must also educate themselves about what to do (and what not to do) if a fire actually occurs. For example, do not go back into a fire for any reason. Have a meeting place where family members can be accounted for. Do not try to put out a fire; instead, have someone notify the fire department immediately. In addition, adults should take the responsibility for getting children involved in fire prevention. Many children learn best by example. Handouts, displays, and videotapes are especially helpful. Demonstration and practice of exit drills in the home and of "Stop, Drop, and Roll" are also useful, particularly during special fire hazard periods such as Halloween and Christmas. Participating in drawing escape plans and making inspections of the home for potential problems also make children feel they are helping. In fact, children can sometimes see things that adults overlook. (Timothy E. Miles, "Fighting Fire with Fire Safety Education")

Practice Choosing Effective Transitions

Each sentence in the passages below has been given a number. Read the passages carefully and then answer the questions that follow them, which refer to sentences by number. Answers and explanations appear on pp. 259–60.

1. The last original-design Volkswagen Beetle was manufactured in Puebla, Mexico, on July 30, 2003. **2.** _____. **3.** Volkswagen started as the "people's car" in Germany in the 1930s, and the low-priced, mass-produced car quickly became popular. **4.** For one thing, mechanically it was simple enough that many drivers could do repairs themselves. **5.** The original Beetle had drawbacks: it was both cramped and noisy, with the engine in the rear compartment drowning out most other sounds inside the car. **6.** _____, as the young VW bug drivers of the 1960s grew older and more prosperous, they left the cars behind. **7.** It was also much smaller and more lightweight than many other vehicles and consequently more dangerous to its occupants in a crash. **8.** The low cost of the car and its very basic engine also appealed to members of the 1960s counterculture; hippies, artists, students, and many others of limited money adopted the "love bug." **9.** However, many retained a nostalgic fondness for the Beetle, in spite—or perhaps because—of its flaws. **10.** Volkswagen stopped making the cars in Europe and the United States in the 1970s. **11.** Because of the car's importance in Mexico, however, the Puebla factory remained open. **12.** The car was called a _vocho_ in Mexico. **13.** At last, however, Volkswagen recognized that the original bug's design, much the same as it had been sixty years earlier, was obsolete. **14.** The final car rolled out of the factory, and the Beetle's era was officially over.

1. Which transition if inserted in blank 6 would make the relationship between 5 and 6 clearer?

   a. Also   b. Not surprisingly   c. Indeed   d. For instance

1. _____. **2.** Bartering is the exchange of goods or services that have approximately the same amount. **3.** Individuals sometimes barter, as two of my neighbors did recently. **4.** Jonathan, a fine artist who also paints houses for extra income, agreed to paint Shamila's garage in exchange for her putting up his Web site and scanning images of his artwork. **5.** Jonathan has no expertise with computers, so he could not

(continued)

create the Web site himself. **6.** The barter arrangement suited both of them, each offering special skills to do an expert job for the other. **7.** Both agreed that each had spent about the same amount of time on his or her project. **8.** _____, neither of them had had to lay out any cash to have the work done. **9.** Business bartering works much like bartered exchanges between individuals, but on a larger scale. **10.** For any business or individual with skills or goods that are not being fully utilized, the barter system may be a lifesaver.

2. Which transition if inserted in blank 8 would make the relationship between 7 and 8 clearer?

a. Best of all

b. On the other hand

c. In comparison

d. In conclusion

1. _____. **2.** The origin of this arrangement of massive stones in southern England has intrigued scholars for centuries. **3.** One common misconception, that Stonehenge was designed as a Druid temple, is demonstrably false. **4.** The carbon dating of digging tools found at the oldest part of the site, a circular outer ditch, shows that it was created about five thousand years ago, before 3000 BCE. **5.** Most scholars believe that work on this second phase occurred between 2800 and 2200 BCE. **6.** The final part of the monument, the ring of eighty smaller outer stones, was probably completed about 1100 BCE. **7.** During the second phase of the monument's construction, the largest stones—including the thirty-five-ton "heel stone" and other parts of the central rectangle—were put in place. **8.** Since Druids did not appear in the area until sometime around twenty-five hundred years ago, they could not have planned or built the site. **9.** But if Stonehenge isn't a Druid temple, what is it? **10.** The simple answer is that it appears to be a calendar. **11.** Of course, it did not have pages and numbers. **12.** The site probably also had a religious significance of some kind, although the exact purpose for which it was used remains unclear. **13.** _____, scholars know only that if Stonehenge had not been created for religious reasons, the society responsible for it would not have continued the heavy and exacting work for two thousand years.

3. Which transition if inserted in blank 13 would make the relationship between 13 and the previous sentences clearer?

a. Hence   b. Similarly   c. Finally   d. However

1. _____. **2.** After winning first prize—a cake—on a local radio station's talent show in 1947, she began to sing for extra money for her schoolbooks, and an encouraging instructor told her that she could succeed financially in the music world. **3.** Cruz never looked back. **4.** Cuban listeners, who resisted her at first when she replaced the popular singer of Cuba's best-loved orchestra, soon made her a star in her native country. **5.** The rise of Fidel Castro led to Cruz's defection from Cuba in 1960, and Castro never allowed her to return. **6.** She and the orchestra played for a time in Mexico. **7.** _____, however, they moved north to try to break into the Latino music market in the United States. **8.** Cruz's traditional style did not immediately attract young listeners, but her long association with Tito Puente and her star turn in the rock opera *Hommy* at Carnegie Hall in 1973 finally helped her win the crowds in New York City, her adopted home. **9.** From then until the end of her life, she performed for multiple generations of Cuban-Americans and other Latinos who revered her as the Queen of Salsa. **10.** In addition to her remarkable voice, the costumes she wore onstage also thrilled audiences. **11.** She was married for over forty years. **12.** Cruz, who had hoped that young women might follow in her footsteps and take up salsa singing, never saw a likely successor. **13.** Her death in 2003 left a noticeable gap in the Latin music world.

4. Which transition if inserted in blank 7 would make the relationship between 6 and 7 clearer?

  a. Soon   b. In addition   c. Moreover   d. Thus

1. The Aral Sea, once the fourth-largest body of water in the world, has shrunk dramatically in the past thirty years. **2.**_____.
3. Under the administration of the Soviet Union, irrigation canals diverted water away from the rivers flowing into the Aral Sea because Soviet agricultural authorities had designated Kazakhstan as the country's cotton production center. **4.** _____, cotton requires a great deal of water, and soon far less water was reaching the Aral Sea than it had in the past. **5.** While cotton makes good cloth, it is not edible. **6.** People in the sea's fishing ports began to watch the water recede and the fish die as the remaining water became increasingly salty. **7.** As the level of the Aral Sea has dropped—about fifty feet since the irrigation project began—the large sea has become two small ones. **8.** The smaller of the two may be saved, but the other will probably never again sustain life. **9.** Even the air quality is bad because wind stirs up the polluted dust. **10.** The life expectancy of people in Aral Sea communities is the lowest in the former Soviet Union. **11.** This land cannot be farmed, and the salt and chemicals have poisoned the drinking water. **12.** The land that has been uncovered by the disappearing water is saturated with salt and heavily polluted with the agricultural chemicals in whatever water the rivers still bring. **13.** This human-made tragedy could have been prevented by better planning, but now many of the people who live in the Aral Sea region face a stark choice: they can leave now, or they can die of starvation, disease, or chemical poisoning later.

5. Which transition if inserted in blank 4 would make the relationship between 3 and 4 clearer?

    a. Also   b. Finally   c. Unfortunately   d. For instance

> **1.** Dirt roads may not strike many people as the ideal driving surface. **2.** They are often uneven, pitted, and rocky, and they may deteriorate badly in rainy weather. **3.** _____, they can be difficult to plow in winter. **4.** _____ _____. **5.** Road conditions that make driving slow and difficult, for example, are not always a negative for people who live along the road. **6.** Speeding cars in a residential area can be a danger to pets and small children, and they are often an annoyance to everyone who lives there. **7.** Dirt roads act as natural speed bumps for such vehicles. **8.** Another irritation is drivers who play music so loudly that the whole neighborhood vibrates with the sound. **9.** Furthermore, roads made of gravel or dirt can lend a rural atmosphere to an area.

6. Which transition if inserted in blank 3 would make the relationship between 2 and 3 clearer?

    a. In contrast   b. Strangely   c. Also   d. On the other hand

> **1.** _____. **2.** According to linguist Michael Krauss, up to half of the six thousand or so languages still in use are endangered and likely to disappear entirely by the end of this century. **3.** A language begins to die when speakers stop teaching their children the language and stop using it at home. **4.** Most of these dying languages are spoken by only a few people, often the elderly, in a tribe or other close-knit group. **5.** The younger generation's lack of interest in the group's historical language may stem from a view of it as outmoded and useless for social and economic advancement. **6.** In the communities where native speakers of disappearing languages still live, even finding young people willing to learn can be a problem. **7.** The rarity of non-native speakers of tribal languages allowed Navajo soldiers to use their native tongue to communicate top-secret information during World War II. **8.** In the United States, some native speakers of English object to hearing non-English languages, adding to the stigma of speaking a rare tongue. **9.** Linguists point out that regions where multilingualism is uncommon or unpopular are losing endangered languages the fastest. **10.** _____, the death of a native tongue has a chilling effect on tribal or group culture. **11.** Linguists are scrambling to record all they can of disappearing languages, but the rate of loss is so high that many endangered languages are likely to vanish before much serious work can be done to preserve them.

7. Which transition if inserted in blank 10 would make the relationship between 10 and previous sentences clearer?

a. Gladly   b. Unfortunately   c. Since   d. For example

> **1.** Two or three hundred young people gather suddenly in an expensive New York shoe store and simultaneously make calls on their cell phones. **2.** A large group takes over a San Francisco crosswalk, blocking traffic and doing calisthenics. **3.** Young men and women in Rome descend on a bookstore and all request the same nonexistent book. **4.** _____ _____. **5.** The global happenings follow a certain pattern. **6.** The plan circulates, usually anonymously, by e-mail and cell phone. **7.** Smaller groups gather in prearranged locations before the big get-together. **8.** Indisputably, many members join a flash mob for the sheer delight of doing something silly—a mindless escape from daily uncertainties. **9.** _____, flash mobs remind some participants and observers of performance art, a brief and unrecorded show that leaves spectators intrigued or, perhaps, puzzled. **10.** Still other participants see the phenomenon as a rebellion. **11.** Whatever the reason people have for joining in a flash mob, the events have spread around the world as fast as the electronic word can travel. **12.** Ironically, the computers and cell phones that make flash mobs possible are themselves increasingly disposable.

8. Which transition if inserted in blank 9 would make the relationship between 8 and 9 clearer?

a. On the other hand   b. Subsequently   c. Moreover   d. In addition

> **1.** _____. **2.** The manatee, or sea cow, belongs to a family of marine animals called *Sirenia* after the Sirens, the mythical water-dwelling women in old Greek stories who mesmerized sailors with their songs. **3.** In fact, manatees may have inspired ancient sailors' stories about mermaids. **4.** _____ manatees have whiskery faces and elephant-like skin, their paddle-tailed bodies are said to have fooled lonely—and perhaps nearsighted—mariners who thought the animals were beautiful women. **5.** Manatees' curiosity about people, their gentle nature, and their funny, friendly-looking faces make them popular with Florida's residents and visitors alike. **6.** Manatees have been spotted as far north as Virginia. **7.** With no natural enemies, these half-ton plant-eating creatures are threatened only by human actions. **8.** Water pollution has killed some manatees, but the most common cause of death for the adult mammals is collisions with motorboats and other recreational watercraft. **9.** Commonsense measures supported by a majority of boaters would provide more protection to the manatee. **10.** Manatees have a long history with humans, who are both their chief enemy and their best hope for survival.

9. Which transition if inserted in blank 4 would make the relationship between the parts of the sentence clearer?

    a.   Nevertheless   b.   Thus   c.   Certainly   d.   Although

1. _____. **2.** Before 1917, most people considered the hymn "God Save the Tsar" a national song of sorts, but after the Russian Revolution, when the tsar was executed and religion officially banned, the song obviously no longer suited the country. **3.** Instead, the brand-new Soviet Union adopted "Internationale." **4.** The song had been a popular anthem among communists in many European countries during the Russian Revolution era. **5.** "Internationale" survived until the middle of World War II, when Soviet officials changed it because they wanted a specifically Soviet song instead of one expressing international solidarity. **6.** A new number, "Unbreakable Union of Free-Born Republics," became the official anthem of the Soviet Union in 1943. **7.** The lyrics were written by a poet, Sergei Mikhalkov. **8.** But the union did prove breakable in 1989, so the song was quietly retired two years later. **9.** _____, Russia lacked an anthem altogether. **10.** The need to choose a new song became urgent just before the Olympic Games of 1996. **11.** Unfortunately, "Patriotic Song" never captured the Russian imagination. **12.** Few people outside of the government even recognized the tune as a Russian anthem. **13.** The melody of a nineteenth-century number, "Patriotic Song," was chosen, and since no one could agree on what the new words should say, the song had no lyrics. **14.** Finally, in December of 2000, the Russian Parliament approved new words for the only tune most Russians recognized as their anthem—the song formerly known as "Unbreakable Union of Free-Born Republics."

10. Which transition if inserted in blank 9 would make the relationship between 8 and 9 clearer?

    a.   Surprisingly   b.   Moreover   c.   In contrast   d.   For a while

Language Use

3.2A CHOOSING APPROPRIATE WORDS AND EXPRESSIONS

What Is Appropriate Word Choice?

Appropriate word choice means that the writer has selected the words that express his or her meaning clearly and accurately. Consider the differences between these two sentences:

> The calm lake *showed* the reds and golds of the towering maples.
> The calm lake *mirrored* the reds and golds of the towering maples.

You probably understood what the writer meant by *showed*, but *mirrored* gives a much more precise impression of the scene and of the author's intention.

How Do You Choose Appropriate Words in Context?

To choose the right word, you need to understand its context—the words, sentences, and paragraphs that appear before and after it. This context provides clues to a word's meaning. When you read, you can use context to make educated guesses about the meanings of words you don't recognize.

Suppose you are asked to pick the best word to fill in the blank here:

> We expected Charlie to be _____, but instead we found him stubborn and uncooperative.
>
> a. indifferent   b. compliant   c. obnoxious   d. sleepy

The sentence indicates that "we" expected to find Charlie one way but instead found him "stubborn" and "uncooperative." This means that you need to find a word that expresses the opposite meaning of these adjectives. Going through the choices, you can eliminate "indifferent," "obnoxious," and "sleepy." "Compliant" is the best choice.

You can use such a process of elimination on the test. If one option doesn't leap out at you as the correct one, eliminate the options that just don't make sense in context. (See pp. 73–74 for a more detailed discussion of how to use contextual clues to discern the meanings of words.)

Practice Using Words Correctly in Context

For each sentence, choose the correct word or phrase based on context. Answers and explanations appear on pp. 260–61.

1. Even though the wedding took place in a lush tropical garden, some guests _____ about their outdoor surroundings.

   a. respected   b. complained   c. viewed   d. observed

2. The young attorney was _____ about winning her first major case; this made the other lawyers resentful.

    a. worried   b. implicit   c. greedy   d. boastful

3. The landscape architect _____ the mansion's outdoor garden plans several times before presenting them to his clients.

    a. revised   b. highlighted   c. retracted   d. eliminated

4. The children's athletic coach _____ the kids to play their best in the finals.

    a. threatened   b. encouraged   c. penalized   d. marginalized

5. The house painters refused to apply a primer before the main color, so the walls are now _____.

    a. designing   b. breaking   c. peeling   d. sagging

6. The professor wanted to create a challenging final, so he _____ other colleagues who had taught the course.

    a. berated   b. agreed   c. denied   d. consulted

7. Charlotte's luggage was lost on her flight to San Francisco; I believe she's demanding _____.

    a. compensation   b. installation   c. ratio   d. revision

8. The gourmet dinner at the resort complemented the healthy lifestyle the spa _____.

    a. highlighted   b. underlined   c. capitalized   d. promoted

9. The gourmet food shop _____ fine wines and cheeses from Europe.

    a. corrected   b. imported   c. allotted   d. predicted

10. The boss of the maintenance crew was _____ by his workers' slow progress during the week.

    a. disappointed   b. predictable   c. coerced   d. unnerved

3.2B   IDENTIFYING COMMONLY CONFUSED AND MISUSED WORDS

What Are Commonly Confused and Misused Words?

Confused and **misused words** may look or sound similar to words with different meanings. When writers use a word that resembles or sounds like the one they mean but is spelled differently and has a different meaning, they might confuse their readers.

> **EXAMPLE**
>
> It's colder inside then outside.
>
> [*then* looks and sounds almost like *than* but it is the wrong word here because it is an adverb, not a conjunction, which is needed for this comparison]

Here is a list of common words that sound alike. If you don't know the differences among the words listed together, look them up in a dictionary and familiarize yourself with how each should be used.

a, an, and	peace, piece
accept, except	principal, principle
advice, advise	quiet, quite, quit
affect, effect	right, write
are, our	set, sit
by, buy	suppose, supposed
conscience, conscious	than, then
fine, find	their, there, they're
its, it's	though, through, threw
knew, new, know, no	to, too, two
loose, lose	use, used
mind, mine	who's, whose
of, have	your, you're
passed, past	

Words that do not sound alike can also be misused; for example, many writers wrongly use *disinterested* (which means "objective or impartial") when they mean *uninterested*. The mistake is understandable, but careful writers use a dictionary or thesaurus to check how a word should be used whenever they are not absolutely certain of the correct use.

How Do You Find Commonly Confused and Misused Words?

To prepare to find commonly confused and misused words on the test, review the preceding list. Also, develop a personal list of words you confuse often. Write down the words and their meanings.

In your own writing,

- look for and correct mistakes you make with the commonly confused words in the list. Also, look for words on your personal list.

- double-check words that you do not use regularly.

- look up a word if you are not completely confident about its meaning or about how it should be used.

Practice Finding Commonly Confused and Misused Words

For each sentence, select the option that corrects a confused or misused word in an underlined portion. If no change is necessary, choose d. Answers and explanations appear on p. 261.

1. The baby's bib will come off if you have it that lose.
        A   **B**   **C**

   a.   babys   b.   you're   c.   loose   d.   No change is necessary.

2. The affects of Hurricane Andrew left many, except those with good homeowner's
       A   **B**

   insurance, quite despondent.
             C

   a.   effects   b.   accept   c.   quiet   d.   No change is necessary.

3. Jennifer does seem to be quite and peaceful but she has quite a temper on her!
            A   **B**   **C**

   a.   dose   b.   quiet   c.   quit   d.   No change is necessary.

4. Joanna use to go shopping every day except Sundays.
         A   **B**   **C**

   a.   used   b.   everyday   c.   accept   d.   No change is necessary.

5. Your sometimes surprised at how well people regard their bosses.
    A   **B**   **C**

   a.   You're   b.   good   c.   they're   d.   No change is necessary.

6. The climate and whether changes in North Dakota affected many farmers; many lost
              A   **B**   **C**
   crops.

   a.   weather   b.   effected   c.   loss   d.   No change is necessary.

7. The morning after his bachelor party, Simon had scratches on his arms and an pounding
                                                             A
   headache; he had had too much to drink.
                  B   **C**

   a.   a   b.   two   c.   too   d.   No change is necessary.

8. Swimming and gardening are idea ways to stay in shape; however, gardening beautifies
                           A

   one's surroundings and the former doesn't.
     B   **C**

   a.   ideal   b.   once   c.   latter   d.   No change is necessary.

9. I really can't believe that James lost his keys and then left the baby along in the house!
                                A   **B**   **C**

   a.   loss   b.   than   c.   alone   d.   No change is necessary.

10. Flying these days has become expensive; my sister had to pay an additional $75 for her
          A

    excess baggage on the plain.
      B   **C**

    a.   this   b.   access   c.   plane   d.   No change is necessary.

3.3A USING MODIFIERS CORRECTLY

What Are Modifiers?

A **modifier** is a word or word group that functions as an adjective or an adverb. A modifier describes or limits other words in a sentence. In order to avoid confusing readers, writers should always place a modifier as close as possible to the word or words it modifies—ideally, either directly before or directly after the word or words.

Many word groups that act as modifiers are introduced by present or past participles. A present participle modifier consists of the *-ing* form of the verb along with the words it introduces.

present participle modifier

Steve Jobs, using his garage as a workshop, invented the personal computer.

A past participle modifier consists of the past participle form of the verb (usually ending in *-d* or *-ed*) along with the words it introduces.

past participle modifier

Rejected by Hamlet, Ophelia goes mad and drowns herself.

How Do You Place Modifiers Correctly?

A modifier must be near the sentence element it modifies and must clearly modify only one sentence element. In most cases, the modifier should appear right before or right after that sentence element.

A modifier in the wrong position in a sentence can seem to apply to an element that it cannot logically modify. This error is called a *misplaced modifier*. To identify a misplaced modifier, ask yourself the following questions:

- Is the modifier a limiting word such as *only, almost, hardly, nearly,* and *just*? If so, the modifier must be placed right before, not just close to, the words it modifies.

    almost

    Joanne ~~almost~~ ran ten miles.
    ^
    [Joanne actually ran; she didn't "almost" run.]

- Is the modifier a prepositional phrase? If so, make sure that the phrase appears immediately after the words it modifies.

    for her father

    She was shopping for a present all afternoon. ~~for her father.~~
    ^

- Is the modifier a phrase beginning with a present participle (an *-ing* form of the verb) or a past participle (usually a form ending in *d* or *ed*)? If so, make sure that it is right next to the word or word group it modifies.

> *Using my credit card,*
> I bought the puppy. ~~using my credit card.~~
> ^
> [The puppy was not using the credit card.]

- Is the modifier a clause beginning with *who, whose, that,* or *which*? If so, make sure that the clause appears immediately after the word or word group it modifies.

> *that was infecting my hard drive*
> Joel found the computer virus attached to an e-mail message. ~~that was infecting my hard drive.~~
> ^
> [What was infecting the hard drive, the virus or the message?]

A modifier that does not modify a word or word group in a sentence is known as a *dangling modifier*. Writers often fail to include the word being modified because they think the meaning is clear (or because they have not realized that the thing being modified is not present in the sentence).

> *I drove*
> Distracted by the bright lights, my car ~~drove~~ off the road.
> ^
> [The word being modified, *I*, was not included in the original sentence.]

Writers can correct dangling modifiers either by rewriting the sentence so that the word being modified appears right after the modifier (as in the preceding example) or by rewriting the sentence to get rid of the problem.

> *Because I was*   *I drove*
> d̶I̶stracted by the bright lights, my car ~~drove~~ off the road.
> ^   ^

On the test, eliminate answer options that show illogically placed modifiers like those in the examples.

Practice Finding Correctly Placed Modifiers

For each item, choose the sentence in which modifiers are placed correctly or most effectively. Answers and explanations appear on pp. 262–63.

1. a.   The new camcorder was stolen while on my vacation.

   b.   While I was on vacation, my camcorder was stolen.

   c.   My camcorder while on my vacation was stolen.

2. a. The student driver crashed while driving into a pole and playing loud music on the radio.

   b. While driving and playing loud music, the student driver crashed into a pole on the radio.

   c. While driving and playing loud music on the radio, the student driver crashed into a pole.

3. a. The teens saw exotic wild animals watching a documentary at their uncle's house.

   b. The teens watching exotic wild animals saw a documentary at their uncle's house.

   c. Watching a documentary at their uncle's house, the teens saw exotic wild animals.

4. a. Wearing a crisp white shirt and black pants, the drinks were made by the bartender.

   b. The bartender made the drinks wearing a crisp white shirt and black pants.

   c. Wearing a crisp white shirt and black pants, the bartender made the drinks.

5. a. Lost in a new city, the maps were forgotten by the sorry tourists.

   b. The tourists were sorry to have forgotten their maps, lost in a new city.

   c. Lost in a new city, the tourists were sorry to have forgotten their maps.

6. a. The bathtub filled up fast after we turned on the water.

   b. The bathtub, after we turned on the water, filled up fast.

   c. The fast bathtub filled up after we turned on the water.

7. a. The firefighter saved the little boy stuck in the tree.

   b. Stuck in the tree, the firefighter saved the little boy.

   c. The firefighter stuck in the tree saved the little boy.

8. a. Waiting for the tea kettle to boil, the waitress checked her table's order.

   b. The waitress checked her table's order waiting for the tea kettle to boil.

   c. Waiting for the waitress to check her table's order, the tea kettle boiled.

9. a. Dangling before a colorful fish, the diver noticed a baited line.

   b. Before a colorful fish, the diver noticed a baited line dangling.

   c. The diver noticed a baited line dangling before a colorful fish.

10. a. Without explanation shortly after accepting the position, the newly hired employee broke the contract.

   b. Shortly after accepting the position, the newly hired employee broke the contract without explanation.

   c. The newly hired employee without explanation broke the contract shortly after accepting the position.

What Are Coordination and Subordination?

Coordination and **subordination** are ways to join sentences with related ideas. Coordination can join two sentences when the ideas in each are equally important. Subordination can join two sentences when one idea is more important than the other.

The coordinating conjunctions—words used to join words, phrases, and clauses of equal importance—are *and, but, for, nor, or, yet,* and *so.* Some of the most common subordinating conjunctions—words used to join words, phrases, and clauses when one idea is more important than the other—include those in the following table.

FREQUENTLY USED SUBORDINATING CONJUNCTIONS

after	even though	since	whenever
although	if	so that	where
as	if only	than	whereas
as if	in order that	that	wherever
as though	now that	though	whether
because	once	unless	while
before	provided that	until	
even if	rather than	when	

The relative pronouns *who, whom, whose, which,* and *that* are also used to subordinate one part of a sentence to another. Typically, *that* and *which* refer to objects and *who* and *whose* to people. Note the use of *that* and *who* in the following underlined subordinate phrases.

> The bike *that* was in the window cost $500.
>
> The boy *who* took my bike is in trouble.

The phrases are not set off by commas because they are essential to the meaning of the sentences. In the next examples, however, the phrases provide nonessential information—information that could be taken out without significantly affecting the sentence's meaning. Such phrases are set off by commas.

> Jeanne, who has always done well in math, decided to study accounting in college.
>
> *A Farewell to Arms,* which is one of my father's favorite books, is being made into a new movie.

Note that in sentences like the previous one (in which the subordinate information is not essential), *which* (not *that*) introduces the subordinate clause.

How Do You Use Coordination and Subordination?

There are several ways in which sentences are combined through coordination and subordination.

USING COORDINATION

If the ideas in the sentences are equally important, the best choice is coordination. Writers can join the two sentences in two ways:

- Choose the coordinating conjunction—*and, but, for, nor, or, yet, so*—that makes the most sense of the relationship between the ideas. Then place it, preceded by a comma, between the sentences to be joined.

Equal idea	, and	Equal idea
	, but	
	, for	
	, nor	
	, or	
	, yet	

Antarctica is huge	, and	it is 98 percent ice.
	[*And* simply joins two ideas.]	
It is beautiful	, but	it is very cold.
	[*But* indicates a contrast.]	
It is very dry	, for	it receives only as much rain as a desert.
	[*For* indicates a reason or cause.]	
The vegetation is not lush	, nor	is it leaf-bearing.
	[*Nor* indicates a negative.]	
Perhaps people could live there	, or	it could be used for other purposes
	[*Or* indicates alternatives.]	

- Replace the period between the two sentences with a semicolon or with a semicolon followed by a conjunctive adverb that makes sense, such as *therefore* or *in addition*. In this case, the ideas should be very closely related.

Equal idea	;	Equal idea
Antarctica is a mystery	;	no one knows too much about it.

A semicolon alone does not tell readers much about the relationship between the two ideas. To give more information about the relationship, writers often follow a semicolon with a word that indicates the relationship and put a comma after this word. Here are the most common words that are used this way; they are known as *conjunctive adverbs*.

Equal idea	; also,	Equal idea
	; as a result,	
	; besides,	
	; however,	
	; in addition,	
	; in fact,	
	; instead,	
	; still,	
	; then,	
	; therefore,	

Antarctica is largely unexplored	; as a result,	it is unpopulated.
It receives little rain	; also,	it is incredibly cold.
It is a huge area	; therefore,	scientists are becoming more interested in it.

USING SUBORDINATION

If an idea in one sentence is more important than an idea in the other, writers typically use subordination. Specifically, they

- choose a subordinating conjunction that makes sense of the relationship between the ideas. Then they add the conjunction to the beginning of the sentence with the less important idea.

- place the sentences together. If the clause that begins with the subordinating word appears first in the sentence, writers typically put a comma after that clause. If it appears second in the sentence, however, a comma is not added.

Main idea	after	since	Subordinate idea
	although	so that	
	as	unless	
	as if	until	
	because	when	
	before	where	
	even though	while	
	if		

Scientists study the interior of Mt. Erebus	because	it might provide clues about global of warming.

Note the comma in this variation:

> Because it might provide clues about global warming, scientists study the interior of Mt. Erebus.

On the test, when you are asked to pick words or sentences that achieve effective coordination or subordination, ask, "What is the relationship between the parts of the sentence?" If they are equally important, choose coordination using the guidelines here. If one part is more important than the other, choose subordination.

Practice Using Coordination and Subordination

For each item (1) choose the term that creates effective coordination or subordination in a sentence or (2) choose which of three sentences uses correct coordination or subordination. Answers and explanations appear on p. 263.

1. The young couple wishes to buy the wedding bands in platinum, _____ they can't afford it.
   a. because   b. but   c. if   d. as

2. The swimming instructor did not want to teach the 8 a.m. class, _____ did she want to teach any evening classes.
   a. but   b. for   c. nor   d. and

3. _____ attending a community college has its advantages, it also has its disadvantages.
   a. Because   b. Until   c. Unless   d. Although

4. The new waiter was upset by the rude customers at table 4; _____, he cheered up after being treated kindly—and tipped generously—by the customers at table 5.
   a. hence   b. thus   c. however   d. accordingly

5. The senior citizens were thrilled to get a visit from the young carolers; _____, they appreciated the cookies the children brought.
   a. moreover   b. consequently   c. therefore   d. nonetheless

6. a. The dog whose bit my neighbor's son is a Doberman Pinscher.
   b. The dog which bit my neighbor's son is a Doberman Pinscher.
   c. The dog that bit my neighbor's son is a Doberman Pinscher.

7. a. After the breakup, Cynthia wanted to cry; however, she remained cold and silent.
   b. After the breakup, Cynthia wanted to cry, however, she remained cold and silent.
   c. After the breakup, Cynthia wanted to cry, however; she remained cold and silent.

8. a. The Cheesecake Factory, who is one of her favorite restaurants, has over 25 desserts.

   b. The Cheesecake Factory, which is one of her favorite restaurants, has over 25 desserts.

   c. The Cheesecake Factory, that is one of her favorite restaurants, has over 25 desserts.

9. a. Working as a waiter can be lucrative in South Florida, but working as a chef is definitely better.

   b. Working as a waiter is lucrative in South Florida; but, working as a chef is definitely better.

   c. Working as a waiter can be lucrative in South Florida but working as a chef is definitely better.

10. a. Biology is one of my favorite subjects while it deals with living creatures and how life evolved.

    b. Biology is one of my favorite subjects because it deals with living creatures and how life evolved.

    c. Biology is one of my favorite subjects unless it deals with living creatures and how life evolved.

3.3C UNDERSTANDING PARALLEL STRUCTURE

What Is Parallel Structure?

Parallel structure is a grammatical construction used to present comparable or equivalent ideas. Nouns are used with nouns, verbs with verbs, adjectives with adjectives, phrases with phrases, and clauses with clauses.

Faulty parallelism occurs when different grammatical constructions are used to present comparable or equivalent ideas.

> **EXAMPLE**
>
> **Not Parallel**   On our anniversary, we <u>ate</u>, <u>danced</u>, and <u>were singing</u>.
>
> [Verbs must be in the same tense to be parallel.]
>
> **Parallel**   On our anniversary, we <u>ate</u>, <u>danced</u>, and <u>sang</u>.

How Do You Make Sentences Parallel?

Problems with parallel structure are most likely to occur in the following types of sentence construction:

- Pairs and Lists: When two or more items are presented in a series joined by one of the coordinating conjunctions (*and, but, for, or, nor, yet,* or *so*), every item in the pair or list must be in parallel form.

Not Parallel	The story was <u>in the newspaper</u>, <u>on the radio</u>, and <u>the television</u>.
Parallel	The story was <u>in the newspaper</u>, <u>on the radio</u>, and <u>on the television</u>.

- Comparisons Using *than* or *as*: In comparisons, the items being compared must have parallel structure. Make sure that items on both sides of the words *than* or *as* have parallel structure.

Not Parallel	<u>To admit a mistake</u> is better than <u>denying it</u>.
Parallel	<u>To admit a mistake</u> is better than <u>to deny it</u>.
	<u>Admitting a mistake</u> is better than <u>denying it</u>.

- Constructions with Correlative Conjunctions (Paired Words): When a sentence uses a pair of words known as *correlative conjunctions*, the items joined by the conjunctions must be parallel. The correlative conjunctions are *both . . . and, either . . . or, neither . . . nor, not only . . . but also,* and *rather . . . than.*

Not Parallel	He can *neither* <u>fail the course</u> and <u>quitting his job is also impossible</u>.
Parallel	He can *neither* <u>fail the course</u> *nor* <u>quit his job</u>.

In all of these situations, be especially careful to use parallel forms—nouns with nouns, verbs with verbs (in the same tense), adjectives with adjectives, phrases with phrases, and clauses with clauses.

Practice Recognizing Parallel Structure

For each item, choose the sentence that has no error in structure, or select the word that makes the sentence parallel. Answers and explanations appear on pp. 263–64.

1. a.   Virginia didn't understand that she had to prepare the turkey, make the stuffing, and decorating the table, all before her guests arrived.

   b.   Virginia didn't understand that she had to prepare the turkey, make the stuffing, and decorated the table, all before her guests arrived.

   c.   Virginia didn't understand that she had to prepare the turkey, make the stuffing, and decorate the table, all before her guests arrived.

2. a.   Art has been a major tourist draw in Paris, which is also famous for its varied architecture and has a lot of great restaurants.

   b.   Art has been a major tourist draw in Paris, which is also famous for its varied architecture and great restaurants.

   c.   Art has been a major tourist draw in Paris, which is also famous for its varied architecture, and it has a lot of great restaurants.

3. Raising well-behaved children takes firmness, persistence, and _____.

    a.   being patient   b.   patience   c.   to be patient

4. a.   The new warehouse manager made us restock the shelves, clear out the old boxes, and wanted us to work overtime.

    b.   The new warehouse manager made us restock the shelves, clearing out the old boxes, and wanting us to work overtime.

    c.   The new warehouse manager made us restock the shelves, clear out the old boxes, and work overtime.

5. Her latest hobbies include sewing, _____, and cooking vegetarian meals.

    a.   to garden   b.   gardened   c.   gardening

6. a.   John is looking for a girlfriend with three important qualities: kindness, brains, and she must look like a model.

    b.   John is looking for a girlfriend with three important qualities: she must be kind, must be brainy, and she looks like a model.

    c.   John is looking for a girlfriend with three important qualities: kindness, brains, and good looks.

7. The hardest lessons to learn in grammar are fixing run-ons, eliminating fragments, and _____ verbs.

    a.   conjugated   b.   conjugating   c.   to conjugate

8. a.   Piper Piper, the new local band, has already toured Europe, recorded two CDs, and is planning to release songs in Portuguese.

    b.   Piper Piper, the new local band, has already toured Europe, recorded two CDs, and planned to release songs in Portuguese.

    c.   Piper Piper, the new local band, has already toured Europe, recorded two CDs, and has a plan to release songs in Portuguese.

9. a.   I'm planting my herbs this spring, my carrots this summer, and forget about fall and winter.

    b.   I'm planting my herbs this spring, my carrots this summer, and nothing this fall and winter.

    c.   I'm planting my herbs this spring, my carrots this summer, and forgetting about fall and winter.

10. a.   Three things make Mom lose her temper: laziness, sloppiness, and being late.

    b.   Three things make Mom lose her temper: laziness, being sloppy, and being late.

    c.   Three things make Mom lose her temper: laziness, sloppiness, and tardiness.

What Are Fragments?

A sentence is a group of words that has a subject and a complete verb and expresses a complete thought, independent of other sentences. A **fragment** is a group of words that looks like a sentence—beginning with a capital letter and ending with a period or other end punctuation—but lacks a subject or a complete verb or fails to complete a thought. A fragment is only a piece of a sentence.

EXAMPLE

Sentence   I got home late, so I ate some cold pizza and drank a whole liter of Pepsi.

Fragment   I got home late, so I ate some cold pizza. <u>And drank a whole liter of Pepsi.</u>

["And drank a whole liter of Pepsi" contains a verb ("drank") but no subject.]

How Do You Find Fragments?

Sentence fragments almost always appear in paragraphs and longer passages, right beside complete sentences.

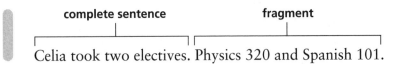

complete sentence   fragment

Celia took two electives. Physics 320 and Spanish 101.

Five trouble spots often signal fragments. To find fragments, look for word groups that begin with the following elements, which are underlined in the examples:

1. a preposition such as *at, in, on,* and *with*

    The order of one's birth in a family has a strong influence. <u>On</u> one's personality.

2. a word group containing a dependent clause
    —The word group may start with a subordinating conjunction such as *after, because,* and *when.*

    The group is meeting this morning. <u>After</u> my first class ends.

    —The word group may include a relative pronoun such as *who, which,* and *that.*

    Novelist Richard Wright, <u>who</u> came to Paris in 1947.

3. a word group that starts with a participle

   —A present participle starts with an *-ing* verb form.

   > The twins spent most of the day outside. <u>Looking</u> for trouble.

   —A past participle starts with an *-ed* verb form.

   > The first full-length animated film was Walt Disney's *Snow White and the Seven Dwarfs*. <u>Released</u> originally in 1937.

4. a word group that starts with *to* and a verb

   > I asked my professor for help. <u>To understand the difficult concept.</u>

5. a word group that starts with an example or explanation of something mentioned in the previous sentence

   > Employees need to know of all exits from the building. <u>For instance, the nearest fire exit.</u>

Sentences that are missing a part of the verb are also fragments. A sentence that contains a present or past participle without a helping verb (a form of *be* or *have*) lacks a complete verb.

> The letter hidden behind the sofa pillow.

You can correct a fragment either by joining it to the sentence before or after it (choose the sentence that makes sense with the fragment added) or by adding the missing parts to the fragment so that it can stand alone as a complete sentence.

Fragment	A quinceañera, which celebrates a Latina's fifteenth birthday.
Sentence	A quinceañera celebrates a Latina's fifteenth birthday.
Sentence	A quinceañera, which celebrates a Latina's fifteenth birthday, signifies her entrance into womanhood.

Practice Correcting Fragments

For each sentence, select the option that corrects a fragment. If no change is necessary, choose option d. Answers and explanations appear on pp. 264–65.

1. We really didn't know where we were going in the decrepit mansion, so we decided
   <u>know where</u> <u>going in</u>
       A   **B**

   to follow our <u>instincts. And</u> open the first door on the left-hand side.
                    C

   a.   know. Where   b.   going. In

   c.   instincts and   d.   No change is necessary.

2. The group of teenagers smoking on the street <u>corner. Were</u> <u>accused of</u> throwing rocks
                                                   A   **B**
   at the <u>buses driving</u> by the schoolyard.
             C

   a.   corner were   b.   accused. Of

   c.   buses. Driving   d.   No change is necessary.

3. However the Girl Scouts plan to organize their <u>hike. Is</u> their business; all we know is
                                                    they must reach the camp site by dusk.

   a.   hike is   b.   hike; is

   c.   hike, is   d.   No change is necessary.

4. The couple decided to end the <u>marriage when</u> they returned from their <u>trip; they</u> needed
                                    A   **B**

   time <u>away. To</u> make the decision.
          C

   a.   marriage. When   b.   trip, they

   c.   away to   d.   No change is necessary.

5. Since raising four children on her own was difficult for <u>Sarah. She</u> decided to remarry
                                                              A

   and give her children and herself one last chance at happiness.

   a.   Sarah, she   b.   Sarah she

   c.   Sarah; she   d.   No change is necessary.

6. He knew the mail carrier would be delivering a very important <u>package to</u> his <u>home,</u> so
                                                                   A   **B**
   at 5:30 p.m. <u>he rushed</u> home from work.
                  C

   a.   package. To   b.   home so

   c.   he was rushing   d.   No change is necessary.

7. Before I go to <u>bed.</u> I check all the doors and windows to make sure they're locked.

   a.   bed, I   b.   bed I

   c.   bed; I   d.   No change is necessary.

8. I had to pay a late <u>fee. Since</u> my library books were <u>overdue.</u> I didn't <u>care, though;</u>
                             A   **B**   **C**

    I finished my report on time.

    a.   fee since   b.   overdue, I

    c.   care. Though   d.   No change is necessary.

9. Florida has many <u>attractions;</u> it is a wonderful <u>place to visit.</u> <u>And</u> a great place to live.
                             A   **B** **C**

    a.   attractions, it is   b.   place. To

    c.   visit and   d.   No change is necessary.

10. After the lumberjack crew cut down all the <u>trees, the</u> crew leader sent them home
                                                           A

    <u>early. Because</u> he didn't want <u>them just</u> standing around.
              B   **C**

    a.   trees the   b.   early because

    c   them; just   d.   No change is necessary.

3.3E   AVOIDING COMMA SPLICES AND FUSED SENTENCES

What Are Comma Splices and Fused Sentences?

Comma splices and **fused sentences** are errors that occur when two complete sentences (independent clauses) are made into one. When the sentences are joined with only a comma, the resulting error is a comma splice. When the two sentences are joined without punctuation, the error is called a fused sentence.

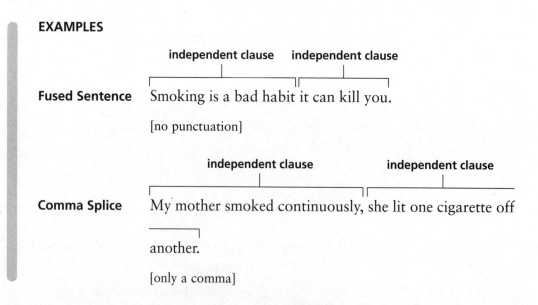

EXAMPLES

independent clause   independent clause

Fused Sentence   Smoking is a bad habit it can kill you.

[no punctuation]

independent clause   independent clause

Comma Splice   My mother smoked continuously, she lit one cigarette off

another.

[only a comma]

How Do You Find and Correct Comma Splices and Fused Sentences?

To find comma splices and fused sentences, ask yourself the following questions about any sentence that you think might contain one of these errors:

- Does the sentence have more than one subject and more than one verb?
- Does the sentence contain at least two complete thoughts?

If the answer to both questions is yes, ask these questions:

- Are the two sentences joined with a comma and a coordinating conjunction (*and, but, for, nor, or, yet*, or *so*)?
- Are they joined with a semicolon?
- Are they joined with a semicolon and a conjunctive adverb (such as *however*) or a transitional expression (such as *for example*)?

If the answer to all of these questions is no, ask these questions:

- Are the two sentences joined without punctuation between them? If so, the sentence is fused.
- Are the two sentences joined with a comma alone? If so, the sentence is a comma splice.

Comma splices and fused sentences can be fixed by adding the proper punctuation and perhaps a joining word. You can also make one sentence subordinate to the other.

Fused Sentence	Boston has a couple of unusual holidays Evacuation Day is one of them.
Revised	Boston has a couple of unusual holidays. Evacuation Day is one of them.
	[sentences separated with a period]
Revised	Boston has a couple of unusual holidays; Evacuation Day is one of them.
	[sentences separated with a semicolon]
Comma Splice	I missed the bus, I had to get a ride.
Revised	I missed the bus, so I had to get a ride.
	[sentences joined with comma and a coordinating conjunction]
Revised	Because I missed the bus, I had to get a ride.
	[first part of sentence made subordinate to the other]

You can also join sentences with a semicolon and a conjunctive adverb (like *therefore* and *however*) followed by a comma.

Comma Splice	I can't figure out how to solve this problem, I'm going to ask for advice.
Revised	I can't figure out how to solve this problem; therefore, I'm going to ask for advice.

Practice Correcting Comma Splices and Fused Sentences

For each sentence, select the option that corrects a comma splice or fused sentence. If no change is necessary, choose option d. Answers and explanations appear on p. 265.

1. Lila didn't try out for the soccer team this year she plans to do so next year, assuming

    A   B   C

her knee heals.

    a.   Lila didnt   b.   year, but she

    c.   year; assuming   d.   No change is necessary.

2. No one knows how to cook a roast better than my Uncle Dean, therefore he ends up

                                                                          A   B

doing a lot of the cooking on holidays.

                                              C

    a.   roast, better   b.   Dean; therefore,

    c.   cooking, on   d.   No change is necessary.

3. Careful attention to foot placement is important for rock climbing, and balance is also key.

    a.   climbing and   b.   climbing; and

    c.   climbing: and   d.   No change is necessary.

4. After a busy day, Roberta picked her clothes up at the cleaners she forgot to get takeout food for herself and her roommates.

    a.   cleaners: she   b.   cleaners, but she

    c.   cleaners, and she   d.   No change is necessary.

5. The Coast Guard searched all day and far into the night, the vanished boat and its crew

                    A   B

were not recovered, and rescuers' hopes began to fade.

                    C

    a.   Coast Guard searched,   b.   night; however, the

    c.   recovered; and   d.   No change is necessary.

6. Tina and Paulo were surprised to find they had a very good friend in common a week later, all three of them met for coffee.

    a.   common, but a   b.   common. A

    c.   common: a   d.   No change is necessary.

7. The customer service department received multiple <u>calls about</u> the faulty remote-
                                                                                A

control <u>device, they</u> never passed on the <u>complaints to</u> the engineering department.
       B   **C**

    a.   calls. About   b.   device, but

    c.   complaints—to   d.   No change is necessary.

8. My sister didn't like <u>beets until</u> she tasted my beet-and-leek <u>risotto, now</u> she raves
                          A   **B**

about <u>them, and</u> she's planning to add them to her garden.
      C

    a.   beets, until   b.   risotto; now

    c.   them. And   d.   No change is necessary.

9. I made it to the theater an hour before the show <u>time I</u> had to park several blocks
                                                     A

<u>away, so</u> I nearly missed the <u>start of</u> the performance.
 B   **C**

    a.   time; however, I   b.   away. So

    c.   start, of   d.   No change is necessary.

10. Human-resources managers are <u>busy, they</u> may become annoyed if a résumé is longer
                                   A

than one or two <u>pages or</u> if an applicant calls several times to <u>check on</u> a position.
                B   **C**

    a.   busy; therefore, they   b.   pages. Or

    c.   check, on   d.   No change is necessary.

3.4A USING STANDARD VERB FORMS

What Are Standard Verb Forms?

Verb forms are the different ways a verb can be spelled and pronounced. Verbs have different forms to indicate that they are singular or plural, past or present tense, second or third person, and so on.

Most verbs in English are regular verbs—their forms follow standard rules. Regular verbs have two forms for the present tense, an *s* ending for the third-person singular (with *he, she, it,* and singular nouns), and a base form (without an ending) for other first- and second-person singular (*I, you*) and all plural uses.

REGULAR VERB FORMS IN THE PRESENT TENSE		
	Singular	**Plural**
First person	I jump.	We jump.
Second person	You jump.	You jump.
Third person	She (he, it) jumps.	They jump.
	The child jumps.	The children jump.

Regular verbs have one past-tense form, which ends in *ed*.

REGULAR VERB FORMS IN THE PAST TENSE		
	Present Tense	**Past Tense**
First person	I avoid her.	I avoided her.
Second person	You help me.	You helped me.
Third person	He walks fast.	He walked fast.

Regular verbs have one past-participle ending, which is the same as the past-tense form (with an *ed* ending).

REGULAR VERB FORMS IN THE PAST-PARTICIPLE TENSE	
Past-Tense Form	**Past-Participle Form**
My kids watched cartoons.	They **have watched** cartoons before.
George visited his cousins.	He **has visited** them every year.

Many English verbs do not follow the regular patterns. A few—including two very common verbs, *be* and *have*—are irregular in the present tense.

PRESENT-TENSE FORMS OF TWO IRREGULAR VERBS			
Be		**Have**	
I am	we are	I have	we have
you are	you are	you have	you have
he, she, it is	they are	he, she, it has	they have
the editor is	the editors are		
Denise is	Denise and Sarah are		

Irregular verbs have unusual forms in the past tense, in the past participle, or both.

COMMON IRREGULAR VERBS		
Present Tense	**Past Tense**	**Past Participle**
am/are/is	was/were	been
bring	brought	brought
do	did	done
go	went	gone
have/has	had	had
lay (put or place)	laid	laid
lie (recline)	lay	lain

There are many more irregular verbs than we are able to list here. If you are having trouble with these verbs, it is best to get a grammar handbook and study the more comprehensive lists there.

How Do You Find Nonstandard Verb Forms?

There is no simple rule for identifying an irregular verb or for determining how an irregular verb forms the past tense and past participle, so the only way to be certain of the forms of English irregular verbs is to memorize lists like the preceding one.

To find nonstandard verb forms, ask the following questions:

- Is the verb regular? If so, is it in the correct form? Regular verbs add endings only in the third-person singular present tense (the *s* form), the past tense (the *ed* form), and the past-participle form (the *ed* form again). Memorize the list of irregular verbs so that you can be sure how each verb changes form.

- If the verb is irregular, how does it form the past tense and past participle (and the present tense, in the case of *be* or *have*)? Is the correct form used?

- If the verb is irregular and in the past tense, does it use the appropriate form? In the simple past tense, the past-tense form is used; in the perfect tenses, the past participle is used with one or more helping verbs. Check the way the verb is used to be sure that the appropriate form appears.

EXAMPLES

begun
Lately, many businesses have ~~began~~ to hire temporary workers.
        ^

ed
Online classes have appears at many colleges.
          ^

is
The company ~~be~~ part of a fast-growing industry.
        ^

Practice Correcting Nonstandard Verb Forms

For each sentence, select the option that corrects the underlined verb. If the verb is correct as is, choose option d. Answers and explanations appear on p. 266.

1. Rebecca was <u>chosen</u> from the seven candidates.

   a.   chosed   b.   choosen   c.   choose   d.   No change is necessary.

2. Old letters from the family's business dealings <u>fallen</u> from the worn-out Bible.

   a.   fell   b.   falls   c.   felled   d.   No change is necessary.

3. During the challenging routine, some of the gymnasts <u>hurted</u> their feet upon landing.

   a.   hurts   b.   hurting   c.   hurt   d.   No change is necessary.

4. The vegetarian family upstairs doesn't eat meat or chicken; they <u>prefers</u> fish.

   a.   prefer   b.   preferring   c.   preferred   d.   No change is necessary.

5. I should <u>have went</u> directly to the emergency room after <u>injuring</u> my foot instead of
             A   **B**
<u>waiting</u> for the pain to get worse.
   C

   a.   have gone   b.   injured   c.   waited   d.   No change is necessary.

6. The children who live next door to us <u>waken</u> up before seven a.m. and turned on the
television.

   a.   wakened   b.   wake   c.   woke   d.   No change is necessary.

7. The news report <u>stated</u> that the island government <u>spended</u> hundreds of thousands of
                A   **B**
dollars to <u>attract</u> new tourists.
           C

   a. state   b.   spent   c.   attracted   d.   No change is necessary.

8. After last night's delicious home-cooked meal, the housekeeper <u>frozen</u> the leftovers.

    a.   freezed   b.   freezing   c.   froze   d.   No change is necessary.

9. I like to <u>lay</u> on the couch and <u>dream</u> of what I'll do when summer <u>comes</u>.
           A   **B**   **C**

    a.   lie   b.   dreamt   c.   is coming   d.   No change is necessary.

10. After <u>wearing</u> her new blouse only once, Sharon <u>shrunk</u> it by <u>throwing</u> it into the
               A   **B**   **C**

washer and dryer.

    a.   worn   b.   shrank   c.   threw   d.   No change is necessary.

(3.4B) AVOIDING INAPPROPRIATE SHIFTS IN VERB TENSE

What Is Consistency of Verb Tense?

Consistency of verb tense means that all verbs in the passage that describe actions happening at the same time are in the same tense. If all of the actions happen in the present tense or at the same time, all of the verbs should be in the present tense. If all of the actions happened in the past, all verbs should be in the past tense.

When a writer shifts from one tense to another for no apparent reason, the verb tenses are inconsistent. Illogical shifts can confuse readers by making it difficult to understand when actions happened in relation to one another.

	EXAMPLE
Illogical Tense Shift	The dog <u>walked</u> to the fireplace. Then, he <u>circles</u> twice and <u>lies</u> down in <u>front</u> of the fire.
	[past to present]
Revised	The dog <u>walked</u> to the fireplace. Then, he <u>circled</u> twice and <u>lay</u> down in <u>front</u> of the fire.
	[consistent past]
Revised	The dog <u>walks</u> to the fireplace. Then, he <u>circles</u> twice and <u>lies</u> down in <u>front</u> of the fire.
	[consistent present]

How Do You Find Shifts in Verb Tense?

Ask the following questions about the verbs in a passage to find illogical shifts in verb tense:

* What is the tense of each verb in the passage?
* Are the tenses the same throughout?
* If the tenses are all the same, do all of the actions described happen at the same time? If your answer is no, look for verbs whose tense seems illogical.

- If the tenses are not the same throughout the passage, does the passage describe actions that occur at different times? If your answer is no, look for places where the verb seems to shift illogically from one tense to another.

EXAMPLE

Past
When Beverly Harvard became the chief of the Atlanta police

was
force, she ~~is~~ the first African American woman ever to hold
^

that title in a major US city.

Past
She started on the police force when she was twenty-two, at

_ed_
a time when mostly white men work as Atlanta police officers.
^

Present
Now, more than half the department is African American,

make
and women ~~made~~ up about a quarter of the force.
^

Practice Correcting Shifts in Verb Tense

For each sentence, select the option that corrects an underlined verb if its tense doesn't make sense. If the sentence is correct as is, choose option d. Answers and explanations appear on pp. 266–67.

1. Maria never <u>likes</u> to drive at night when it's raining; she drove only during the day.

   a. liking   b. liked   c. liken   d. No change is necessary.

2. We never <u>found</u> out where Michael was yesterday, though we <u>look</u> in every room and
        A   **B**
eventually <u>called</u> his home.
       C

   a. find   b. looked   c. calling   d. No change is necessary.

3. After finishing her internship this coming August, Harriet <u>goes</u> on safari with two friends.

   a. went   b. going   c. will go   d. No change is necessary.

4. It didn't occur to me until much later that Jack <u>is</u> the man I'd seen leaving the building with Audrey.

   a. was   b. has been   c. would be   d. No change is necessary.

5. Even though little Paolo <u>likes</u> bananas, he <u>spit out</u> every bite his mother fed him
A   B

because he <u>was</u> grouchy.
C

 a. used to like b. spits out c. has been d. No change is necessary.

6. When my grandfather, Antonio Ricci, became president of Cecil's French-American Club, he <u>is</u> the first Italian to hold that post in the town's history.

 a. were   b. is becoming c. was   d. No change is necessary.

7. My grandfather <u>tells</u> us stories about that time. He especially likes to tell the one about
A

how, many years ago, he <u>sings</u> France's national anthem flawlessly when a French diplo-
B

mat <u>came</u> into the club.
C

 a. is telling b. sang   c. comes d. No change is necessary.

8. He joined the French-American Club in 1964, when most of the members <u>are</u> French immigrants or of French descent; now many nationalities are represented.

 a. is   b. was   c. were   d. No change is necessary.

9. During his summer vacation, Gerard swam every morning, napped every afternoon, and <u>goes</u> for ice cream every evening.

 a. went   b. is going c. has gone d. No change is necessary.

10. George Washington <u>is</u> well-known for his strengths as a general and president. Many
A

people <u>don't realize</u>, however, that he <u>is</u> also an excellent soldier.
B   C

 a. was   b. didn't realize c. was   d. No change is necessary.

3.4C MAKING SUBJECTS AND VERBS AGREE

What Is Subject-Verb Agreement?

The subject of a sentence or clause is the person, place, or thing that the sentence or clause is about.

> <u>Bill</u> drives to school everyday.
>
> ["Bill" is the subject. The verb "drives" indicates what Bill does.]

A sentence's subject and its verb must agree in number. A singular subject—one person or thing—must match a singular verb (as in the sentence about Bill), and a plural subject—

more than one person or thing—must have a plural verb. A subject can be a single word (a noun or a pronoun) or a compound of two or more words joined by *and* or *or*.

How Do You Find Problems with Subject-Verb Agreement?

Most subject-verb agreement problems occur in the present tense, where third-person singular subjects require special verb forms. Regular verbs form the third-person singular by adding *s* or *es* to the base form. (For a review of standard verb forms, see section 3.4A.)

To find problems with subject-verb agreement, look for the following special cases:

- Compound subjects in which two or more words are joined with *and* or *or*: A compound subject joined with *and* is treated as a plural subject. When the compound subject is joined with *or*, the verb should agree with noun or pronoun closer to the verb.

- The irregular verbs *be, have,* and *do*: The forms of these common irregular verbs do not follow the usual pattern for third-person singular verbs in the present tense. The particular verb form must agree with the particular subject.

- Words that come between the subject and the verb: Identify the subject and ignore any prepositional phrases or other words that appear between it and the verb. The verb must agree with the subject regardless of anything that comes between the subject and the verb. (On the test, you might want to cross out intervening words.)

- Indefinite pronouns such as *everyone*: Most indefinite pronouns are singular and take a singular verb, even though their meanings may seem plural. (See section 3.4D, p. 184, for a list of singular indefinite pronouns.)

- Verbs that come before the subject: In questions and constructions such as *there is* and *there are*, the verb must agree with the subject that follows it. *There* is not a subject.

- Dependent clauses: The relative pronouns *who, which,* and *that* can be either singular or plural. The verb must agree with the word to which the relative pronoun refers.

Be aware of words—such as *mathematics, United States, news,* and *physics*—that end in *s* but are singular. Often, these words refer to a field or discipline. For example, the following sentence is correct: *Physics is Stephanie's favorite subject.*

Also, constructions that include the phrase *one of the* can be tricky. Note the correction in the following sentence:

> Organizing files is one of the tasks that takes the longest.

"That" actually refers to "tasks," not "one"; therefore, the verb should be "take" to agree with "tasks."

Practice Correcting Problems with Subject-Verb Agreement

For each sentence, select the option that corrects an underlined problem with subject-verb agreement. If no change is necessary, choose option d. Answers and explanations appear on pp. 267–68.

1. Mayor Green <u>has always said</u> that the banking industry and regulatory agencies

            A

<u>makes</u> strange bedfellows, and he <u>vows</u> to investigate their dealings.

 B   **C**

    a.   have always said   b.   make   c.   vow   d.   No change is necessary.

2. Of all the courses the graduate students <u>has taken</u>, physics <u>has been</u> the most difficult,

                                      A   **B**

and psychology <u>has been</u> the easiest.

             C

    a.   have taken   b.   have been   c.   have been   d.   No change is necessary.

3. Sheila has yet to register for her fall classes, but she already knows that aerobics <u>are</u> a
fun class to take in the mornings.

    a.   was   b.   were   c.   is   d.   No change is necessary.

4. Although TV news <u>helps</u> the public <u>keep up</u> with current events, few would dispute

                 A   **B**

that news <u>sensationalize</u> local and world events.

           C

    a.   help   b.   keeps up   c.   sensationalizes   d.   No change is necessary.

5. The competition was fierce between the two candidates who <u>was running</u> for the
congressional seat; however, either of them would be a good choice.

    a.   is running   b.   were running

    c.   has been running   d.   No change is necessary.

6. At the end of the long, dark hallway <u>stand</u> a shadowy figure who <u>reminds</u> me of a

                                      A   **B**

character in one of the novels <u>written</u> by Edgar Allan Poe.

                           C

    a.   stands   b.   remind

    c.   were writing   d.   No change is necessary.

7. Marco is one of those students who <u>make</u> every teacher smile since he always <u>does</u> his

                                A   **B**

work, <u>participates</u> in class discussions, and asks pointed questions.

      C

    a.   makes   b.   do   c.   participate   d.   No change is necessary.

8. The cheerleaders and their coach <u>has</u> already left for the competition, and they believe
that the principal from the school <u>is</u> also on her way up to join them.

    a.   having   b.   have

    c.   is having   d.   No change is necessary.

9. Although most participating organizations <u>has filled out</u> the Walk-a-Thon forms,
A

many others <u>have</u> yet to <u>turn in</u> the forms.
B   C

   a. have filled out   b. has
   c. turned in   d. No change is necessary.

10. Almost everyone <u>love</u> to go the zoo—everyone but my sister Claire.
   a. loving   b. loves   c. to love   d. No change is necessary.

11. Studying for final exams, taking care of elderly parents, and spending quality time with
his family <u>has taken</u> their toll on Tony, for he <u>has had</u> little time for his hobbies, which
A   B

<u>keep</u> him centered and stress-free.
C

   a. have taken   b. have had   c. keeps   d. No change is necessary.

12. Five singles or a five-dollar bill <u>are</u> all I need for my cash register.
   a. were   b. be   c. is   d. No change is necessary.

13. There, on the table, <u>is</u> the passport and entry visa that Max <u>needs</u> to enter the country,
A   B

which has borders that <u>lie</u> close to the Swiss Alps.
C

   a. are   b. need   c. lies   d. No change is necessary.

14. Grandparents who take care of a grandchild often <u>faces</u> many challenges given the
differences between generations.
   a. facing   b. face   c. is facing   d. No change is necessary.

15. When young people first <u>enter</u> college, they must deal with a variety of situations that
A

<u>are</u> surprising and difficult; usually, these obstacles <u>are quickly overcome</u>.
B   C

   a. enters   b. is
   c. is quickly overcome   d. No change is necessary.

16. Neither Jessica nor her sister <u>have decided</u> what she wants to wear to the Halloween
party.
   a. has decided   b. is decided
   c. has been deciding   d. No change is necessary.

17. Mark <u>has had</u> his eyes on the new computer models for some time, but the cost of these
     A

  <u>were</u> more than his budget would allow; recently, however, the prices of the computers
  B

  <u>have been reduced</u>.
      C

    a.   have had   b.   was

    c.   has been reduced   d.   No change is necessary.

18. Nobody in the company has been able to figure out why Julie and Karen <u>has both quit</u> their jobs.

    a.   has quitted   b.   have both quit

    c.   is quitting   d.   No change is necessary.

19. Most of the architecture class <u>had reviewed</u> the chapter in the design textbook; thus,
                       A

  no one <u>was surprised</u> when Professor Roy pointed out that the problem with Maria's
       B

  designs <u>was described</u> on page 150.
       C

    a.   have reviewed   b.   were surprised

    c.   were described   d.   No change is necessary.

20. At the book fair, there <u>was</u> six tables covered with dusty volumes from the Edmonds family's personal history.

    a.   be   b.   were   c.   is   d.   No change is necessary.

3.4D MAKING PRONOUNS AND ANTECEDENTS AGREE

What Is Pronoun-Antecedent Agreement?

A pronoun is a word that replaces a noun.

> **EXAMPLES**
>
> David is the best pitcher I've seen.
> <u>He</u> is the best pitcher I've seen.

In the second sentence, the pronoun "he" replaces "David."
Many pronouns have antecedents, nouns to which pronouns refer.

> **EXAMPLE**
>
> David forgot <u>his</u> glove at practice.

The pronoun "his" refers back to the antecedent "David."

The pronoun must agree with its antecedent in number and gender. A singular pronoun, which refers to just one person or thing, must have a singular antecedent; a plural pronoun, which refers to more than one person or thing, must have a plural antecedent. Feminine or masculine singular pronouns must also match the gender of their antecedents (if the antecedents have a gender).

Inconsistent	Any student can tell you what <u>their</u> least favorite course is.
	["Student" is singular, but the pronoun "their" is plural.]
Consistent	Any student can tell you what <u>his</u> or <u>her</u> least favorite course is.
	["Student" is singular, and so are the pronouns "his" and "her."]

How Do You Find Problems with Pronoun-Antecedent Agreement?

The main problem areas for pronoun-antecedent agreement are indefinite pronouns; singular, generic nouns such as "student" in the preceding example; and collective nouns.

To find problems with pronoun-antecedent agreement, ask yourself the following questions:

- Is the antecedent an indefinite pronoun?

INDEFINITE PRONOUNS

Singular

another	everybody	no one
anybody	everyone	nothing
anyone	everything	one
anything	much	somebody
each	neither	someone
either	nobody	something

Plural

both	others
few	several
many	

If the indefinite pronoun antecedent is singular, the pronoun must be singular. If the antecedent is plural, the pronoun must be plural.

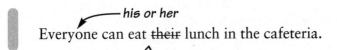

> Everyone can eat ~~their~~ lunch in the cafeteria.

- Is the antecedent a generic singular noun, such as *person* or *professor*, that can be either masculine or feminine? If so, a singular pronoun must be used. To avoid using a masculine pronoun such as *he*, which is widely considered sexist, you may use two pronouns, as in *he or she*; you may also recast the singular noun as a plural noun (changing *professor* to *professors*, for example) so that a plural, genderless pronoun such as *they* can be used.

> Each employee at a company pays only about half as much toward social
>
> *he or she*
> security as ~~they~~ would pay if self-employed.
>
> *Employees*
> ~~Each employee~~ at a company pays only about half as much toward social secur-
>
> ity as they would pay if self-employed.

- Is the antecedent a collective noun that names a group, as in *committee*, *jury*, and *team*? If so, you must determine whether the collective noun is singular or plural in any given case: if the members of the group are acting as a unit, the noun is singular and the pronoun must also be singular; if the members of the group are acting as individuals, the noun is plural and the pronoun must also be plural.

> The band played on, but it never played our song.

- Is there a two-part antecedent connected by *or* or *nor* (or by *either/or* or *neither/nor*)? If so, the pronoun needs to agree with the closer antecedent.

> Neither Ellen nor her sisters lost their keys.

Practice Correcting Problems with Pronoun-Antecedent Agreement

For each sentence, select the option that corrects an underlined problem with pronoun-antecedent agreement. If no change is necessary, choose option d. Answers and explanations appear on pp. 268–69.

1. An instructor always enjoys seeing one of their students do well on final exams.
   a. his or her   b. its   c. our   d. No change is necessary.

2. The chamber of commerce is publishing a fancy new brochure with large headlines; their message will certainly get out.
   a. they're   b. there   c. its   d. No change is necessary.

3. The couple drove its cars in separate directions.
   a. it's   b. their   c. his   d. No change is necessary.

4. The attorney and his legal assistant decided to rewrite the proposal and submit them to the defendant.
   a. it   b. their   c. they're   d. No change is necessary.

5. Either the campus center or the libraries will have <u>its</u> floors cleaned this month.

    a. his   b. it's   c. their   d. No change is necessary.

6. Patricia, one of the engineers assigned to the project, takes pride in <u>her</u> designs.

    a. their   b. his   c. its   d. No change is necessary.

7. At 3:00 p.m., the toddlers eagerly awaited <u>her</u> parents.

    a. their   b. its   c. hers   d. No change is necessary.

8. The rain or the protest may delay the baseball game, but Carlos will not let <u>either one</u>
                                                                           A
dampen <u>his</u> spirits or drive <u>him</u> away.
         B   **C**

    a. it   b. their   c. them   d. No change is necessary.

9. The warts on Mabel's fingers seem to be getting worse. <u>She</u> wants to have <u>it</u> removed
                                                     A   **B**
before <u>her</u> brother's wedding.
        C

    a. Her   b. them   c. she   d. No change is necessary.

10. Not one of the buildings set for demolition had <u>their</u> permits pulled.

    a. them   b. its   c. they're   d. No change is necessary.

11. Every planet and every star in the universe has <u>its</u> place.

    a. their   b. our   c. it's   d. No change is necessary.

12. Neither skateboarding nor soccer seems to be losing <u>their</u> popularity with today's youth.

    a. its   b. our   c. his   d. No change is necessary.

13. Many environmentalists are now saying that the gray wolf is no longer in danger of
losing <u>their</u> habitat.

    a. our   b. its   c. they're   d. No change is necessary.

14. By the time the ballet dancers were halfway through <u>their</u> recital, most of the audience
                                                                 A
had left <u>its</u> seats and had returned to <u>their</u> cars.
          B   **C**

    a. its   b. their   c. its   d. No change is necessary.

15. Ling Phong or her cousins will submit <u>their</u> recipes for the cookbook.

    a. them   b. our   c. she   d. No change is necessary.

16. The company can't possibly expect me to move to Alaska! <u>They</u> just can't!

    a. You   b. Us   c. It   d. No change is necessary.

17. One of the gymnasts twisted <u>their</u> ankle while dismounting the balance beam.

    a. her   b. our   c. its   d. No change is necessary.

18. The mouse worked <u>its</u> way through the wall and is now hiding behind the trash can.

    a. their   b. they're   c. our   d. No change is necessary.

19. After leaving <u>their</u> rallying place, the mob crossed the park and demanded to be admitted to the statehouse.

    a. its   b. our   c. they're   d. No change is necessary.

20. She is an honor student who always studies for <u>its</u> tests.

    a. our   b. their   c. her   d. No change is necessary.

3.4E   AVOIDING SHIFTS IN PRONOUN PERSON

What Is Consistency in Pronoun Person?

Person is the point of view a writer uses—the perspective from which he or she writes. Pronouns may be in the first person (such as *I*), the second person (such as *you*), or the third person (such as *she*). The writer's perspective throughout a passage should be consistent; a passage that begins with the first person should not shift to the second or third person, for example.

Inconsistent Person	As soon as a <u>shopper</u> walks into the store, <u>you</u> can tell it is a weird place.
	[The sentence starts with the third person ("a shopper") but shifts to the second person ("you").]
Consistent Person	As soon as a <u>shopper</u> walks into the store, <u>he</u> or <u>she</u> can tell it is a weird place.
Consistent Person, Plural	As soon as <u>shoppers</u> walk into the store, <u>they</u> can tell it is a weird place.

How Do You Find Shifts in Person?

To find shifts in person, which might confuse a reader, check each pronoun in a passage. Are they all in the same person, or do you find shifts from first to third person, third to second person, or other shifts? If you find illogical shifts, the passage uses inconsistent pronoun person.

EXAMPLE

first person   second person

I have gone to the writing center at my school because sometimes you need a second pair of eyes to look over a paper.

Practice Correcting Shifts in Person

For each sentence, select the option that corrects an underlined problem with shifts in person. If no change is necessary, choose option d. Answers and explanations appear on pp. 269–70.

1. When people get up in the morning, we should focus on the positive; they should
                                               A   **B**

take a deep breath and count their blessings.
                                   C

    a.   they   b.   we   c.   his or her   d.   No change is necessary.

2. No one expects his car to be stolen from the driveway, his garage to be broken into,
                       A   **B**

and his belongings to be scattered in the streets.
     C

    a.   their   b.   their   c.   their   d.   No change is necessary.

3. Dana and the other architects should combine our efforts and present their proposal to
the board for its final approval.   **A**   **B**
                         C

    a.   their   b.   its   c.   their   d.   No change is necessary.

4. We are reading several books by Toni Morrison, a prodigious African American author;
 A

however, you don't always understand the complex themes woven into her work.
        B   **C**

    a.   They   b.   we   c.   their   d.   No change is necessary.

5. When voters enter the polling place, they need to specify their ward and precinct and
                                           A   **B**

show identification; otherwise, you will not be allowed to vote.
                             C

    a.   you   b.   your   c.   they   d.   No change is necessary.

6. The students want to be recognized for their hard work, but we'd rather get a good
grade than hear their praises sung.   **A**   **B**
                    C

    a.   his or her   b.   they'd   c.   your   d.   No change is necessary.

7. Every horticulturalist at the fair knows that James is a man who always stands by his
word, and that he takes his plants very seriously.   **A**
                B   **C**

    a.   their   b.   you   c.   our   d.   No change is necessary.

8. The drivers took <u>their</u> time making <u>their</u> way to work along the foggy route; <u>you</u>
                 A   **B**   **C**

couldn't see more than ten yards into the distance.

    a.   your   b.   our   c.   they   d.   No change is necessary.

9. After the shuttle failed to take off, the engineers studied its mechanical problems, and
<u>they</u> reviewed <u>their</u> previous assumptions; however, <u>you</u> will never be certain what went
A   **B**   **C**

wrong.

    a.   you   b.   our   c.   they   d.   No change is necessary.

10. Some hikers have taken cell phones on dangerous treks, counting on being able to dial
911 if <u>they</u> need help; <u>they</u> do not consider the dangers a rescue team would face or the
            A   **B**

fact that <u>you</u> might have to pay the costs of the rescue.
           C

    a.   you   b.   we   c.   they   d.   No change is necessary.

3.4F MAINTAINING CLEAR PRONOUN REFERENCES

What Is Clear Pronoun Reference?

A pronoun should always refer clearly to one, and only one, antecedent. When the reader can't be certain what noun or pronoun a pronoun refers to, the sentence lacks **clear pronoun reference**, and the meaning of the sentence may not be apparent.

There are two types of unclear pronoun reference. Ambiguous pronoun references could refer to more than one antecedent in a sentence.

> **Ambiguous**   Michael told Jim <u>he</u> needed a better résumé.
>
> [Did Michael tell Jim that Michael himself needed a better résumé? Or did Michael tell Jim that Jim needed a better résumé?]

Vague pronoun references do not refer clearly to anything in the sentence.

> **Vague**   On the evening news, <u>they</u> said a baseball strike was inevitable.

How Do You Find Unclear Pronoun References?

To find unclear pronoun references, find every pronoun in the passage. Then ask the following questions about each pronoun:

- Is there a noun or pronoun in the sentence to which the pronoun refers? If the answer is no, then the pronoun reference is vague.
- If there is a noun or pronoun to which the pronoun refers, is it the *only* possible pronoun reference? If you can find more than one possibility, then the pronoun reference is ambiguous.

EXAMPLES

Refers to price—not mentioned in the sentence

When I first looked at the car, the salesman told me it was far below the actual value.

Could refer either to loan officer or customer service rep

The loan officer told the customer service representative to make sure he had a full report by tomorrow.

Practice Correcting Unclear Pronoun References

For each sentence, select the option that corrects an underlined problem with pronoun reference. If no change is necessary, choose option d. Answers and explanations appear on pp. 270–71.

1. Regina told Mary that she needed to pick up the cake for the party.
   a. she, Regina,   b. her   c. it   d. No change is necessary.

2. In every class you take, they say that listening carefully, taking notes, and asking questions will improve your grade.
   a. you   b. instructors   c. them   d. No change is necessary.

3. Jackie's parents called out to her at the same moment her shoelace broke, which caused her to lose the race.
   a. broke. They   b. Broke. It
   c. broke. These misfortunes   d. No change is necessary.

4. The man who caused the accident told Bob that he would have to fill out an accident report.
   a. him   b. us   c. he, Bob,   d. No change is necessary.

5. When you dress for a job interview, choose the suit jacket over the jean jacket. This can make you look unprofessional.
   a. It   b. Such clothing
   c. Casual clothing   d. No change is necessary.

6. Marco told his roommates that they needed to leave so he could get some sleep.
                 A   **B**   **C**
   a. its   b. we   c. him   d. No change is necessary.

7. In almost every magazine, they show racy pictures of celebrities; readers are left
                           A

   to wonder whether they will ever escape the long reach of Hollywood and its many stars.
                    B   **C**
   a. articles   b. you
   c. their   d. No change is necessary.

8. When you move out of your parents' house, you are able to stay out as late as you want
   __A__   __B__

   and eat whatever you want. Over time, this isn't always beneficial.
                                       __C__

   a. we   b. us
   c. such a lifestyle   d. No change is necessary.

9. As she was leaving for lunch, Bernadette told Mary that she would have to stay late to
   __A__   __B__

   finish the report that was due the next day. The women's boss had insisted that the
   report be finished on time so he could present it at a conference.
                                      __C__

   a. her   b. she, Bernadette,
   c. him   d. No change is necessary.

10. While showing the Lombardos the house, the real estate agent said it was lower than
                                                                    __A__

    typical for the neighborhood, but she couldn't explain why. Because the Lombardos were
                                       __B__

    suspicious about the lack of an explanation, they did not make an offer.
                                                __C__

    a. its price   b. her   c. we   d. No change is necessary.

3.4G USING PROPER CASE OF PRONOUNS

What Are Proper-Case Pronouns?

A personal pronoun refers to a particular person or thing. Personal pronouns change form according to the way they function in a sentence. They can be in the **subjective case**, the **objective case**, or the **possessive case**.

Subjective-case pronouns function as the subject of a sentence or clause:

Finally, she realized that dreams could come true.

	Subjective Case	Objective Case	Possessive Case
First-person singular/plural	I/we	me/us	my, mine/ our, ours
Second-person singular/plural	you/you	you/you	your, yours/ your, yours
Third-person singular	he, she, it	him, her, it	his, her, hers, its
Third-person plural	they who/who	them whom/whom	their, theirs, its, whose

Objective-case pronouns function as either the direct object of a verb or a preposition or as indirect objects.

Direct Object of a Verb	If Joanna hurries, she can stop <u>him</u>.
Object of a Preposition	Mark threw the ball to <u>them</u>.
Indirect Object	Professor Miller sent <u>us</u> information about his research.

Possessive-case pronouns show ownership.

Debbie and Kim decided to take <u>their</u> lunches, too.

How Do You Find Case Problems with Pronouns?

Often, pronoun-case problems happen in sentences that contain a compound subject or object or the word *who* or *whom*.

To find case problems with pronouns, ask the following questions:

- Does the sentence contain more than one subject or object joined by a conjunction such as *and* or *or*, and is one subject or object a pronoun? If so, you can choose the correct case for the pronoun in the compound subject or object by omitting the other part of the compound and trying the pronoun alone.

  The car was headed right for ~~Chuck and~~ (she/(her)).

  [*Think*: The car was headed right for *her*.]

- Does the sentence use *who* or *whom*? If so, use *who* as a subject and *whom* as an object. If the pronoun performs the action, use *who*. If the pronoun does not perform an action, use *whom*. In sentences other than questions, when the pronoun is followed by a verb, use *who*. When the pronoun is followed by a noun or pronoun, use *whom*.

***Who* Is Subject**	I would like to know <u>who</u> caused this problem.
***Whom* Is Object**	He told me to <u>whom</u> I should report.

Practice Correcting Case Problems with Pronouns

For each sentence, select the option that corrects an underlined problem with pronoun case. If no change is necessary, choose option d. Answers and explanations appear on p. 271.

1. The contest took on a different tone when the host and <u>his</u> crew announced that <u>they</u>
                                                      A   **B**

   would give a million dollars to <u>whomever</u> correctly answered the puzzle.
                                          C

     a.   him   b.   them   c.   whoever   d.   No change is necessary.

2. I had just entered the living room when I spotted my Cousin Alva, <u>whom</u> I was mad at.

  a. whose   b. her   c. who   d. No change is necessary.

3. Ricardo and Beth recently came back from <u>their</u> trip to Korea; the child <u>whom</u> the

   A**B**

  couple adopted there never knew <u>his</u> parents.

   C

  a. they're   b. who   c. he   d. No change is necessary.

4. I would like to go with <u>them</u>, as long as they don't mind.

  a. they   b. their   c. these   d. No change is necessary.

5. There are no secrets between Rita and <u>I</u>; we share everything in our lives.

  a. me   b. we   c. mine   d. No change is necessary.

6. Lucas and <u>me</u> would like to finish this project before <u>we</u> move into the next one;

   A**B**

  however, <u>we're</u> sure we'll meet the deadline.

   C

  a. I   b. us   c. we were   d. No change is necessary.

7. Since Dorrie and Nick are so busy, <u>I</u> agree that <u>we</u> need to help <u>them</u> take care of the kids.

   A**B****C**

  a. Me   b. us   c. they   d. No change is necessary.

8. Even though I asked five people, no one could tell me <u>who</u> I had to see about registering
   for the class.

  a. whose   b. that   c. whom   d. No change is necessary.

9. I know that Bill wants to go to the conference with Ming and <u>I</u>, but there isn't room for
   A**B**

  <u>him</u> in <u>my</u> car.

   C

  a. Me   b. me   c. their   d. No change is necessary.

10. Paul and <u>me</u> always get in trouble when we take more than $20 to the race track.

  a. them   b. I   c. us   d. No change is necessary.

3.4H USING ADJECTIVES AND ADVERBS CORRECTLY

What Are the Proper Forms of Adjectives and Adverbs?

Adjectives describe or modify nouns (words that name people, places, or things) and pronouns (words that replace nouns). They answer questions about *what kind, which one,* or *how many.* **Adverbs** describe or modify verbs (words that tell what happens in a sentence), adjectives, and other adverbs. They answer questions about *how, how much, when, where, why,* or *to what extent.*

Many adverbs are formed by adding *ly* to the end of an adjective.

Adjective	**Adverb**
She received a <u>quick</u> answer.	Her sister answered <u>quickly</u>.
The <u>new</u> student introduced himself.	The couple is <u>newly</u> married.
That is an <u>honest</u> answer.	Please answer <u>honestly</u>.

People are often confused about whether to choose *good* or *well. Good* is an adjective, so it should be used to describe a noun or pronoun. *Well* is an adverb, so it should be used to describe a verb or an adjective. However, *well* is also an adjective when it is used to describe a person's health.

Adjective	Fred Astaire was a <u>good</u> dancer.
	["Good" modifies the noun "dancer."]
Adverb	He danced especially <u>well</u> with Ginger Rogers.
	["Well" modifies the verb "danced."]

Be careful when a modifying word follows verbs that refer to senses or emotions (for example, *feel, look, smell, sound, taste*) and so-called linking verbs (for example, *be, appear, seem*). In both these cases, use the adjective form—for instance *good* instead of *well* and *bad* instead of *badly.*

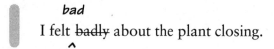

bad

I felt ~~badly~~ about the plant closing.

It can help to remember that you never say "I feel happily" when you feel happy.

How Do You Find Improperly Used Adjectives and Adverbs?

The similarity of adjectives and adverbs can make it difficult to choose between them. To decide whether to use an adjective or an adverb, find the word it is describing or modifying. If that word is a noun or pronoun, use an adjective. If it is a verb, adjective, or another adverb, use an adverb.

Adjective   Let me give you one <u>quick</u> reminder.

["Quick" modifies the noun "reminder."]

Adverb   He <u>quickly</u> changed the subject.

["Quickly" modifies the verb "changed."]

Adjective   Tell me your <u>real</u> name.

["Real" modifies the noun "name."]

Adverb   It was <u>really</u> rude of her to ignore me.

["Really" modifies the adjective "rude."]

Practice Correcting Improperly Used Adjectives and Adverbs

For each sentence, select the option that corrects an underlined problem with adjectives or adverbs. If no change is necessary, choose option d. Answers and explanations appear on pp. 271–72.

1. I was <u>real</u> happy to discover that the car performed <u>well</u>, even during the <u>extremely</u>
   A   **B**   **C**

   cold weather we had last winter.

   a. really   b. good   c. extreme   d. No change is necessary.

2. Doug left in an old <u>red</u> truck and came home with a <u>bright</u> new car. He must have made
                        A   **B**

   a <u>good</u> trade somewhere.
     C

   a. reddish   b. brightly   c. well   d. No change is necessary.

3. Because we all did so <u>good</u> on the test, the teacher <u>proudly</u> explained that we would
                          A   **B**

   not have a pop quiz this week. We were <u>very</u> glad to hear the news.
                                           C

   a. well   b. proud   c. verily   d. No change is necessary.

4. I was <u>restlessly</u> all day Monday after hearing that Tuesday would be my first day as a
   starting pitcher.

   a. restfully   b. resting   c. restless   d. No change is necessary.

5. Get over here <u>quick</u> and tell me if I have to cook this lobster any longer. It looks <u>done</u>

  A   **B**

to me, but last time we had lobster, it was <u>undercooked</u>.

                                                 C

  a.   quickly   b.   donely

  c.   undercooked   d.   No change is necessary.

6. Elena was <u>awful</u> pleased to hear she'd won the jackpot; now she could afford the vacation she'd always dreamed about.

  a.   awestruck   b.   awfully   c.   awesome   d.   No change is necessary.

7. It's nice to hear that we don't have to wear the <u>old</u> uniform anymore; the <u>newly</u> waiter's

                                                           A   **B**

costume—a <u>white</u> shirt with black tie and black pants—is much more flattering to

          C

everyone.

  a.   oldly   b.   new   c.   whitely   d.   No change is necessary.

8. Last night, Luis played the piano <u>beautiful</u>, and Dora accompanied him with her <u>sweet</u>

                                        A   **B**

voice. Listening to them, we were <u>entranced</u>.

                                   C

  a.   beautifully   b.   sweetly   c.   entrancing   d.   No change is necessary.

9. After I came down with the flu, I felt <u>badly</u> for about a week.

  a.   baddish   b.   poorly   c.   bad   d.   No change is necessary.

10. A <u>long</u> walk on a <u>warm</u> spring morning can often lift a <u>bad</u> mood.

     A   **B**   **C**

  a.   longly   b.   warmly   c.   badly   d.   No change is necessary.

3.41 USING COMPARATIVE AND SUPERLATIVE ADJECTIVES AND ADVERBS

What Are Comparative and Superlative Forms?

Sometimes an adjective or adverb describes something by comparing it to something else. The **comparative form** of an adjective or adverb compares two people or things. Adjectives and adverbs form the comparative either with an *er* ending or with the addition of the word *more*. The **superlative form**, which compares more than two, is formed with an *est* ending or with the addition of the word *most*.

Four common adjectives and adverbs have irregular comparative and superlative forms: *good, well, bad,* and *badly.*

COMPARATIVE AND SUPERLATIVE ADJECTIVES AND ADVERBS	Comparative	Superlative
Adjective		
good	better	best
bad	worse	worst
Adverb		
well	better	best
badly	worse	worst

How Do You Find Problems with Comparative and Superlative Forms?

Most adjectives and adverbs follow a few simple rules for forming comparatives and superlatives.

ADJECTIVES

- One-syllable adjectives generally form the comparative by adding *er* and the superlative by adding *est*.

  great   greater   greatest

- Adjectives with two or more syllables form the comparative with *more* and the superlative with *most*.

  wonderful   more wonderful   most wonderful

  Exception: Two-syllable adjectives ending in *y* add *er* or *est* after changing the *y* to an *i*.
  funny   funnier   funniest

ADVERBS

- All adverbs ending in *ly* form the comparative with *more* and the superlative with *most*.
  efficiently   more efficiently   most efficiently

- Some other adverbs form the comparative with *er* and the superlative with *est*.

  soon   sooner   soonest

To find problems, ask the following questions about any comparative or superlative form of an adjective or adverb:

- Are exactly two things being compared? If so, use the comparative form, not the superlative.
- Are more than two things being compared? If so, use the superlative form, not the comparative.
- Are both the *er* ending and the word *more* used to make a modifier comparative? Do not use both together. Use the preceding table to determine the correct one, and drop the other.

- Are both the *est* ending and the word *most* used to make a modifier superlative? Do not use both together. Use the preceding table to determine the correct one, and drop the other.

- Is an *er* form such as *quicker* used as a comparative adverb, or is an *est* form such as *quickest* used as a superlative adverb? Check whether the word being modified is a noun or pronoun (in which case the comparative adjective *quicker* and the superlative adjective *quickest* are correct) or a verb, adjective, or adverb (in which case the comparative adverb *more quickly* and the superlative adverb *most quickly* must be used). Remember that all adverbs ending in *ly* form the comparative with *more* and the superlative with *most*.

- Are the comparative and superlative forms of the irregular adjectives *good* and *bad* or of the irregular adverbs *well* and *badly* being used correctly? The comparative forms of both adjectives and adverbs are *better* and *worse*; the superlative forms are *best* and *worst*.

Practice Correcting Problems with Comparative and Superlative Forms

For each sentence, select the option that fixes an underlined error in comparative or superlative forms, or fill in the blank with the correct form. Answers and explanations appear on pp. 272–73.

1. Among all the entries in the engineering contest, Maria's drawing was one of the best the judges had ever seen.

    a. goodly   b. goodest   c. good   d. No change is necessary.

2. Both the delegates from Korea and the delegates from France wanted to open a new consulate near downtown, but the French had a _____ proposal for the city.

    a. best   b. better   c. more better   d. more bestest

3. Of all of the flowers in her garden, the roses have grown the tallerer.

    a. taller   b. most tall   c. tallest   d. No change is necessary.

4. Victor once told me that the view from his new Manhattan apartment is the _____ in the world.

    a. beautiful   b. beautifuller   c. beautifullest   d. most beautiful.

5. During the high school pep rally, the principal promised a pizza party to the groups that cheered the more loud.

    a. louder   b. louderer   c. loudest   d. more loud

6. Cindy loves to buy electronic gadgets, but her latest acquisition is by far the better interesting.

    a. interesting   b. more interesting

    c. most interesting   d. No change is necessary.

7. When Alexander walked into the room, everyone commented that his shirt was the <u>most</u> <u>reddest</u> they had ever seen.

    a.   redder   b.   most red   c.   reddest   d.   No change is necessary.

8. Once the new courthouse is built downtown, it will be _____ than most of the buildings there now.

    a.   more big   b.   biggest   c.   more bigger   d.   bigger

9. Between the two cousins, everyone always liked Patricia <u>better</u> than her sister Sara.

    a.   most   b.   more better   c.   bestest   d.   No change is necessary.

10. The neon sign above the new restaurant said, "We Serve the _____ Steaks in Town."

    a.   Most Best   b.   Best   c.   Better   d.   Bestest

3.4J   USING STANDARD SPELLING

Understanding Spelling Conventions

Although English spelling often seems to be made up entirely of exceptions, a few **spelling rules** will help you avoid many spelling errors.

1. *I* before *e* except after *c*, or when pronounced like *a* as in *neighbor* and *weigh*. Memorize this rule.

i before *e*	except after *c*	or when *ei* is pronounced *ay*
achieve	ceiling	eight
believe	conceive	freight
friend	deceive	neighbor

Exceptions to the "*i* before *e*" Rule

There are some exceptions to the "*i* before *e*" rule. The exceptions follow no pattern, so you must memorize them.

ancient	either	leisure	seize
caffeine	foreign	neither	species
conscience	height	science	weird

2. If a word ends in a silent *e*, drop the *e* if you are adding an ending that begins with a vowel (*a, e, i, o, u*).

Drop the e

hope + <u>i</u>ng = hoping   dance + <u>er</u> = dancer

continue + <u>ou</u>s = continuous   insure + <u>a</u>ble = insurable

Exceptions

change + able = changeable   courage + ous = courageous

notice + able = noticeable   replace + able = replaceable

Keep the *e* if the ending begins with a consonant (a letter that is not a vowel).

Keep the e

hope + ful = hopeful	bore + dom = boredom
excite + ment = excitement	same + ness = sameness

Exceptions

argue + ment = argument	true + ly = truly
judge + ment = judgment	nine + th = ninth

3. When adding an ending to a word that ends in *y*, change the *y* to *i* when a consonant comes before the *y*.

Change y to i

beauty + ful = beautiful	busy + ly = busily
try + ed = tried	friendly + er = friendlier

Exceptions

- Keep the *y* if the suffix starts with an *i*.

cry + ing = crying	baby + ish = babyish

- Keep the *y* when you add a suffix to some one-syllable words.

shy + er = shyer	dry + ness = dryness

When a vowel comes before the *y*, do not change the *y*.

Keep the y

annoy + ance = annoyance	enjoy + ment = enjoyment
play + ful = playful	display + ed = displayed

Exceptions

day + ly = daily	say + ed = said
gay + ly = gaily	pay + ed = paid

4. When adding an ending that starts with a vowel to a one-syllable word, follow these rules:

- Double the final consonant only if the word ends with a consonant-vowel-consonant pattern.

trap + ed = trapped	occur + ence = occurrence
prefer + ed = preferred	commit + ed = committed

- Do not double the final consonant if the word ends with some other pattern.

Vowel-Vowel-Consonant	**Vowel-Consonant-Consonant**
clean + est = cleanest	slick + er = slicker
poor + er = poorer	teach + er = teacher
clear + ed = cleared	last + ed = lasted

5. When adding an ending that starts with a vowel to a word with two or more syllables, follow these rules:

- Double the final consonant only if the word ends with a consonant-vowel-consonant pattern and the stress is on the last syllable.

  sub**mit** + ing = submitting

  con**trol** + er = controller

  ad**mit** + ed = admitted

- Do not double the final consonant in other cases.

  problem + atic = problematic

  understand + ing = understanding

  offer + ed = offered

6. Add *s* to form a regular plural of most nouns, including words that end in *o* preceded by a vowel.

Most Words	Words That End in Vowel Plus *o*
book + s = books	video + s = videos
college + s = colleges	stereo + s = stereos
jump + s = jumps	radio + s = radios

7. Add *es* to words that end in *o* preceded by a consonant and to words that end in *s*, *sh*, *ch*, or *x*.

Most Words That End in Consonant + *o*	Words That End in *s*, *sh*, *ch*, or *x*
potato + es = potatoes	class + es = classes
hero + es = heroes	push + es = pushes
go + es = goes	bench + es = benches
tomato + es =tomatoes	fax + es = faxes

Other ways to improve spelling are using a spell-checker—although you will still have to make sure you have not misspelled one word by substituting another word that is correctly spelled—and consulting a dictionary. In addition, keep a list of words you commonly misspell and check your work against it when you proofread. Finally, familiarize yourself with the following list of commonly misspelled words.

Frequently Misspelled Words

across	disappoint	loneliness	reference
all right	early	medicine	restaurant
a lot	embarrass	minute	roommate
already	entrance	necessary	secretary
argument	environment	noticeable	sentence
beautiful	everything	occasion	separate
becoming	exercise	occur	speech
beginning	experience	occurred	studying

believe	finally	occurrences	surprise
benefit	forty	occurring	tomato
calendar	fulfill	occurs	tomatoes
cannot	generally	personnel	truly
careful	government	possible	until
careless	grammar	potato	usually
cemetery	harass	potatoes	Wednesday
certain	height	prejudice	weird
conscience	holiday	prescription	window
definite	integration	privilege	withhold
definitely	intelligence	probably	woman
dependent	interest	professor	women
describe	interfere	receive	writing
develop	judgment	recognize	written

Practice Correcting Spelling

For each sentence, select the option that corrects an underlined spelling error. If no change is necessary, choose option d. Answers and explanations appear on p. 273.

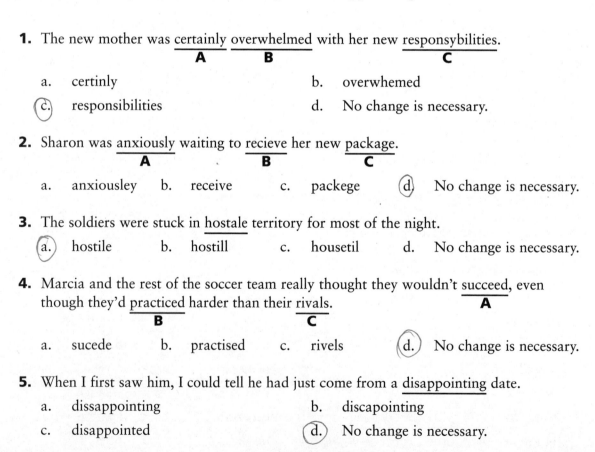

1. The new mother was certainly overwhelmed with her new responsybilities.
                                    A   **B**   **C**

    a.   certinly   b.   overwhemed

    (c.) responsibilities   d.   No change is necessary.

2. Sharon was anxiously waiting to recieve her new package.
                  A   **B**   **C**

    a.   anxiousley   b.   receive   c.   packege   (d.) No change is necessary.

3. The soldiers were stuck in hostale territory for most of the night.

    (a.) hostile   b.   hostill   c.   housetil   d.   No change is necessary.

4. Marcia and the rest of the soccer team really thought they wouldn't succeed, even
    though they'd practiced harder than their rivals.   **A**
                 B   **C**

    a.   sucede   b.   practised   c.   rivels   (d.) No change is necessary.

5. When I first saw him, I could tell he had just come from a disappointing date.

    a.   dissappointing   b.   discapointing

    c.   disappointed   (d.) No change is necessary.

6. That Saturday, everyone <u>volunteered</u> to clean up the <u>poverty-stricken</u> <u>nieghborhood</u>.
                         A   **B**   **C**

    a.   voluntered   b.   povertey

    (c.)   neighborhood   d.   No change is necessary.

7. The <u>ausome</u> task ahead of the construction crew overwhelmed the crew members.

    a.   allsome   **(b.)**   awesome   c.   alsome   d.   No change is necessary.

8. The <u>prossecuting</u> attorney <u>ignored</u> the judge's <u>advice</u>, so he lost the case.
           A   **B**   **C**

    a.   prosecuting   b.   egnored   c.   advise   **(d.)**   No change is necessary.

9. The <u>colorful</u> drawings on the kitchen table were later <u>compiled</u> to make the <u>broshure</u>.
        A   **B**   **C**

    a.   colorfull   b.   compilled   **(c.)**   brochure   d.   No change is necessary.

10. It never <u>occured</u> to me that my brief <u>absence</u> from the office would result in such an
              A   **B**

<u>extensive</u> backlog of work.
  C

    a.   occurred   b.   absense   c.   extenseve   **(d.)**   No change is necessary.

3.4K   USING STANDARD PUNCTUATION

Understanding Punctuation Conventions

Following are some guidelines and examples to help you understand punctuation and identify punctuation errors on the test.

COMMAS (,)

Use commas in the following situations:

- before a coordinating conjunction (*and, but, or, nor, for, yet, so*) that joins two independent clauses (An independent clause has a subject, verb, and other sentence parts that make it complete, and it can stand alone. A dependent clause cannot stand alone and can serve as a modifier or noun.)

> I called my best friend, <u>and</u> she agreed to drive me to work.

- after introductory word groups

> <u>While I waited outside,</u> Susan went backstage.

- after transitional expressions like *for example*, *however*, and *therefore*

  Trisha's salmon dish was overcooked; <u>however</u>, her pear tart was delicious.

- around appositives that rename a noun or pronoun directly preceding or following the appositive

  I have visited only one country, <u>Canada</u>, outside the United States.

- around interrupters, such as *as a matter of fact*, that stop the flow of a sentence without affecting its meaning

  My sister, <u>incidentally</u>, has very good reasons for being late.

- around nonrestrictive relative clauses that start with *who, which*, or *that* and that can be removed from the sentence without changing its meaning

  Telephone calling-card fraud, <u>which costs consumers and phone companies four billion dollars last year</u>, is increasing.

- to separate the elements of an address

  The office of the famous fictional detective Sherlock Holmes was located at <u>221b Baker Street</u>, <u>London</u>, <u>England</u>.

- to separate the day and the year in a date

  The first Cinco de Mayo we celebrated in the United States was <u>Tuesday, May 5, 1998</u>.

- around the name of a person being addressed directly

  Unfortunately, <u>Marie</u>, you need to finish the report by next week.

- around *yes* or *no* in a response

  <u>Yes</u>, I believe you are right.

Do *not* use commas in the following situations:

- before a coordinating conjunction that joins two parts of a compound verb with one subject

Incorrect	The transit workers voted to strike, and walked off the job.
Correct	The transit workers voted to strike and walked off the job.

- before a coordinating conjunction that joins two parts of a compound subject (which has two parts, like *Mary and Ann*)

Incorrect	The transit workers, and the sanitation workers voted to strike.
Correct	The transit workers and the sanitation workers voted to strike.

- to set off a restrictive clause that starts with *who, which,* or *that* and that cannot be removed from the sentence without changing its meaning

Incorrect	People, who live in glass houses, should not throw stones.
Correct	People who live in glass houses should not throw stones.

- before a dependent clause that follows an independent clause

Incorrect	He was exhausted, because he had driven all night.
Correct	He was exhausted because he had driven all night.

- between a subject and a verb, unless they are separated by an interrupter, a modifying word group, or another word group that should be set off with commas

Incorrect	The boy and his dog, wandered around for several hours before returning home.
Correct	The boy and his dog wandered around for several hours before returning home.

Note: Make sure you place the comma correctly after introductory expressions.

Incorrect	Although, Tina was the best swimmer she came in last.
Correct	Although Tina was the best swimmer, she came in last.

APOSTROPHES (')

Use apostrophes in the following situations:

- before an *s* at the end of a singular noun that shows possession—even if the singular noun already ends in *s*

  > This class's syllabus is hard to read.

- at the end of a plural noun ending in *s* that shows possession

  > The twins' father was building them a playhouse.

- before an *s* at the end of a plural noun not ending in *s* that shows possession

  > The children's toys were all broken.

- to show where letters have been omitted in a contraction

  > *I'll* see you there. = *I will* see you there.

Do *not* use apostrophes in the following situations:

- with a possessive pronoun such as *hers* and *its*

  > **Incorrect**   Is that bag your's?
  >
  > **Correct**   Is that bag yours?

- to form a plural

  > **Incorrect**   The Velez's live on Maple Drive.
  >
  > **Correct**   The Velezes live on Maple Drive.

QUOTATION MARKS ("")

Use quotation marks in the following situations:

- to mark a direct quotation

  > Lauren said, "My brother and Tina have gotten engaged."

- for titles of short works

  > "America the Beautiful"
  >
  > "The Tell-Tale Heart"

Do *not* use quotation marks in the following situations:

- to mark an indirect quotation

> **Incorrect**   He said that "I should get the downtown bus."
>
> **Correct**   He said that I should get the downtown bus.

- for titles of long works (italicize or underline these)
- for emphasis or to mark slang

> **Incorrect**   We didn't want her to "hang out" with us.
>
> **Correct**   We didn't want her to hang out with us.

END PUNCTUATION (. ? !)

- Use a period to end a sentence unless it is a direct question or an exclamation.

> The first day of July was sweltering, so we went swimming.

- End a direct question with a question mark.

> What did you do?

- End an exclamation with an exclamation mark.

> I can't believe he said that!

SEMICOLONS (;)

Use semicolons

- to join two closely related independent clauses into one sentence.

> In an interview, hold your head up and don't slouch; it is important to look alert.
>
> I always liked shrimp; however, after my allergic reaction, I realized I could never eat it again.

Practice Correcting Punctuation

For each sentence, select the option that corrects an underlined punctuation error, or choose the correctly punctuated sentence from the four given options. Answers and explanations appear on pp. 273–74.

3

1. However you want to look at <u>it, New</u> York is one of the <u>world's</u> most exciting <u>cities and</u>

                            A   **B**   **C**

it will always be considered that way.

    a.   it; New   b.   worlds'   c.   cities, and   d.   No change is necessary.

2. Even though, cellular phones are helpful in today's busy <u>world, some individuals</u> use

         A   **B**   **C**

them excessively.

    a.   though cellular   b.   world some

    c.   individual's   d.   No change is necessary.

3. While listening to his favorite opera <u>singers, Vittorio</u> enjoys making <u>dishes like</u> lasagna

                                        A   **B**

and <u>manicotti. Sometimes,</u> he makes spaghetti with meatballs.

                C

    a.   singers Vittorio   b.   dishes; like

    c.   manicotti, sometimes   d.   No change is necessary.

4. From the <u>childrens</u> reactions, I'm not so sure the book <u>fair's</u> tot alley was as huge a

              A   **B**

success as the <u>adults</u> claimed.

                   C

    a.   children's   b.   fairs'   c.   adults'   d.   No change is necessary.

5. The mechanic told <u>Denise she</u> needed to change the oil in her car <u>regularly and</u> check the

                            A   **B**

tires; <u>however she</u> didn't follow this advice.

         C

    a.   Denise; she   b.   regularly, and

    c.   however, she   d.   No change is necessary.

6. a.   Can you believe that Billy's Fish Shack is closing.

    b.   Can you believe that Billy's Fish Shack is closing;

    c.   Can you believe that Billy's Fish Shack is closing?

    d.   Can you believe that Billy's Fish Shack is closing!

7. a.   The snake, that bit Jimmy's sister, was not poisonous.

    b.   The snake that bit Jimmy's sister was not poisonous.

    c.   The snake, that bit Jimmy's sister was not poisonous.

    d.   The snake that bit Jimmy's sister, was not poisonous.

8. a. I can't bear to go to the dentist again, I know the bill is going to be huge.
    b. I can't bear to go to the dentist again; I know the bill is going to be huge.
    c. I can't bear to go to the dentist again? I know the bill is going to be huge.
    d. I can't bear to go to the dentist again: I know the bill is going to be huge.

9. a. Thinking about her upcoming wedding, Julia tried to keep her parents wishes in mind.
    b. Thinking about her upcoming wedding, Julia tried to keep her parent's wishes in mind.
    c. Thinking about her upcoming wedding, Julia tried to keep her parents' wishes in mind.
    d. Thinking about her upcoming wedding, Julia tried to keep her parents's wishes in mind.

10. a. My brother who has always liked fishing was thrilled to get a new rod and reel for his birthday.
    b. My brother, who has always liked fishing was thrilled to get a new rod and reel for his birthday.
    c. My brother who has always liked fishing, was thrilled to get a new rod and reel for his birthday.
    d. My brother, who has always liked fishing, was thrilled to get a new rod and reel for his birthday.

3.4L USING STANDARD CAPITALIZATION

Understanding Capitalization Conventions

Capitalization is not as complicated as spelling. The following guidelines will help you use capital letters correctly.

Always capitalize

- the personal pronoun *I*.
- the first letter of every sentence.
- the first letters of proper nouns—particular people, animals, places, objects, and ideas. Proper nouns include the following names of races, ethnic groups, tribes, nationalities, languages, and religions.

> The census data revealed a diverse community of Caucasians, African Americans, and Asian Americans, with a few Latino and Navajo residents. Native languages include English, Korean, and Spanish. Most people identified themselves as Catholic, Protestant, or Muslim.

- names of people and titles that accompany them—but not the titles used without a name.

  > In 1994, President Nelson Mandela was elected to lead South Africa.
  >
  > The newly elected fraternity president addressed the crowd.

- names of specific family members and their titles—but not those that identify family relationships.

  > The twins, Aunt Edna and Aunt Evelyn, are Dad's sisters.
  >
  > My aunts, my father's sisters, are twins.

- names of countries, cities, towns, bodies of water, streets, and so on.

  > The Seine runs through Paris, France.
  >
  > The river runs through the city.

- names of geographical regions—but not words that specify direction.

  > William Faulkner's novels are set in the American South.
  >
  > Turn right at the golf course, and go south for about a mile.

- names of buildings and monuments—but not general references to buildings and monuments.

  > He drove past the Liberty Bell and looked for a parking space near City Hall.
  >
  > He drove past the monument and looked for a parking space near the building.

- names of groups, clubs, teams, and associations—but not general references to those groups.

  > The Teamsters Union represents workers who were at the stadium for the Republican Party convention, the Rolling Stones concert, and the Phillies-Astros game.
  >
  > The union represents workers who were at the stadium for the political party's convention, the rock group's concert, and the baseball teams' game.

- names of historical periods, events, and documents.

> The Emancipation Proclamation was signed during the Civil War, not during Reconstruction.
>
> The document was signed during the war, not during the postwar period.

- names of businesses, government agencies, schools, and other institutions—but not general references to such institutions.

> The Department of Education and Apple Computer have launched a partnership project with Central High School.
>
> A government agency and a computer company have launched a partnership project with a high school.

- brand names.

> Kleenex, Toyota, Rollerblade, Xerox

- titles of academic courses—but not the names of general academic subject areas, except for proper nouns such as the name of a language.

> Are Introduction to American Government and Biology 200 closed yet?
>
> Are the introductory American government course and the biology course closed yet?

- days of the week, months of the year, and holidays—but not the names of the seasons.

> The Jewish holiday of Passover usually falls in April.
>
> The Jewish holiday of Passover falls in the spring.

- the first word and all important words in titles of books, movies, television programs, stories, poems, and so on. The only words that do not need to be capitalized (unless they are the first word) are *the, a, an,* coordinating conjunctions (*and, but, for, nor, or, yet, so*), and prepositions (such as *about, in,* and *to*).

> "Once More to the Lake" is one of Chuck's favorite essays.

Practice Correcting Capitalization

For each sentence, select the option that corrects an underlined capitalization error. If no change is necessary, choose option d. Answers and explanations appear on pp. 274–75.

1. The girls from the <u>junior class</u> asked the <u>saleslady</u>, <u>"do</u> you have any size eight dresses?"

                          A   **B**   **C**

    a. Junior class   b. Saleslady
    c. Do   d. No change is necessary.

2. The <u>Haitian</u> <u>family</u> on <u>Third Avenue</u> cooks delicious food every night.

           A   **B**   **C**

    a. Haitian   b. Family
    c. third avenue   d. No change is necessary.

3. <u>You</u> don't know how hard <u>i</u> have worked on this <u>project</u>.

    A   **B**   **C**

    a. you   b. I   c. Project   d. No change is necessary.

4. My courses this semester include <u>accounting I</u>, <u>mathematics</u>, and <u>Psychology for Teachers</u>.

                                  A   **B**   **C**

    a. Accounting I   b. Mathematics
    c. psychology for teachers   d. No change is necessary.

5. The application given to <u>International</u> students asked if they were <u>American</u> Indian or

                                 A   **B**
<u>Caucasian</u>.

    C

    a. international   b. American indian
    c. caucasian   d. No change is necessary.

6. After visiting the <u>Vietnam Memorial</u> and the <u>Lincoln Memorial</u>, I finally understood

                        A   **B**
many things I was taught in <u>high school</u>.

                               C

    a. Vietnam memorial   b. Lincoln memorial
    c. High School   d. No change is necessary.

7. All the <u>American</u> diplomats were unaware that the delegates from <u>Europe</u> spoke both

           A   **B**
<u>french and spanish</u>.

       C

    a. american   b. europe
    c. French and Spanish   d. No change is necessary.

8. My family enjoys visiting <u>New England</u> in <u>October</u>; the <u>fall</u> is perfect for watching the

                             A   **B**   **C**
leaves turn.

    a. new england   b. october
    c. Fall   d. No change is necessary.

9. <u>will</u> you please close the door of the <u>daycare center</u> after <u>you</u> leave?
   A   **B**   **C**

   a.   Will   b.   Daycare Center

   c.   You   d.   No change is necessary.

10. My <u>Aunt</u> from Russia and <u>Uncle Leonid</u> will be visiting some major cities in the South
          A   **B**

next <u>summer.</u>
     C

   a.   aunt   b.   uncle Leonid

   c.   Summer   d.   No change is necessary.

4 Self-Check Post-Tests

4.1 Reading Post-Test

Read each passage and answer the questions that follow. (An answer form is included on p. 297, and pp. 276–78 provide explanations for answers.)

James Boswell, the son of a Scottish nobleman, moved to London as a young man in the hope of making something of himself. His plans for a military career did not work out, and he quickly became much too fond of drinking heavily and spending time with actresses—habits that haunted him for the rest of his life. But Boswell, seemingly bent on self-destruction, did two things right: he befriended 5 one of eighteenth-century London's best-known writers, Samuel Johnson, and eventually completed the *Life of Johnson*, a book that remains one of the greatest biographies ever written.

Against his father's wishes, Boswell went to London in 1762 at the age of twenty-two. He hoped to become an officer in the army because such a position 10 struck him as the easiest way to live full-time in London, away from his strict family in Scotland. Unfortunately, Boswell seemed to lack the necessary money and powerful friends to get a commission. Instead, he lived cheaply. He entertained himself by writing, going to the theater, and carousing with hard-drinking young noblemen and actors, members of a profession seen as scandalous at that 15 time.

On May 16, 1763, Boswell was drinking tea in a shop when Samuel Johnson came in. Boswell was introduced to the great man, and from that moment on, the lives of the two were intertwined. They became close friends. For years, the great Johnson allowed Boswell, who had no significant accomplishments to 20 his name, to accompany him almost everywhere. Some of Johnson's contemporaries found Boswell an inappropriate companion for the famous man—Boswell was much younger, and he was extravagantly fond of wine and women. But Johnson liked him, so Boswell remained. From their first meeting until Johnson's death in 1784, Boswell collected notes about almost everything Johnson did 25 and said.

(continued)

The sheer volume of material Boswell had collected nearly defeated him. In poor health from years of alcoholism and venereal disease, saddened by the death of his long-suffering wife, short of money, and mocked by detractors, Boswell struggled to piece together his biography of Johnson. In the decade be- 30 tween Johnson's death and his own, Boswell came close to giving up many times, but a few loyal supporters kept him at work. Boswell's *Life of Johnson* appeared in 1791, and the ridicule immediately stopped. Even those who had never considered Boswell fit for the task of chronicling Johnson's life had to admit that his book was a masterpiece. 35

Boswell's name today remains linked with Johnson's, much as it was in his own time. Now, however, Boswell's talents are recognized. Although Boswell never managed to overcome his own worst impulses, he nevertheless ensured that those impulses did not doom the work that created a lasting monument to Johnson, to Boswell, and to their surprising friendship. 40

1. Which sentence best states the main idea?

   a.   Although James Boswell led a self-destructive life, he was successful in writing one of the greatest biographies ever written.

   b.   Samuel Johnson's contemporaries disapproved of his close relationship with James Boswell.

   c.   From the day they met, May 16, 1763, James Boswell and Samuel Johnson were close friends.

   d.   Today James Boswell's talents are recognized.

2. According to the passage

   a.   Boswell met Samuel Johnson in London in 1762.

   b.   Boswell was not able to become an officer in the army due to lack of money and connections.

   c.   Boswell's book *Life of Johnson* is the only book he wrote that was ever published.

   d.   James Boswell was born into poverty.

3. The author's primary purpose is to

   a.   provide a biography of James Boswell.

   b.   persuade the reader that James Boswell was the most successful biographer in the world.

   c.   entertain the reader with an anecdote about James Boswell's life.

   d.   describe how James Boswell created a literary masterpiece despite his personal shortcomings.

4. Paragraphs 2 and 3 are organized by

    a.   simple listing.

    b.   illustration.

    c.   time order.

    d.   comparison.

5. What is the relationship of the parts in the following sentence?

> "In poor health from years of alcoholism and venereal disease, saddened by the death of his long-suffering wife, short of money, and mocked by detractors, Boswell struggled to piece together his biography of Johnson."

    a.   cause and effect

    b.   time order

    c.   example

    d.   comparison

6. What is the overall tone of this passage?

    a.   admiring

    b.   pessimistic

    c.   sarcastic

    d.   objective

7. "Unfortunately, Boswell seemed to lack the necessary money and powerful friends to get a commission."
    This a statement of

    a.   fact.

    b.   opinion.

8. A conclusion that can be drawn from the passage is that

    a.   Boswell drank heavily because he had tremendous insecurities about his ability as a writer.

    b.   On May 16, 1763, Boswell was in the teashop in order to meet Samuel Johnson.

    c.   Boswell's wife overlooked his shortcomings, although they were many and significant.

    d.   Boswell was unable to control the desires that led to much of his destructive behavior.

9. In this passage, the author expresses a biased attitude in favor of

a.   James Boswell's having totally ruined his life as a result of his excessive drinking.

b.   Samuel Johnson's literary masterpiece, his autobiography titled the *Life of Johnson*.

c.   James Boswell's recognition as one of the world's greatest biographers.

d.   the significance of biographies written in the 1800s.

Over many generations, successful species of preyed-upon animals develop defenses that help them avoid becoming a predator's dinner. Some creatures of prey survive by being quick or agile. Others rely on camouflage that helps them blend in with their surroundings. One of the defense mechanisms is mimicry, an evolutionary advantage that helps creatures by making them resemble other, sometimes more dangerous creatures. 5

Batesian mimicry is named for Henry Walter Bates, a British naturalist who studied butterflies in the Amazon in the nineteenth century. In one region, Bates found different species of butterflies that closely resembled each other. He learned that birds who ate some of the butterflies became ill from the toxins in 10 the butterflies' bodies, but birds who ate other, nearly identical butterflies enjoyed a pleasant meal. The theory of Batesian mimicry argues that the good-tasting insects—the mimics—evolve to resemble the bad-tasting or poisonous ones—the models—in order to have a better chance of not being eaten. The mimic gains an evolutionary advantage from looking more like the model be- 15 cause predators are less likely to consider the mimic an appetizing meal. However, Batesian mimicry may cause problems for the model because predators who cannot tell the difference may attack a toxic or bad-tasting insect after learning that the mimic tastes good. Therefore, Batesian models benefit from evolving to look less like their mimics. 20

Müllerian mimics, in contrast, gain an evolutionary advantage from not changing their appearance over time. Fritz Müller, a German scientist who studied Amazonian insects about thirty years after Bates did, identified several species of toxic or bad-tasting butterflies that had evolved to look very much alike. Predators that taste one species learn to leave all of them alone—but unlike 25 Batesian mimics, the Müllerian mimics really are all inedible. The appearance of Müllerian mimics is not deceiving. None of the species, therefore, suffers from its resemblance to others.

In both Batesian and Müllerian mimicry, a predator's refusal to eat creatures with a particular appearance allows the uneaten creatures to pass on their looks 30 to their offspring. Those offspring will also tend to inspire disgust in a predator. Mimicry, then, is an unusual evolutionary defense; creatures that use it rely for their survival not on their own abilities to run, fight, or hide, but on the fact that predators learn to avoid them.

Prey animals may appear to be at a disadvantage in the cycle of life, but na- 35
ture has provided every prey species with some means of defense. Mimics in the
insect world are just one example of apparently helpless creatures with a well-
developed and very effective way of turning the tables on predators.

10. Which sentence best states the main idea?

   a.   In both Batesian and Mullerian mimicry, a predator's refusal to eat creatures with a
        particular appearance allows the uneaten creatures to pass on their looks to their
        offspring.

   b.   One of the defense mechanisms is mimicry, an evolutionary advantage that helps
        creatures by making them resemble other, sometimes more dangerous creatures.

   c.   Prey animals may appear to be at a disadvantage in the cycle of life, but nature has
        provided every prey species with some means of defense.

   d.   Over many generations, successful species of prey animals develop defenses that
        help them avoid becoming a predator's dinner.

11. According to the passage,

   a.   in Batesian mimicry, the mimics resemble the models to have a better chance of
        surviving.

   b.   Müllerian mimics change their appearances over time.

   c.   Henry Walter Bates was a British naturalist who studied butterflies in the Amazon
        in the twentieth century.

   d.   Fritz Müller studied Amazon butterflies prior to Henry Walter Bates' work.

12. The author's primary purpose is to

   a.   define the defense mechanisms employed by species of prey animals.

   b.   clarify the difference between species of prey and predators.

   c.   discuss the defense mechanism of mimicry.

   d.   persuade the reader that mimicry is the most successful defense mechanism.

13. For this passage, the author uses an overall organizational pattern that

   a.   compares and contrasts Batesian and Müllerian mimicry.

   b.   illustrates species of prey animals.

   c.   summarizes evolutionary advantages.

   d.   shows the order of importance of two types of mimicry.

14. What is the relationship of the parts in the following sentence?

> "In both Batesian and Müllerian mimicry, a predator's refusal to eat creatures with a particular appearance allows the uneaten creatures to pass on their looks to their offspring."

    a.   example

    b.   comparison

    c.   clarification

    d.   addition

15. As used in line 3, the word *agile* means

    a.   slow.

    b.   famished.

    c.   nimble.

    d.   ready.

16. Identify the relationship between these two sentences from paragraph 4.

> "Those offspring will also tend to inspire disgust in a predator. Mimicry, then, is an unusual evolutionary defense; creatures that use it rely for their survival not on their own abilities to run, fight, or hide, but on the fact that predators learn to avoid them."

    a.   cause and effect

    b.   time order

    c.   contrast

    d.   clarification

17. A conclusion that can be drawn from this passage is that

    a.   Batesian mimicry is more effective than Müllerian mimicry.

    b.   Mimicry is the most effective of all defense mechanisms.

    c.   Henry Walter Bates and Fritz Müller collaborated to develop their mimicry theories.

    d.   The defense mechanism of mimicry serves all Müllerian mimics equally well.

18. The author's statement that "Mimics in the insect world are just one example of apparently helpless creatures with a well-developed and very effective way of turning the tables on predators" is

    a.   adequately supported by factual evidence.

    b.   inadequately supported by personal opinion.

Twenty years ago, the Japanese economy seemed unstoppable, but the slump that began in Japan more than a decade ago shows no sign of ending. Partly because of the declining economy, an increasing number of Japanese women work outside the home. However, the economic power of women in Japan lags far behind that of women in most industrialized nations. Corporate resistance to women in positions of power in Japan keeps too many women from contributing all they could to the nation's economy.

Women in corporate Japan do not have the opportunities for advancement available to men. Only nine percent of the management positions in Japan are filled by women; in the United States, women make up forty-five percent of business managers. Forty percent of Japanese women work outside the home, but a majority are the so-called office ladies who do clerical work or serve tea. Even the title "office ladies" suggests that women are not taken seriously in the workplace in Japan.

Japanese corporate culture discourages women who do work from having children. Day care is almost unknown. In addition, while maternal leave is theoretically permitted, many women report being illegally fired when they take time off during pregnancy or after the birth of a child. When women with children do remain on staff, they find that they are expected to work late into the evening and sometimes to join colleagues for socializing after work, leaving little time for raising, or even seeing, their children. Japan's falling birthrate means that the country will face a severe population drop—and labor shortages—in the decades ahead.

Japanese women are highly educated, and many Japanese now believe that the lack of input from, and encouragement for, women in the corporate world is holding the country's economy back. A 2003 study by Japan's Economy Ministry found that companies with a high percentage of female workers earn, on average, twice the profits of companies where less than ten percent of the workforce is female. Another study estimates that the country's annual growth is smaller than it should be because women are not full participants in the economy.

Japan is a strongly traditional society, and corporate culture reflects the still-common belief that women should remain in traditional roles. However, many Japanese understand that respect for tradition should not stand in the way of corporate respect for the brains and skills of Japanese women. All willing participants—male and female—should be encouraged to contribute to Japan's economy. The country's economic recovery demands such encouragement.

19. The stated main idea of paragraph 3 is

    a.   Japanese women in the workforce are able to choose flexible work hours.

    b.   Japanese corporate culture discourages women who do work from having children.

    c.   Japanese women who are employed at high levels in corporations enjoy the benefit of joining colleagues for socializing after work.

    d.   Japanese women who are employed outside the home generally have meaningful jobs that contribute to their sense of well-being.

20. Studies concerning Japanese women in the workplace have shown that

    a..   it is beneficial for corporate success to have a majority of male employees.

    b.   Japanese women, in general, lack sufficient education to contribute meaningfully to the corporate culture.

    c.   Japan's society is antitradition.

    d.   "Office ladies" in Japan basically do clerical work and serve tea.

21. The author's primary purpose is to

    a.   convince the reader that the Japanese economy would be improved with more female employees.

    b.   compare the Japanese workforce with the workforce of other industrialized nations.

    c.   clarify the role of the Japanese woman in traditional Japanese culture.

    d.   praise the ability of Japanese women.

22. Paragraph 3 is organized by

    a.   generalization and examples.

    b.   contrast.

    c.   spatial relationship.

    d.   order of importance.

23. Identify the relationship between these two sentences in paragraph 4.

> "A 2003 study by Japan's Economy Ministry found that companies with a high percentage of female workers earn, on average, twice the profits of companies where less than ten percent of the workforce is female. Another study estimates that the country's annual growth is smaller than it should be because women are not full participants in the economy."

    a.   contrast

    b.   cause and effect

    c.   spatial order

    d.   addition

24. As used in lines 16–17, the word *theoretically* most nearly means

    a. always.

    b. supposedly.

    c. never.

    d. sometimes.

25. The author's statement that "Corporate resistance to women in positions of power in Japan keeps too many women from contributing all they could to the nation's economy" is

    a. adequately supported.

    b. inadequately supported.

26. The author is biased

    a. against Japanese women entering the workforce in positions of power.

    b. in favor of Japanese women entering the workforce in positions of power.

27. "All willing participants—male and female—should be encouraged to contribute to Japan's economy."
    This is a statement of

    a. fact.

    b. opinion.

Most of the eight hundred or so movies made in India every year contain musical numbers in which the characters sing. However, an Indian film star does not need to carry a tune. Film songs are sung by professionals known as playback singers, who receive onscreen credit and are often famous in their own right. The most famous playback singer of them all, Lata Mangeshkar, has had a stellar career lasting more than fifty years.   5

Mangeshkar, born in 1929, began taking singing lessons from her father, who was a classical singer, when she was five years old. He recognized her musical talent and worked with her to train her voice. But after her father's death in 1942, Mangeshkar was expected to support her mother and four siblings. She   10 acted in her first film that year and began trying to get work as a playback singer.

In the 1940s, as today, the popularity of the songs in an Indian film was of primary importance: a poor film could be a box-office smash if the songs were good, and bad songs could doom an otherwise fine film. Mangeshkar's high voice did not resemble that of the typical playback singer of 1940s Indian cin-   15 ema, and she had difficulty getting playback work because filmmakers feared that her singing would not win the necessary public attention. Her first break came with a song in a 1947 film. Her number did not sell, but fortunately, her work attracted the attention of a few film composers who continued to hire her.

(continued)

In 1949, Mangeshkar suddenly struck gold, creating several hits in three films. 20
She became a playback star at the age of twenty.

Mangeshkar, who has recorded almost continuously since the late 1940s, has been phenomenally successful even in an industry that is filled with success stories. When the Filmfare Awards—Indian cinema's version of the Academy Awards—created the category of Best Playback Singer in 1958, no one was sur- 25 prised that she won the first award. Mangeshkar also earned a place in the *Guinness Book of World Records* as the most-recorded singer of all time, having recorded more than thirty thousand songs when the category was retired in 1991. Some estimate that she has recorded another ten thousand since then.

Lata Mangeshkar has dominated playback singing in Indian films for over 30 fifty years, outlasting generations of actors. Her piping voice has brought to life the songs of countless young screen heroines. The sound of Lata Mangeshkar's singing is familiar to almost every fan of Indian cinema, and decades of hits have made her name a household word.

28. The implied main idea of paragraph 2 is

   a. Mangeshkar was the most famous movie actress in India's history.

   b. The death of Mangeshkar's father was a serious setback to her singing career.

   c. Mangeshkar resented the family responsibility she had due to her father's death.

   d. A combination of natural talent and necessity was the impetus for Mangeshkar's career.

29. According to the passage

   a. Mangeshkar performed in her first film at the age of 13.

   b. Mangeshkar won the Best Playback Singer award in 1959.

   c. India produces more than one thousand films each year.

   d. Mangeshkar's first movie song in 1947 was a hit and marked the beginning of her successful career.

30. The author's primary purpose is to

   a. persuade the reader that Lata Mangeshkar is the most talented vocalist in the world.

   b. inspire the reader to buy recordings by Lata Mangeshkar.

   c. provide a biography of Lata Mangeshkar.

   d. describe the vocal career of Lata Mangeshkar.

31. The tone of this passage can best be described as

   a. ironic.

   b. nostalgic.

   c. admiring.

   d. reverent.

32. Mangeshkar's first major success was in

    a.   1947.

    b.   1949.

    c.   1958.

    d.   1991.

33. "Her piping voice has brought to life the songs of countless young screen heroines." This is a statement of

    a.   fact.

    b.   opinion.

34. As used in line 5, the word *stellar* most nearly means

    a.   outstanding.

    b.   dramatic.

    c.   long-lasting.

    d.   tragic.

35. What is the relationship between the parts of the following sentence?

> "Her number did not sell, but fortunately, her work attracted the attention of a few film composers who continued to hire her."

    a.   comparison

    b.   time order

    c.   contrast

    d.   example

36. The author's claim that "The most famous playback singer of them all, Lata Mangeshkar, has had a stellar career lasting more than fifty years" is

    a.   adequately supported by factual evidence.

    b.   inadequately supported with personal opinion.

Each sentence in the following passage has been given a number. Read the passage carefully and then answer the questions, which refer to sentences by number. (An answer form is included on p. 299, and pp. 279–82 provide explanations for answers.)

1. _____. **2.** Tomatoes are now one of the most popular vegetables in the United States, second only to the potato. **3.** In other parts of Europe, however, tomato plants were viewed with suspicion. **4.** The plant is native to South America, and European explorers first discovered it in Central America, where local people were eating it happily without being poisoned. **5.** Spanish travelers brought tomatoes back to their homeland in the early sixteenth century. **6.** Far from considering the fruit of the tomato plant toxic, Spanish and Italian cooks soon developed many recipes for tomatoes. **7.** _____, tomatoes are a member of the nightshade family, which has many poisonous members. **8.** Belladonna, for example, is a highly toxic plant related to the tomato. **9.** Although tomato fruits are not only edible but highly nutritious, the leaves and roots of the tomato plant actually contain the same nerve poison found in other members of the nightshade family. **10.** The Europeans who believed that tomatoes were poisonous may not have been correct, but their initial reluctance to eat the fruit of this popular plant is at least understandable.

1. Which sentence if inserted into the blank labeled 1 makes the best main idea or topic sentence for the selection?

   a.   Did Europeans five hundred years ago really believe that tomatoes were poisonous?

   b.   The tomato and its plant have been considered controversial throughout time.

   c.   Spanish and Italian cuisines base many of their recipes on tomatoes.

   d.   There are many reasons why tomatoes are still eaten today.

2. Which of the following sentences is not supported by specific evidence?

   a.   3   b.   4   c.   7   d.   10

3. Which arrangement of sentences provides the most logical sequence?

   a.   Tomatoes are now one of the most popular vegetables in the United States, second only to the potato. The plant is native to South America, and European explorers first discovered it in Central America, where local people were eating it happily without being poisoned. Spanish travelers brought tomatoes back to their homeland in the early sixteenth century. Far from considering the fruit of the tomato plant toxic, Spanish and Italian cooks soon developed many recipes for tomatoes. In other parts of Europe, however, tomato plants were viewed with suspicion.

b. Far from considering the fruit of the tomato plant toxic, Spanish and Italian cooks soon developed many recipes for tomatoes. In other parts of Europe, however, tomato plants were viewed with suspicion. Tomatoes are now one of the most popular vegetables in the United States, second only to the potato. The plant is native to South America, and European explorers first discovered it in Central America, where local people were eating it happily without being poisoned. Spanish travelers brought tomatoes back to their homeland in the early sixteenth century.

c. The plant is native to South America, and European explorers first discovered it in Central America, where local people were eating it happily without being poisoned. Tomatoes are now one of the most popular vegetables in the United States, second only to the potato. Spanish travelers brought tomatoes back to their homeland in the early sixteenth century. Far from considering the fruit of the tomato plant toxic, Spanish and Italian cooks soon developed many recipes for tomatoes. In other parts of Europe, however, tomato plants were viewed with suspicion.

d. Spanish travelers brought tomatoes back to their homeland in the early sixteenth century. Tomatoes are now one of the most popular vegetables in the United States, second only to the potato. The plant is native to South America, and European explorers first discovered it in Central America, where local people were eating it happily without being poisoned. Far from considering the fruit of the tomato plant toxic, Spanish and Italian cooks soon developed many recipes for tomatoes. In other parts of Europe, however, tomato plants were viewed with suspicion.

4. Which sentence is the least relevant to the passage?

   a. 8   b. 7   c. 2   d. 3

5. Which transitional device if inserted in blank 7 would show the relationship between sentences 6 and 7?

   a. Because   b. Thus   c. However   d. As it happens

In the following sentences, you will need to do one of the following three things to answer the questions correctly: (1) choose the most effective word or phrase in the suggested context, (2) select the option that corrects an error in an underlined portion, or (3) choose the correct version of a sentence (from a selection of three).

6. The judge's ruling _____ the legal team, which thought it had mounted an excellent defense.

   a. infuriated   b. burned out   c. inspired   d. tormented

7. Because the paint in the church's interior dome was chipped and _____, the parish decided that the dome should be repainted.

   a. bright   b. ruddy   c. etched   d. faded

8. I use to use a special paint brush for my paintings that I used to sell.
   <u>A</u>   <u>B</u>   <u>C</u>

    a.   used   b.   used   c.   use   d.   No change is necessary.

9.   a.   Swerving in front of him, Jim noticed a car just before the accident occurred.

      b.   Jim noticed a car swerving in front of him just before the accident occurred.

      c.   Jim noticed a car just before the accident occurred swerving in front of him.

10.   a.   An angel holding a horn just to the left of the entrance is my favorite painting in the exhibit.

      b.   Holding a horn, an angel just to the left of the entrance is my favorite painting in the exhibit.

      c.   Just to the left of the entrance is my favorite painting in the exhibit: an angel holding a horn.

11. Janet knows how to swim, _____ she likes to play tennis.

    a.   and   b.   but   c.   yet   d.   nor

12. Louise's purse was stolen, _____ it was soon recovered.

    a.   and   b.   so   c.   yet   d.   for

13.   a.   At last night's book signing, the author met with her fans, read from her latest novel, and signed copies of her poster.

      b.   At last night's book signing, the author met with her fans, read from her latest novel, and she signed copies of her poster.

      c.   At last night's book signing, the author met with her fans, was reading from her latest novel, and signed copies of her poster.

14. Exhausted from the <u>hike the camp counselor</u> still managed <u>to set up the tents</u> for the
                       A   **B**

<u>girls participating</u> in the daylong campout.
      C

    a.   hike, the camp counselor   b.   to set up; the tents

    c.   girls, participating   d.   No change is necessary.

15. Ginger knows all kind of <u>dances. For instance,</u> the tango, the twist, and the fox trot.

    a.   dances; for instance   b.   dances, such as

    c.   dances. For example   d.   No change is necessary.

16. My first trip to <u>Colombia was</u> an unforgettable <u>experience,</u> I learned a lot about my
　　　　　　　　　　A　　　　　　　　　　　　　　　**B**

　　family's <u>heritage in South America.</u>
　　　　　　　　　　　C

　　　a.　Colombia, was 　　　　　　　b.　experience, for I

　　　c.　Heritage. In South America 　d.　No change is necessary.

17. The fact that he <u>forgot</u> his fifteenth wedding <u>anniversary</u> did not plague his <u>conscious.</u>
　　　　　　　　　　　　A　　　　　　　　　　　　　　**B**　　　　　　　　　　　**C**

　　　a.　forget　　　b.　date　　　c.　conscience　　　d.　No change is necessary.

18. The new boutique that <u>opened</u> on the fashionable street <u>have attracted</u> many celebrities
　　　　　　　　　　　　　　A　　　　　　　　　　　　　**B**

　　and wealthy clients <u>looking</u> for exclusive items.
　　　　　　　　　　　C

　　　a.　opening　　　b.　has attracted　c.　look　　　d.　No change is necessary.

19. Either the coach or the members of the athletic board <u>decides</u> what teams the Rockville
　　Raiders will play each season.

　　　a.　deciding　　　b.　has decided　　　c.　decide　　　d.　No change is necessary.

20. Perkins Produce is one of the stores that <u>caters</u> to vegetarians.

　　　a.　catering　　　b.　have catered　　c.　cater　　　d.　No change is necessary.

21. We <u>went</u> to every store along the street, but we never <u>find</u> the paint that Taylor <u>wanted.</u>
　　　　　A　　　　　　　　　　　　　　　　　　　　**B**　　　　　　　　　　　**C**

　　　a.　go　　　b.　found　　　c.　wanting　　　d.　No change is necessary.

22. The new gardener <u>deciding</u> to try a new fertilizer on our lawn this spring.

　　　a.　be deciding　b.　decide　　　c.　has decided　d.　No change is necessary.

23. The backpacks that <u>went</u> on sale this past Friday have gold thread on the side panels.

　　　a.　gone　　　b.　be　　　c.　been gone　d.　No change is necessary.

24. The company hasn't given raises or bonuses for five years, and <u>their</u> benefits are poor too.

　　　a.　they're　　　b.　its　　　c.　our　　　d.　No change is necessary.

25. Carlotta, Monica, and <u>me</u> have been the best of friends for years.

　　　a.　I　　　b.　we've　　　c.　them　　　d.　No change is necessary.

26. Would you like to go to the moves with Jose and <u>I</u>?.

　　　a.　we　　　b.　he　　　c.　me　　　d.　No change is necessary.

4

27. The girl <u>whom</u> works as a hostess lost <u>her</u> job at Waffle-mania. <u>It</u> was all she had to
      A   **B**   **C**

make ends meet.

    a.   who   b.   hers   c.   Its   d.   No change is necessary.

28. My grandmother was as energetic as any <u>teenager she</u> always had at least four projects going at once.

    a.   teenager, she   b.   teenager, which
    c.   teenager. She   d.   No change is necessary.

29. Leanne told April that <u>she</u> needed to move her car.

    a. herself   b. her   c. she, April,   d. No change is necessary.

30. When I see a nice pair of jeans, I buy a second pair because <u>you</u> never know if the style
        A   **B**   **C**

will be discontinued.

    a. one   b. you   c. I   d. No change is necessary.

31. Gina felt <u>badly</u> about what she had done to Mary.

    a. badder   b. more bad   c. bad   d. No change is necessary.

32. Of the triplets, Johanna is the _____.

    a. smarter   b. smartest   c. more smart   d. most smart

33. This is the _____ garden I have ever seen.

    a. beautifullest   b. most beautiful   c. more beautiful   d. best beautiful

34. Jill's favorite month is <u>october</u>; she loves the beautiful <u>fall</u> weather and the spookiness of
                            A   **B**

<u>Halloween.</u>
    C

    a. October   b. Fall   c. halloween   d. No change is necessary.

35. Jonah always was <u>afraid. To</u> go to the movies by himself.

    a. afraid: to   b. afraid; to   c. afraid to   d. No change is necessary.

36. For her civics project, Mary decided to <u>voluntier</u> in Senator Jones's reelection <u>campaign.</u>
                                      A   **B**

He wasn't <u>supposed</u> to win, but she was a big fan.
            C

    a. volunteer   b. campiagn   c. suppose   d. No change is necessary.

37. The officials of the <u>foreign</u> <u>goverment</u> knew it was important to act <u>professionally</u> at
                          A   **B**   **C**

the gathering.

    a. foriegn   b. government   c. proffesionally   d. No change is necessary.

38. "Is this bag <u>your's</u>, Madame?" the waiter asked. "No," <u>she</u> replied, pointing to her left,
A   B

"It's <u>hers</u>."
      C

   a.   yours   b.   her   c.   her's   d.   No change is necessary.

39. The summer classes I took included <u>algebra I</u>, <u>physics</u>, and <u>economics</u>.
                                              A   B   C

   a.   Algebra I   b.   Physics   c.   Economics   d.   No change is necessary.

40. I <u>laid</u> in bed with a fever all day Monday, but I feel much better today.

   a.   lie   b.   lay   c.   layed   d.   No change is necessary.

Appendix · Succeeding on the Writing Sample

An additional component of the Florida College Basic Skills Exit Test is a writing sample, a paragraph or essay about an assigned topic. You will have fifty minutes to plan, write, and proofread the paragraph or essay,* which will test your ability to

- clearly establish a main idea
- back up the main idea with adequate and relevant support
- organize ideas logically and coherently
- choose effective vocabulary and sentence structures
- follow the conventions of standard American English (grammar, spelling, capitalization, and punctuation)

Your writing will be scored from 6 (highest) to 1 (lowest), based on how well it meets these criteria. (See pp. 237–38 for details on scoring.)

The best way to succeed on this part of the test is to practice writing a paragraph or brief essay within fifty minutes, on a topic like one you will receive on the test. (On the actual test, you will be given two topics and asked to choose one.) In addition to subjects you might like or that your instructor might suggest, you can practice on the following topics:

- a current issue that you feel strongly about
- challenges of juggling school and other responsibilities
- your favorite pastime
- a place you enjoy visiting

PLANNING, DRAFTING, AND PROOFREADING YOUR WRITING SAMPLE

These steps will help you to write a successful writing sample under pressure.

1. Pace yourself.

Bring a watch to the exam, and use it to pace yourself. Make sure to leave enough time for planning, writing, and proofreading. Here's a suggestion for how to allocate your time:

- *First ten minutes:* Planning (from focusing on the topic to writing a rough outline)
- *Thirty minutes:* Drafting
- *Last ten minutes:* Reviewing and correcting your work

---

*The processes for writing paragraphs and essays are very similar, and for both types of writing you'll need to write a sound statement of the main point and back it up with adequate supporting details. The main idea of an essay is called a *thesis statement*, and the main idea of a paragraph is called a *topic sentence*. For more explanations and examples, see section 3.1A, pp. 113–21.

2. Focus on the topic.

Suppose you are asked to write an essay about the challenges of juggling school and other responsibilities. Focus on what the topic calls for in an essay by circling or underlining key words such as "challenges," "school," and "other responsibilities."

3. Generate ideas.

Although you may be tempted to begin your paragraph or essay immediately, it's wise to spend five minutes or so jotting down some ideas related to the key words you circled or underlined. This will help you come up with a solid main idea and the beginnings of support for that idea.

For the topic described in point 2, you might write "challenges" on a sheet of scratch paper and then jot down some of the challenges related to school and other responsibilities. Don't censor yourself; write down all ideas that occur to you.

> Challenges
> Not enough time, never enough time!
> Homework, kids, job, laundry
> Sometimes have to work late
> Makes me stressed
> ~~Too many birthdays lately—no time for shopping~~
> Can't focus on anything because I'm so busy
> Always something else to do
> Want to talk to friends instead of study—I need a break!
> Scheduling has helped me—read about it in a magazine and tried it
> Students need a break—but when?

You might quickly look over the list to see if any ideas are clearly off point, or whether you need to add more details. Cross out ideas that don't seem relevant.

4. Develop a main idea.

Look over your list of ideas and ask yourself, "What general conclusion can I draw from these thoughts?" or "What is most significant or interesting about these ideas?" Also, you might group ideas to help draw conclusions. For example, you might realize that several of the ideas listed have to do with the fact that budgeting time is a serious issue for busy students.

Looking over the list, you decide you want to focus on the three challenges that you see as most important: budgeting time, focusing on tasks, and avoiding stress. You will be evaluated on your ability to state your main point clearly, so try to do so now. Don't worry if the statement isn't perfect; you can come back to it later.

> The three main challenges of juggling school and other responsibilities are budgeting time, focusing on the task at hand, and managing stress.

5. Write a quick outline.

This is another step that may feel like a waste of time, but it's not. You will be evaluated on your ability to provide adequate and relevant support for your main idea and to organize that support logically and coherently. Writing an outline will get you off to a good start and save you time in the end.

The sample main-idea statement sets out three challenges, so you might flesh these out in a quick outline.

<u>Budgeting time</u>
—Difficult for students with jobs, spouses, children
—One part of life can cut into another
—Scheduling can help

<u>Focusing on task at hand</u>
—Distractions a serious problem for busy people
—Need to remove distractions to focus

<u>Managing stress</u>
—Life unpredictable—learn to live with that
—Relax and take a break now and then
—Schedule has to be put aside sometimes

6. Draft your paragraph or essay.

Using your main-idea statement and rough outline, begin to draft your paragraph or essay. Write as legibly as you can so that evaluators can read your work easily, and write on every other line so that you'll have room to make corrections and add sentences as needed. It's OK to cross out words and sentences as long as your writing is legible.

If you are writing a paragraph, indent it. If you are writing an essay, indent the first paragraph, and start a new paragraph whenever you begin to develop another major point of support for your main idea. (See the example on p. 236.) If you forget an indentation, insert a paragraph symbol (¶) later.

You may find that you occasionally veer away from your outline, adding new points or dropping old ideas that no longer seem to work. That's fine; just make sure that any points that you add are relevant to your main idea and that you aren't taking your paragraph or essay in a completely new direction.

7. Reread your writing, refining the ideas and correcting any problems.

If possible, take the last five to ten minutes to review your paragraph or essay, keeping the following questions in mind:

- Is your main idea clearly stated and clearly connected to the paragraph or essay that has evolved from it? You may need to refine the statement to make it more reflective of the ideas you've developed.

- Do all the supporting points relate directly to the main idea? Do you provide enough details to back up your main idea?

- Is the order of supporting points logical and coherent? (Consider adding transitions like *for example*, *in addition*, and *also* to clarify the connections between your ideas.)

- Are your word choices effective? If you find words that don't fit your intended meaning, try to find more exact words.

- Are your sentences varied? Look over the essay to see if there are groups or strings of sentences that follow the same structure—for example subject, verb, object/modifying phrase (*I went to the store. I brought a blouse. I returned home.*). If there are, can you find a way to combine sentences or otherwise vary the structure? (For instance, *After buying a blouse at the store, I returned home.*)

- Is your writing free of errors in grammar, spelling, capitalization, and punctuation?

If you find an error or if you want to rewrite a section of the paragraph or essay, simply cross out the problem text and write the new text above it. If you want to move a sentence or passage to another section, circle it and draw an arrow indicating where it should go.

Following is an example of a completed essay, annotated for key writing features, including main idea (p. 234) and support (pp. 234–35).

SAMPLE ESSAY

Main idea (sets up clear organization)

Both new and experienced students can develop ways to cope with three challenges of juggling school and other responsibilities: budgeting time, focusing on the task at hand, and managing stress.

Major support

Budgeting time can be a problem even for full-time students with no families. However, it is even more difficult for students with jobs, spouses, and children. For example, they

Supporting details

may have to work late at a job, cutting into their family and studying time, or they may have to stay up late with a sick child, leaving them exhausted the next day. Although time-budgeting issues are sometimes beyond students' control, students can manage time better by setting a schedule for school, work, and family activities and trying to stick to it. For instance, a student might set a regular studying appointment for six until eight every evening and, if possible, arrange childcare for this time. Setting aside the time—and telling friends and family that this is study time—can help the student establish a routine and avoid interruption.

Major support

Focusing on tasks during the scheduled time is another challenge. Often, busy students who try to focus on a task find their minds racing ahead to all the other things they

Supporting details

need to do. Such students might remove any distractions that are interfering with their inability to focus. For example, if they want to focus on schoolwork, they might shut off the ringer on their cell phone and clear their desks of anything not related to their studies. At night, during family time, they might put their books in a book bag and stash the bag out of view.

Major support

The third challenge is managing stress—an unavoidable result of juggling multiple responsibilities. One of the most important strategies for managing stress is to be flexible.

Supporting details

Although a schedule is a helpful tool for managing time, sometimes it has to be violated. For example, there will be times when students have to miss school to care for a child, or when they will have to miss study time because of work. At those times, it can help to take a deep breath, relax, and say, "That's life." It also helps to take a break from time to time. Busy students might not be able to take a week off, but they need occasional breaks (such as an afternoon "power nap") to keep up their energy.

Conclusion

Although these three challenges may seem daunting, they can be managed effectively with some thoughtfulness, planning, and a little determination.

A final note: After you've written a practice paragraph or essay, review it based on the five criteria described on p. 233. (If possible, have your instructor, a peer, or a writing-center tutor review it as well.) If you note any areas of weakness, revise those sections. Although you won't have an opportunity to revise the test paragraph or essay after you've handed it in, the revision practice will help you when it comes time to take the test.

UNDERSTANDING HOW THE WRITING SAMPLE IS SCORED

Your paragraph or essay will be scored from 6 (highest) to 1 (lowest) based on the degree to which it meets the five criteria described on p. 233. After you have written a practice paragraph or essay, you might want to check it against this chart. Does it deserve a score of 6? If not, what would you need to do to improve it?

MEANING OF SCORE BASED ON TEST CRITERIA					
Score	**Main Idea**	**Support**	**Organization**	**Vocabulary and Sentence Structures**	**Correctness (according to Standard English)**
6	Clearly established	Adequate—main idea is fully developed with specific details and examples	Logical and coherent	Varied and effective	Few errors in grammar, spelling, capitalization, and punctuation
5	Clearly established	Adequate—main idea is developed and recognizable through specific details and examples	Logical and coherent	Mostly varied and effective	Occasional errors in grammar, spelling, capitalization, and punctuation. However, these errors do not interfere with the writer's ability to get the message across.
4	Adequately stated	Main idea is developed with some specific details and examples	Mostly logical and coherent	Somewhat varied and effective	Occasional errors in grammar, spelling, capitalization, and punctuation. These errors may interfere with the writer's ability to get the message across. *(continued)*

Score	Main Idea	Support	Organization	Vocabulary and Sentence Structures	Correctness (according to Standard English)
3	Stated	Main idea developed through generalizations or lists	Occasional lapses in logic and coherence—paper may be "mechanical"	Repetitious and often ineffective	Variety of errors in grammar, spelling, capitalization, and punctuation. These errors sometimes interfere with the writer's ability to get the message across.
2	Incomplete or ambiguous	Main idea developed through generalizations and lists	Occasional lapses in logic and coherence—organization is "mechanical"	Word choice is simplistic, and sentence structure is disjointed	Errors in grammar, spelling, capitalization, and punctuation frequently interfere with the writer's ability to get the message across.
1	Not evident	Inadequate or irrelevant	Illogical or incoherent	Garbled and confusing	Significant and numerous errors in grammar, spelling, capitalization, and punctuation interfere with the writer's ability to get the message across.

This chart and the descriptions of criteria have been adapted from information from the State of Florida, Department of Education.

GETTING MORE HELP

Although writing a timed paragraph or essay is the best way to prepare for the writing-sample portion of the test, you may find that you need additional instruction in the five criteria tested. The following chart shows where you can get help in this book. If you still feel that you need help in any of these areas, see your instructor or a writing-center tutor, if one is available.

WHERE TO GET MORE HELP IN THIS BOOK	
Skill	**Relevant Section**
Establishing a main idea	Section 3.1A, pp. 113–21
Backing up a main idea with adequate and relevant support	Section 3.1B, pp. 122–34
Organizing ideas logically and coherently	Section 3.1C, pp. 134–45
Choosing effective vocabulary and sentence structures	Sections 3.2A, pp. 153–54, and 3.3, pp. 157–73
Following the conventions of standard American English (grammar, spelling, capitalization, and punctuation)	Section 3.4, pp. 174–213

Answer Key for Pre-Tests

PART ONE. DIAGNOSTIC PRE-TESTS

1.1 **READING PRE-TEST**

Question Number	Answer	Where to Get More Help in This Book
1.	A	Section 2.1A, pp. 23–31
2.	D	Section 2.1A, pp. 23–31
3.	B	Section 2.1C, pp. 38–51
4.	C	Section 2.2B, pp. 64–72
5.	A	Section 2.1B, pp. 32–37
6.	B	Section 2.3A, pp. 73–78
7.	D	Section 2.2B, pp. 64–72
8.	D	Section 2.3B, pp. 78–85
9.	B	Section 2.2A, pp. 52–64
10.	D	Section 2.1A, pp. 23–31
11.	A	Section 2.3A, pp. 73–78
12.	D	Section 2.1B, pp. 32–37
13.	A	Section 2.2A, pp. 52–64
14.	C	Section 2.1C, pp. 38–51
15.	D	Section 2.2B, pp. 64–72
16.	C	Section 2.3C, pp. 85–93
17.	A	Section 2.3B, pp. 78–85
18.	A	Section 2.4A, pp. 94–97
19.	B	Section 2.1A, pp. 23–31
20.	D	Section 2.1B, pp. 32–37
21.	B	Section 2.3A, pp. 73–78
22.	C	Section 2.1C, pp. 38–51
23.	A	Section 2.2B, pp. 64–72
24.	C	Section 2.3C, pp. 85–93
25.	D	Section 2.4B, pp. 97–102
26.	A	Section 2.4C, pp. 103–11
27.	B	Section 2.4A, pp. 94–97
28.	B	Section 2.3C, pp. 85–93
29.	A	Section 2.1B, pp. 32–37
30.	A	Section 2.4A, pp. 94–97
31.	A	Section 2.1B, pp. 32–37

32.	A	Section 2.1C, pp. 38–51
33.	B	Section 2.2A, pp. 52–64
34.	C	Section 2.2B, pp. 64–72
35.	A	Section 2.4C, pp. 103–11
36.	B	Section 2.3B, pp. 78–85

1.2 WRITING PRE-TEST

Question Number	Answer	Where to Get More Help in This Book
1.	D	Section 3.1A, pp. 113–21
2.	C	Section 3.1B, pp. 122–34
3.	A	Section 3.1C, pp. 134–45
4.	B	Section 3.1B, pp. 122–34
5.	D	Section 3.1D, pp. 145–52
6.	B	Section 3.2A, pp. 153–54
7.	C	Section 3.2A, pp. 153–54
8.	A	Section 3.2B, pp. 154–56
9.	B	Section 3.2B, pp. 154–56
10.	B	Section 3.3A, pp. 157–59
11.	B	Section 3.3B, pp. 160–64
12.	D	Section 3.3B, pp. 160–64
13.	C	Section 3.3C, pp. 164–66
14.	A	Section 3.3C, pp. 164–66
15.	B	Section 3.4K, pp. 203–9
16.	D	Section 3.4K, pp. 203–9
17.	B	Section 3.3D, pp. 167–70
18.	B	Section 3.3E, pp. 170–73
19.	A	Section 3.4C, pp. 179–83
20.	C	Section 3.4A, pp. 174–77
21.	D	Section 3.4A, pp. 174–77
22.	C	Section 3.4A, pp. 174–77
23.	C	Section 3.4B, pp. 177–79
24.	D	Section 3.4F, pp. 189–91
25.	B	Section 3.4G, pp. 191–93
26.	C	Section 3.4D, pp. 183–87
27.	B	Section 3.4E, pp. 187–89
28.	B	Section 3.4D, pp. 183–87

K

29.	B	Section 3.4E, pp. 187–89
30.	B	Section 3.4H, pp. 194–96
31.	C	Section 3.4I, pp. 196–99
32.	B	Section 3.4J, pp. 199–203
33.	C	Section 3.4J, pp. 199–203
34.	B	Section 3.4L, pp. 209–13
35.	D	Section 3.4L, pp. 209–13
36.	B	Section 3.4K, pp. 203–9
37.	A	Section 3.4K, pp. 203–9
38.	B	Section 3.4L, pp. 209–13
39.	C	Section 3.4K, pp. 203–9
40.	C	Section 3.3D, pp. 167–70

Answer Key for Practice Items

PART TWO. MASTERING THE READING TEST

2.1A **IDENTIFYING THE MAIN IDEA**

1. **C**—Choice A is a broad generalization and, therefore, untrue. This passage relates two incidents from the 1970s and does not discuss the current point of view, so the reader does not have enough information to choose choice B. Likewise, the reader does not have enough information to judge the validity of choice D and, if true, it would be a specific detail. Choice C sums up the main idea of the passage.

2. **A**—Choice B is an incorrect inference. The reader has no information about the popularity of horse racing today. C cannot be the main idea because we cannot know this. Choice D is false. Riggs was older than King, but both of the horses were three years old.

3. **D**—Choice A is wrong because this idea is not expressed in this passage. In addition, body scans are not foolproof. Choices B and C are points in the passage but not the author's main point. They are details. D states the main idea of the passage. The passage discusses the problems with patients putting too much faith in self-prescribed body scans and the importance of having a good doctor.

4. **A**—The rest of the passage explains why a patient's faith in full-body scans can be problematic and even dangerous. B is a specific detail, as are choices C and D.

5. **D**—The topic of this paragraph is radiation exposure, and choice D discusses the concept of radiation in relation to good health. Choice A is a general statement. B and C are specific details.

6. **C**—The author describes the poor driving habits of people who think they are better-than-average drivers. These poor driving habits prove that the drivers are mistaken about their ability. Choices B and D are specific details. Choice A cannot be correct because the author does not discuss any studies. If an idea is not discussed, it cannot be the main idea.

7. **A**—A driver who is not paying attention is a distracted driver. Choice B is a false statement. The author doesn't imply that listening to music is in and of itself a bad choice. Likewise, the author does not suggest choice C. D is a false generalization.

8. **A**—Choice B is true but a specific detail. Choice D is true according to the author but also a detail. Choice C is not discussed. Choice A is the best choice because the author claims that ice cream making should be a social endeavor and that the finished product is superior when handmade.

9. **D**—A is true but a specific detail. B is an unproved supposition not stated in the passage, and C is not supported by the passage. The reader has no idea whether this is a true statement so it can certainly not be considered a main idea.

10. **C**—Choices A and B are specific details, and D is not discussed in the passage.

1. **A**—The passage refers to Lamar Mervine as the "current mayor." Therefore, the reader knows that A is correct. There is no way for the reader to know when Mervine's term began (B). We cannot infer that he was or was not the mayor when the fire started (C), nor do we know how concerned other mayors have been (D).

2. **B**—Route 61 collapsed after twenty-one years, but the fire continued, so choice A is incorrect. The passage states that the fire has enough coal fuel to burn for at least 100 to 250 more years. The last specific date of reference in the passage is 1983. Adding a minimum of 100 years would mean the fire would burn until at least 2083. Therefore, choice B is correct. Choice C is incorrect because the passage offers no information about how long coal fires generally last. Choice D is a false statement. The passage states the coal fire was ignored for several months, not years.

3. **C**—Choice A is a false statement. Trenches were dug to attempt to contain the fire but were unsuccessful. Choice B is false also. Fly ash is mentioned as a material used unsuccessfully in an attempt to smother the fires. Choice C is stated in the first sentence of paragraph 4 and is the correct answer. Choice D is incorrect because it is the measurement of the coal fire as stated in paragraph 6.

4. **A**—The passage states that Centralia had approximately eleven hundred residents. Therefore, choice A is a correct statement. The town has never been totally shut down, and 1983 is the date of the collapse of Route 61, so choice B is incorrect. Paragraph 1 states that there are thirty-six coal fires in Pennsylvania. Choice C, two dozen, or 24, is incorrect. Choice D is also an incorrect statement. Centralia now has only about twenty citizens as a result of a mass paid exodus.

5. **D**—The first sentence in paragraph 2 states that planets have elliptical, or oval, orbits as they travel around the sun. Therefore, D is the correct answer.

6. **A**—The most recent perihelic opposition was in 2003, and the passage states that the next one is due in about 280 years. Therefore, 2283 is correct.

7. **A**—The passage states that there have been no significant differences in what astronomers are able to see because the distance between Earth and Mars in perihelic oppositions stays relatively the same. Several kilometers do not make a difference regarding visibility. Therefore, choice A is the correct choice. Choices B and C are disputed in the passage, and choice D is factually incorrect.

8. **C**—Line 20 explains the direction of water flow. Therefore, the correct choice is C. Paragraph 3 explains that the Coriolis force is insignificant in small containers, so choice A is incorrect. Choice B is the opposite of the correct answer, and choice D is false and not even discussed.

9. **B**—The correct answer is B because Gaspard de Coriolis was a famous nineteenth-century mathematician. The nineteenth century refers to the 1800s.

10. **D**—The dimensions of the tank are stated in paragraph 4. Choices A, B, and C are false statements.

1. **D**—The author presents a strong case for the idea that intellectual property (literature, symbols, images, and ideas) should be available to all and not owned or copyrighted by individuals or corporations. The author's primary purpose is not to entertain or amuse the reader with stories, so choice A is incorrect. Although the author does mention different examples of intellectual property (Pepperidge Farm crackers, certain types of yoga), listing them is not the author's main purpose (C). Likewise, the author explains or informs the reader of the importance of intellectual property, but most of all, the author is trying to build a case or persuade the reader to adopt his position. That makes choice D the best answer.

2. **A**—The author is describing what a weed is and giving a great deal of explanation to illustrate the point. The author does not attempt to convince the reader that weeds are dangerous (B) or that they should all be eliminated (C). The author does not discuss weeds in terms of their importance (D).

3. **B**—The author primarily wants to inspire or persuade readers to reevaluate their attitudes toward income and goals. The author's point is that too many Americans measure their worth in terms of money when there are other equally or more important aspects to life. The author does mention some ways Americans spend money (houses, cars) but those are specific details, not the purpose. Likewise, the author describes spending habits but then criticizes them in attempting to inspire readers to make changes. Therefore, choice B is the best answer.

4. **D**—The author explains at length how communication can be misleading and even destructive. The author takes a very negative position regarding damaging communication. Therefore, he is criticizing those tactics. To illustrate, discuss, and teach are objective or factual. This is a very subjective, or opinionated, passage. Therefore, choices A, B, and C are incorrect answers.

5. **A**—The author goes into great detail describing Van Gogh's painting *The Night Café* and examines its relationship to his depression. Therefore, choice A is the best description of the author's purpose. Choices B and D are much too broad, and choice C is incorrect because the author does not discuss in detail any other work of Van Gogh.

6. **B**—The author begins by defining the Coriolis force but then continues throughout the passage to explain the misconceptions about the theory. Therefore, choice A is not the overall purpose of this passage. Ascher Shapiro was trying to prove the Coriolis theory, so choice C makes no sense. Since the author does not discuss other scientific theory, choice D is incorrect.

7. **C**—This passage uses satire to make the point that all drivers have weaknesses in their styles of driving, and they need to be aware of these potential problems. Therefore, choice C is the best expression of the author's purpose. Although the author seems to be funny at times, it is satiric or tongue-in-cheek humor. Choice A is incorrect because the author is not trying to be funny. The author does describe driving styles (B) and does illustrate dangers involved with driving (D), yet these are not the purpose of the passage.

8. **A**—The author clearly praises her grandmother by talking about her many talents and attributes. Therefore, choice A is the main purpose. Grandma Anna's hobbies

are discussed (B), but that is not the purpose of the passage. The author does not compare Grandma Anna with other grandmothers, nor does she contrast her hobbies. Because choices C and D are not discussed, they cannot be the purpose of the passage.

9. **B**—This passage begins with a discussion of the interest in cave art. It continues with a discussion of a newly discovered cave in Australia and how the inaccessibility safeguards the cave's preservation. Therefore, choice B is the best answer for the author's purpose. This passage does not analyze the history of cave art (A), nor does it list the elements of cave art (C) or build a case for the Australian government to encourage more visitors to the cave (D).

10. **A**—The author tells the story of the town of Centralia in order to show the reader how amazingly destructive and long-lasting the effects of a coal fire can be. Choices B and D are not discussed. Although the author does describe the problems that Centralia suffered, choice C is not the best expression of the author's purpose. The author discusses the problems in Centralia to make a point about the severity of the coal fires.

2.2A IDENTIFYING PATTERNS OF ORGANIZATION

1. **C**—The organizational pattern is one of cause and effect. The author discusses how limiting the rights to intellectual property (literature, symbols, images, ideas) is detrimental to the American consumer. The author does not merely list examples of intellectual property (A). Choice B is not discussed. Although the author does define intellectual property and give examples (D), that is not the organizational pattern for the overall passage.

2. **A**—Although the author does, in paragraph 3, discuss the four basic types of pasta (B), overall, the author is listing the many shapes that pasta can have. Therefore, choice A is the best answer. Choice C is not discussed, and D is a specific detail.

3. **B**—In the first paragraph, the author suggests Americans look for ways to make their lives more satisfying. In the next two paragraphs, the author describes the sequence of first identifying goals and then achieving them. Choice B best describes this pattern of organization. The first paragraph lists some of the purchases American workers make with high salaries, but this is a specific detail, so choice A is incorrect. Choices C and D are not discussed.

4. **A**—The author defines a weed and then lists numerous examples. Choices B and D refer to specific details rather than an overall organizational pattern. Choice C is not discussed.

5. **C**—Clearly, the author is describing in detail the spatial relationships of all the people and objects that van Gogh painted in *The Night Café*. The author vividly explains the position of each element in the painting in relation to every other element. Choices A and B are incorrect because they do not describe the overall organization. Although the author does mention or list the people and objects in the painting (D), the prominent aspect of the passage's organization is the physical arrangement.

6. **A**—The overall pattern of organization for this passage is a statement that full-body scans can be harmful, followed by explanations and examples of why this is so.

Choices B and C are not discussed. Although the author does state at the end of the passage that a good doctor is the most important factor in health care, choice D does not describe the pattern of the overall passage.

7. C—Paragraph 2 describes the myth of the Coriolis force, and then paragraph 3 contrasts the myth with the truth. Therefore, choice C is the correct answer. Although the author describes the impact of the Coriolis force (B) in the first paragraph, that is not the organization of paragraphs 2 and 3. Choice D is not discussed, and choice A is not relevant to the organization of paragraphs 2 and 3.

8. A—The references to time ("after two hours," "after twenty-four hours," . . .) indicate that the organizational pattern is one of sequence. Shapiro's experiment is described in sequence, or time order. Therefore, choice A is the correct answer. This passage does not describe the Coriolis force with examples (B), summarize multiple myths about the Coriolis force (C), or classify Shapiro's experiment as an important scientific discovery (D).

9. D—Paragraph 2 begins with "One reason . . . ," and paragraph 3 begins with "A more important reason. . . ." Therefore, the organizational pattern for the two paragraphs is order of importance (D). The two paragraphs do list reasons why citizens are apathetic about voting (A), but the reasons are discussed in terms of importance. There is no definition of voter apathy (B), and choice C deals with specific details discussed in paragraph 3, not a pattern of organization.

10. A—In this passage the author describes the two gender battles in detail and shows what they have in common and the very different outcomes. Therefore, A is the best answer. The author does connect the King-Riggs match to the popularity of women's tennis, but that is a specific detail in the second paragraph (B). The author does discuss two gender battles, but there is no list of recent battles (C). The author does not discuss choice D.

11. B—The author raises the issue of "incomprehensible or misleading language" and gives examples of bad academic writing, poor business language, and political and military jargon. Choices A, C, and D are not discussed.

12. D—In this passage, the author classifies three types of poor driver and gives the characteristics of each. Choices A, B, and C are not discussed.

2.2B IDENTIFYING RELATIONSHIPS WITHIN AND BETWEEN SENTENCES

1. D—The yoga master's action is the cause, and the consumer's having to pay more is the effect. The author is not adding information (A) or showing how two things are related in physical space (B). A comparison (C) shows how two things are alike. This relationship does not apply to the two parts of this sentence.

2. C—The coyote is mentioned as an example of a weed animal (C). There is no time element (B), nor is there a cause-and-effect element (D). There is no comparison to show how two elements are alike (A).

3. A—The word *after* often signifies a time-order relationship, as it does in this instance. Contrast (B) shows differences between two items. There is no contrast in this sentence. The author is not giving an example (C) or adding information (D).

4. **C**—The author is showing where the wall is in relation to the foreground. This is an example of spatial relationship. There is no contrast, or showing differences between two items (B). No time relationship is stated (A), and no example is given (D).

5. **B**—This one is tricky. At first glance, the word *when* might lead you to guess that this is a time-order relationship. However, it is actually a cause-and-effect relationship. The cause is the access to politicians that the corporations, lobbyists, and interest groups get based on money, and the effect is that citizens who do not make large contributions believe that their votes don't count. There is no comparison (C) or example (D).

6. **C**—The author is talking about the workers applying for the loan. They are classified as poor candidates. To explain why, or to *clarify* why, the author explains about the collateral and credit, and the amount of a loan request. All of that information further explains the initial statement. Therefore, choice C is the best answer. The author is not contrasting two ideas (A), discussing issues in time order (B), or showing a cause-and-effect relationship (D).

7. **A**—The word *while* may suggest time order. However, when the sentence is read in its entirety, the reader sees the author is acknowledging the popularity of spaghetti and macaroni but commenting that many other shapes are available to the consumer. Spatial relationship (B) and time order (C) do not apply here. Although "spaghetti and meatballs and macaroni and cheese" are examples of pasta, the relationship between the two parts of the sentence is not one of example.

8. **B**—The author is telling the reader how parts of the picture are related to each other in terms of physical space. Clue words are "left," "rear corner," "top left," and "in front of." The author is not comparing (A) or showing cause and effect (D). The relationship does not involve a statement with examples (C).

9. **B**—Don't be fooled! Just because a date is mentioned does not mean there is a relationship of time order (C) in the sentence. That is just a specific detail. The word "like" is a clue that the author is comparing two items. When the author shows how two issues are different, that is contrast (A). There is no cause-and-effect relationship in this sentence (D).

10. **D**—The author talks about the CSPI testing popular foods and then lists examples, so D is correct. Although the author mentions "the past few years," there is no time-order relationship (B) in this sentence. There is no additional information about the testing (C), and the author is not comparing two items (A).

11. **D**—The transition words "as a result" should give you a clue. The relationship here is cause and effect (D). The consequence of the legal discussions and disputes has been the unavailability of intellectual property for the public. There is no time order (A), contrast (B), or example (C) relationship.

12. **A**—The author is talking about approval of a loan and then adds information about the interest rate. Comparison (B), time order (C), and example (D) do not apply.

13. **C**—The author is showing the timing involved in the race. The words "At the start" and "then" in the first sentence express time relationships. Then the word "when" in the second sentence gives the reader a clue that the author is talking about the time.

14. **A**—The author is talking about the person who thinks he or she is a better-than-average driver. The author gives the example of tailgating and then adds information

by explaining the driver's reaction when a light turns green. There is no contrast (B), spatial relationship (C), or time-order relationship (D) between the two sentences.

15. **A**—The author states a premise and then uses an example about cars and snakes to prove the point.

16. **C**—The relationship within the first sentence is cause and effect. The connection between eating the jelly beans and waking up with a virus results in an aversion to a former favorite treat. However, the word "similar" is a clue to the reader that the author is comparing the first situation to others that are much the same. Therefore, choice C is the correct answer.

17. **B**—The author states that Grandma Anna can catch a fish, and then gives additional information about Grandma Anna's skills relating to fish.

18. **A**—The author mentions the "elliptical orbit" of the planets in the first sentence. Then in the second sentence the author clarifies or explains what this means. The words "this means" should provide a clue to the reader.

19. **C**—The words "farther left" indicate to the reader where, physically, the curtain and back room are in relationship to the hanging lamps.

20. **B**—The author mentions interesting characters in the first sentence and then gives the example of the character Max in the second sentence. There is no comparison (A), sequence (C), or addition (D).

2.3A IDENTIFYING WORD MEANING BASED ON CONTEXTUAL CLUES

1. **A**—*Mundane* means "ordinary, routine, or boring." In this sentence, the phrase "disguise mundane ideas as innovative" is a clue that "mundane" and "innovative" are opposites. If mundane is the opposite of innovative (new, creative), then the best definition is "ordinary."

2. **C**—*Jargon* means "specialized or technical language." The clue is found in the preceding sentence, which contains the examples of the jargon "on the same page" and "vision statement."

3. **B**—*Gloss over* means "to disregard or ignore." The sentence is explaining that the new language (jargon) ignores or makes light of the facts and issues.

4. **B**—*Offensive* means "distasteful, unpleasant, or insulting." The author gives examples of positions that candidates take that will appeal to everyone. No voter will find those views to be offensive or unlikable.

5. **A**—*Reputable* means "trustworthy, well-thought-of, or decent." The author states that trustworthy newspapers give comprehensive profiles of the candidates and their positions, not just sound bites or remarks taken out of context.

6. **D**—*Apathy* means "lack of interest or lack of concern." The author is talking about eligible voters who choose not to vote and their reasons. A major reason for their apathy or lack of concern is that citizens don't think their votes matter.

7. **C**—The word *hordes* means "crowds, masses, multitudes, or groups." The author is claiming that it isn't likely that large groups of tourists will descend on the Australian cave because it is difficult to reach.

8. B—The word *aboriginal* means "indigenous, native, or original." If the drawings date back 200 to 4000 years, they would be native drawings.

9. A—The word *arduous* means "strenuous, hard, or tiring." The trip involved a trek or hike through the desert. That would be a strenuous trip.

10. D—The word *precaution* means "safety measure, preventive measure, or safeguard." Restricting access to the cave and keeping its location secret are safeguards that keep too many people from visiting.

2.3B IDENTIFYING BIASED LANGUAGE

1. B—The author clearly states in the last paragraph that intellectual property should "remain free." The passage expresses a definite bias in favor of ideas remaining available to everyone (B). Specifically, the author renounces the ownership of intellectual property by either corporations (A) or individuals (C).

2. A—The author is very much against limiting competition in the corporate world by allowing ownership of ideas or intellectual property (A). The author is in favor of consumers' having free choice (B), of competition in the business world (C), and of creativity (D).

3. C—The author strongly suggests simplifying one's life in order to fully enjoy what is really important. Earning as much money as possible (A) and seeking promotions (B) can create a great deal of stress. Retirement (D) and preparation for it are not discussed in this passage.

4. D—In the second paragraph, the author discusses different pleasures in life and is highly in favor of readers' reevaluating goals and determining what makes them happiest. The author suggests hobbies (A), travel (B), and family (C) as possibly worthy goals. In the second-to-last paragraph, the author speaks out against using high-tech entertainment in place of simple pleasures. Therefore, the correct answer is D.

5. A—Although health insurance is mentioned in passing in paragraph 3, the author is not showing a general bias against all health insurance (D). The author is opposed to unnecessary surgery but not all surgery (B) and is certainly not against physicians (C). However, the author suggests that full-body scans can be detrimental for several reasons. Therefore, the author has a bias against them.

6. D—The author is clearly opposed to patients' having unnecessary medical tests (B) and is specifically opposed to routine full-body scans (C). In paragraph 4, the author discusses the danger of exposure to radiation (A) and the serious ramifications. In the last paragraph, patients are urged to have a physician whom they can trust (D).

7. B—Choices A, C, and D are too broad. The author is definitely biased in favor of the CSPI. In the last paragraph, the author states, "CSPI offers data that Americans need but do not want to hear."

8. A—The author believes people should have healthy diets and take advantage of information from the CSPI, which recommends that Americans avoid excess calories and fats. Therefore, A is the correct answer. The author is in favor of the CSPI reporting honest and helpful information, so choice B is incorrect. Choices C and D are too broad.

9. **C**—The author clearly prefers socialization (C) to isolation (A). The author favors the ice cream social partly because it encourages people to spend time together doing something that is enjoyable, as opposed to using a time-saving appliance like a modern motorized ice cream freezer (B and D).

10. **C**—The author values hard work (A). The reader will remember the mention of black-and-white TV (B), but it is mentioned as another example of something old-fashioned like the ice cream social. The author is not biased against it. Nor is the author biased against "child's play," which is mentioned in paragraph 3 (D). The author states that new types of ice cream makers are too easy, thus "child's play." However, there is no bias against child's play. The correct answer is C because the author mentions in paragraph 3 that some food critics don't appreciate the value of hard work to produce a superior product.

2.3C IDENTIFYING TONE

1. **B**—Choice B is the best answer because the author is primarily giving factual information about weeds. There is no argument regarding the issue, so choice A is incorrect. *Compassionate* means "sympathetic," and the author shows no emotion here for the ecosystems that weed organisms affect. Therefore, choice C is wrong. *Bitter* means "resentful." Choice D is wrong because the author does not take the position that weeds are at fault.

2. **C**—The author presents an optimistic, or positive, view of how microlending can help relatively poor people achieve success in business ventures, so C is the best choice. *Neutral* (A) means the author is neither positive or negative, and *ambivalent* (B) means the author doesn't care. Sarcasm (D) involves ridiculing the subject.

3. **A**—The passage describes the author's doubts about taking a prize at the bake-off; therefore, the tone is pessimistic. *Excited* (B), which means "thrilled or animated," is not appropriate for this passage, nor is *flattering* (C), which means "complimentary." *Confident* (D) is not correct; in fact, the author is the opposite of confident.

4. **B**—This tone of this passage is cautionary because it warns that Americans have questionable values regarding money. *Optimistic* (A) means "bright and cheerful," and that is not the tone of this passage. The writing is not sentimental or emotional in a romantic way (C). *Self-pitying* (D) means "feeling sorry for oneself." The author does not use this tone in the passage.

5. **D**—This passage is related in the manner of a news story. The author does not give an opinion. Therefore, the tone is objective (D), or factual, as opposed to subjective (C), which means "opinionated." Although there are entertaining images in this passage, like the arrival of Riggs with bikini clad women, the overall tone is not humorous (B), nor is it regretful (A).

6. **C**—The author is being sarcastic, or saying the opposite of what he means. He clearly is not grateful to get the rejection letter for financial aid and is using sarcasm to make his point. Therefore, choice C is the best answer. *Straightforward* (B) is a synonym for *objective*. Because this writing is definitely opinionated, choice B cannot be the right answer. *Solemn* (A) means "serious," and although this passage deals with a serious subject, the author is writing in a tongue-in-cheek, or sarcastic,

K

manner. *Impartial* (D) means "neutral." As previously described, the author here is definitely opinionated.

7. **A**—*Ironic* can refer to a contradiction between what is said or believed to be true and the actual truth, or it can refer to a difference between an expected and an actual result. Therefore, this passage's tone can be described as ironic. (Note especially the line, "It's funny how something you think will make your life better doesn't always do so.") The tone is not forgiving (B), nor is it tolerant (C). *Ambivalent* (D) means "indecisive," and the author is not indecisive.

8. **D**—This paragraph evokes a longing for the past, specifically in terms of ice cream socials. Nostalgia is a longing for the past. Therefore, D is the correct choice. *Objective* (A) means "factual, not opinionated." Because this is an opinionated piece, choice A is incorrect. *Humorous* (C) means "funny or entertaining," and that is not the overall tone. *Hesitant* (B) means "unsure or cautious." The author does not express uncertainty or cautiousness.

9. **A**—The author clearly is excited about this movie, urging everyone to see it. The tone, therefore, is enthusiastic. Objective (B) means "factual, not opinionated," but this is a highly opinionated passage. *Tolerant* (C) means "understanding and broad-minded." That is not relevant to this passage. *Mocking* (D) means "disrespectful or derisive." This paragraph does not mock anything.

10. **C**—The author shows tremendous admiration (high regard for and appreciation of) her grandmother; therefore, C is the best choice. *Forgiving* (A) means "overlooking an offense." *Authoritative* (B) means "acting in a position of leadership or authority." This tone is not relevant to the passage. *Impartial* (D) is an incorrect answer because impartial means "neutral or unbiased," and the author takes a strong position in terms of admiring her grandmother.

2.4A DISTINGUISHING FACT FROM OPINION

1. **B**—The words *deluded,* which means "deceived," and *wrong* clearly make this a statement of opinion. There is no way to verify or prove this statement.

2. **B**—There is no way to prove that everyone knows this. Also, the description "more appealing" cannot be proven. Therefore, this is an opinion.

3. **B**—The words "more disgusting" make this a statement of opinion, as do the words "bland and meaningless." These are judgments that cannot be proven.

4. **B**—"Bad" is an example of a qualitative word. Such words—*bad, good, better, worse,* and so on—usually indicate an opinion because they cannot be verified. What is bad to one person may be acceptable or good to another.

5. **C**—Research can be done to verify statements A, B, and D. They can be proven. However, statement C cannot be verified. Therefore, it is an opinion.

6. **A**—This statement can be researched and proven. Therefore, it is a fact.

7. **B**—There is no way to prove that this statement is true. How can you prove the difficulty of imagining something? Therefore, this is an opinion.

8. **A**—This can be verified by looking at the painting. Therefore, this is a fact.

9. **B**—It would be impossible to prove whether this is true of all people. Therefore, it is an opinion.

10. **A**—This statement can be verified by examining the voting records of eligible U.S. citizens and by examining poll activity over the last three decades (thirty years). Therefore, this is a statement of fact.

2.4B DRAWING INFERENCES AND CONCLUSIONS

1. **A**—The passage begins with the statement that Americans favor spaghetti and macaroni, yet other Italian pasta is available. The inference here as well as in the last paragraph is that Americans can now vary the pasta shapes they eat as they become more familiar with the choices available. Choice B is incorrect because the passage compares the number of pasta shapes to the large number of cartoon characters. No connection is made between the shapes of pasta and the shapes of the characters. Choice C is incorrect because the passage provides no information regarding the popularity of pasta in the U.S. compared with other foods. Choice D is also incorrect. The problem here is with the words "most often." The passage states that the pasta can be shaped and named after almost anything. Creatures and body parts, as well as household items, are mentioned as examples. There is no way to know what the pasta shapes are named after "most often."

2. **B**—In the passage, the author refers to the "discovery of pasta novelty." A novelty is something new. In addition, the last paragraph states that "spaghetti and macaroni are no longer the only shapes of pasta available in grocery stores in this country" and that "Americans . . . now have access to an abundance of exotic pasta shapes and sizes." The inference is that these pastas have not always been available to U.S. consumers. Choice A is incorrect because there is no discussion about the quality of dinner choices. Choice C is incorrect because it is a very broad generalization. People's choice of pasta is no indication of their overall creativity. Choice D is incorrect because there is no discussion about how much pasta is or should be eaten. Therefore, this is a false inference.

3. **C**—The author is suggesting that English teachers can be expected to understand good writing, and if they are unable to understand a sentence in a colleague's article, then the writing is bad academic writing. Choice A is incorrect because the intelligence of English teachers is not being compared with that of any other academic group. Choice B is incorrect because the passage doesn't comment on whether English teachers enjoy judging each other's writing. Choice D is a false inference. The passage does not discuss how often English teachers write incomprehensibly.

4. **B**—The second sentence in the paragraph describes how political leaders "manipulate buzzwords designed to make the policies of their political party look good and those of the other party foolish or evil." The author also describes these actions as "attempts to use emotional language to confuse and mislead." Therefore, the truth is misrepresented by unfair or "dirty" tactics. Choice A is a generalization and stereotype. Stereotypes are always incorrect. No statement can be true about all politicians. Choice C is incorrect because there is no information about which group uses misleading communication more often. Choice D is incorrect because there is no information about who uses cover-ups most often.

5. **C**—The author says that to ensure that ice cream making is a social event, people should invest in a hand-cranked ice cream machine—the implication being that such a machine requires group effort. Choice A is incorrect because it is too broad a statement. The author does not imply that modern methods are inferior to old-fashioned methods. For instance, is the automobile inferior to the horse and buggy as transportation? Choice B is also too broad to be a correct inference. The author is speaking about the superiority of socialization in only one specific instance. Choice D is not discussed. The author merely mentions obsolete black-and-white televisions to express how out of fashion hand-cranked ice cream freezers are.

6. **A**—The author talks about making ice cream with good cream, sugar, and vanilla beans. This would create vanilla-flavored ice cream. The words "if they must" with regard to peach or "even" with regard to chocolate show that the author regards those flavors as inferior to vanilla. Therefore, choices B, C, and D are incorrect inferences.

7. **B**—The passage states that twenty citizens remain in Centralia, although the U.S. government paid the residents to leave the area. With future damage a possibility, those who choose to remain are living in a dangerous situation. Choice A is incorrect. The passage tells us the coal fire burned "unhindered" for twenty-one years. No one did anything about it, and it wasn't until 1983—when part of Route 61 collapsed—that the government interceded. We cannot assume there was any major above-ground damage during those twenty-one years. Choice C is incorrect because on the contrary, the government decided it was less expensive to pay citizens to relocate than to put out the fire, which would have cost 663 million dollars. Choice D is incorrect because there is no way to be sure what will take place in the future.

8. **B**—The passage indicates that the residents were "surprised" when the garbage dump fire burned for a month. They then tried to smother the fire but were unsuccessful. Choice A is incorrect because there is no indication that the residents didn't care about the fire. They were ignorant about its serious nature. Choices C and D are both false inferences. The passage states that all but twenty citizens accepted the government's offer to relocate. There is no information, however, as to how they felt about this—whether they were happy or sad. Therefore, the reader cannot make either assumption.

9. **D**—If the student applied for financial aid, it makes no sense to be "grateful" to be rejected or turned down. The student is being sarcastic. Choice A makes no sense. This would be an inappropriate reaction. Choice B is incorrect because there is no reason to believe the student will not be able to attend. Choice C is incorrect because there is no basis for an assumption that the student has lied about his financial status or need.

10. **A**—Based on the information in the passage, the family consists of a father who does not work steadily, a mother who works two part-time jobs, and two children who work on weekends and during the summer. The mother's income pays only the rent. Therefore, the family is having difficulty with its finances. Choice B is incorrect. The reader knows the father was laid off and hasn't found steady employment for two years. However, there is no way to know how hard he has been or is looking for a full-time job. Choice C is also incorrect. The passage states that the mother works two part-time jobs. The reader doesn't know if this is by choice. The reader cannot assume the mother is unable to find a full-time job. Choice D is incorrect because no

information indicates that the children work any time other than summers and weekends.

2.4C ASSESSING SUPPORT FOR REASONING

1. **B**—There is no factual evidence supporting the author's claim. With the examples of both the yoga and crackers, the author states that if the market is limited, consumers "may" have to pay more or prices "may" be higher. No facts are given to support these claims.

2. **D**—Limited creativity and consumer choices result from ownership of intellectual property when "ideas and symbols become unavailable for public use." Such restrictions would would decrease competition in the marketplace. Choices A and B are specific details but not sufficient support. Choice C is irrelevant.

3. **A**—The author gives many specific examples of language throughout the passage to substantiate the claim about confusing and intimidating language. The author does not expect the reader to accept the claims based merely on unsupported opinion.

4. **B**—The author gives an opinion and one example but gives no substantial evidence to support this opinion.

5. **B**—A may be a true statement, but it is irrelevant as support for the author's claim. Choices C and D are not discussed in the passage. This passage states that patients often get scans without physicians' referrals, but it does not say that the patients lack trust in their doctors.

6. **A**—The passage gives specific explanations about the negative features of full-body scans: the cost, the false-positive results, and the risky high doses of radiation.

7. **A**—Clearly, the correct choice is A. The author follows up the claim with facts about a specific experiment conducted by the MIT researcher Ascher Shapiro.

8. **C**—Shapiro's experiment demonstrated the result of forces that are effective on a larger scale. Choice A is irrelevant. Choices B and D are false statements.

9. **D**—The example of the child who is more likely to run from a snake than to pick it up directly supports the notion that fears have a biological component and don't necessarily have to be taught. Choice A is a true specific detail but does not support the claim. Choices B and C are false statements.

10. **A**—The author cites specific experiments conducted by psychologists that prove and substantiate this claim.

PART THREE. MASTERING THE WRITING TEST

3.1A IDENTIFYING THESIS STATEMENTS AND TOPIC SENTENCES

1. **B**—Statement B summarizes the entire passage best. Statement A is too broad. Option C is also incorrect because although the paragraph discusses the car's drawbacks, they are not the focus of the writing. Statement D is too narrow in focus, and it simply states a fact, not an opinion or stance on an issue.

2. **C**—Choice C is the best choice because this statement summarizes the main idea of the passage. Statement A is too narrow, for the passage also talks about positive aspects of bartering. Choice B is incorrect, for the passage does not say that the drawbacks of bartering outweigh its benefits. Statement D is too broad, and the passage is not about the history of bartering.

3. **A**—Statement A addresses the focus of the passage most effectively. Statement B is incorrect because the passage doesn't focus on people's fascination with Stonehenge. Statement C is too narrow, and it is a dead-end statement, which is never a good choice for a thesis statement or topic sentence. Statement D is not the best choice because the passage focuses on the mystery of why Stonehenge was created, not on its construction.

4. **C**—Statement C addresses the passage's main idea most effectively. Choice A is too narrow in focus, merely stating a fact. Choice B is incorrect because the passage is not only about Cruz's fans. Choice D is incorrect because the passage does not concern just the reasons that Cruz was adored by fans.

5. **D**—Statement D most aptly summarizes the main idea of the passage. Statement A focuses on one fact from the passage and does not discuss the larger issues. Statement B is too broad and indicates that the Aral Sea disaster has devastated the former Soviet Union as a whole. In fact, the passage does not support this notion. Statement C is inaccurate; the passage clearly states the reason for the environmental disaster.

6. **B**—Statement B most aptly summarizes both the pros and cons of dirt roads. Statement A is too narrow; it does not account for the positive traits of dirt roads. Likewise, statement C considers only the positive attributes of dirt roads. Statement D is not supported by the passage, and it addresses only drivers.

7. **C**—Statement C addresses the passage's main idea most effectively. Choice A is incorrect because the passage does not focus on preserving dying languages. Choice B is incorrect because the passage never asserts that linguists know why some languages last and others don't. Statement D is too narrow; it simply states a fact from the passage without addressing the larger issues.

8. **A**—Statement A most accurately summarizes the main idea of the passage. Statement B is too broad and doesn't address what "flash mobs" are or do. Statement C is too narrow, and the passage doesn't say that flash mobs are an intricate form of rebellion used mostly by young men and women in Rome. Likewise, statement D is not supported by the passage.

9. **D**—Statement D most aptly addresses the main idea of the passage. Statement A is too narrow and simply defines the manatee. Choice B states a fact that is too narrow to be the main idea. Statement C is inaccurate; it is not supported by the passage.

10. **B**—Statement B most aptly summarizes the main idea of the passage. Statement A is too general and does not accurately reflect the content of the passage. Likewise, statements C and D are inaccurate.

1. **B**—Sentence 3 reads: "Volkswagen started as the 'people's car' in Germany in the 1930s, and the low-priced, mass produced car quickly became popular." Sentence 4 (B) directly supports this statement by giving a reason (ease of repairs) why people loved the vehicle so much.

2. **C**—Sentence 3 reads: "Individuals sometimes barter, as two of my neighbors did recently." Sentence 4 (C) supports this statement by explaining how the neighbors bartered.

3. **A**—Sentence 3 reads: "One common misconception, that Stonehenge was designed as a Druid temple, is demonstrably false." Sentence 8 (A) directly supports this statement by stating that Druids did not appear until after Stonehenge was built.

4. **B**—Sentence 8 reads: Cruz's traditional style did not immediately attract young listeners, but her long association with Tito Puente and her star turn in the rock opera *Hommy* at Carnegie Hall in 1973 finally helped her win the crowds in New York City, her adopted home." Sentence 9 (B) best supports this statement because it addresses the fan base she created and also supports her popularity.

5. **D**—Sentence 3 reads: "Under the administration of the Soviet Union, irrigation canals diverted water away from the rivers flowing into the Aral Sea because Soviet agricultural authorities had designated Kazakhstan as the country's cotton production center." Sentence 4 (D) directly supports this statement by indicating how cotton production drained water resources.

6. **B**—Sentence 5 reads: "Road conditions that make driving slow and difficult, for example, are not always a negative for people who live along the road." Sentence 6 (B) supports this statement by suggesting one benefit of dirt roads—their effects on speeding cars. Sentence 7 further builds on this support.

7. **B**—Sentence 8 reads: "In the United States, some native speakers of English object to hearing non-English languages, adding to the stigma of speaking a rare tongue." Sentence 9 (B) indicates that where multilingualism is uncommon (presumably, where there may be a stigma against speaking rare languages), endangered languages are being lost at the fastest rate.

8. **C**—Sentence 5 reads: "The global happenings follow a certain pattern." Sentence 7 (C) supports this statement because it describes the pattern.

9. **A**—Sentence 3 reads: "In fact, manatees may have inspired ancient sailors' stories about mermaids." Sentence 4 (A) directly supports this statement because it describes how manatees could have been mistaken for mermaids despite these creatures' whiskers, paddle-tailed bodies, and so on.

10. **B**—Sentence 3 reads: "Instead, the brand-new Soviet Union adopted 'Internationale.'" Sentence 4 (B) supports this statement by suggesting why the song was adopted: It had been a popular anthem among European communists during the Russian Revolution.

11. **B**—Sentence 12 (B) is least relevant because the fact that the Beetle was called a *vocho* in Mexico has nothing to do with the larger point: that the Beetle, despite its flaws, was much loved and its loss mourned.

12. **B**—Sentence 9 (B) is not supported by specific detail: The passage does not describe how business bartering works.

13. **C**—Sentence 10 (C) is not supported by specific detail: The author does not provide evidence for the notion that Stonehenge appears to be a calendar.

14. **D**—Sentence 11 (D) is least relevant to the paragraph. The fact that Cruz was married for over 40 years has nothing to do with the larger point: how she won the hearts of fans over her long career.

15. **A**—Sentence 5 (A) is the least relevant to the passage. The fact that cotton makes good cloth but is not edible is unrelated to the larger point: the toll that the cotton industry has taken on the Aral Sea.

16. **B**—Sentence 8 (B) is the least relevant to the paragraph. The comment about drivers who irritate others with their loud music is unrelated to the larger point about the advantages and disadvantages of dirt roads.

17. **C**—Sentence 7 (C) is the least relevant to the paragraph. The fact that Navajo soldiers communicated top-secret information in World War II is unrelated to the larger point about the death of languages.

18. **C**—Sentence 10 (C) lacks adequate supporting detail; the passage never indicates how or why some flash-mob participants see these gatherings as a form of rebellion.

19. **A**—Sentence 9 (A) lacks adequate supporting detail; the passage doesn't provide details on what the commonsense measures might be or how they would protect the manatee.

20. **D**—Sentence 10 (D) lacks adequate supporting detail; the paragraph does not indicate why the need for a new song became urgent just before the Olympic Games of 1996.

3.1C ARRANGING IDEAS IN A LOGICAL PATTERN

1. **C**—Note the logical pattern of choice C: The first sentence describes one advantage (ease of repair), and the second sentence describes another (the car's low cost and basic engine). Note that the second sentence includes "also" to make a link to the first. The next part of choice C moves on to disadvantages, logically discussing them together—first, the fact that the car was cramped and noisy and, second, the dangerousness of the car in crashes. Choice C ends with a logical conclusion based on these disadvantages: young VW drivers eventually left the cars behind. The other choices do not follow this logical order.

2. **B**—Sentence 5 (B) and the sentence-to-be-placed (about Shamila) work well together because the former suggests Jonathan's needs and the latter suggests Shamila's. This sequence sets up sentence 6, which indicates that the bartering arrangement met both of their needs. A clue to where the sentence about Shamila should go is its beginning: "Shamila, on the other hand, ..." The phrase "on the other hand" indicates the second part of a two-part proposition or idea.

3. **B**—Note that this extract is in time order. It moves from the creation of Stonehenge's outer ditch to the placement of the largest stones (the second phase) to the placement of the ring of smaller outer stones. The other choices do not follow this logical order.

4. **A**—Here's another passage that uses time order. Given this order, the fact that Cruz trained to be a literature teacher must go after sentence 1 (in other words, before sentence 2) because sentence 2 describes the start of her musical career. The other choices do not fit the time line.

5. **D**—Note that passage D logically moves from causes to effects—from the saturation of the uncovered land with salt and agricultural chemicals (cause) to the statement that the land can't be farmed, the drinking water is poisoned, and so on (effects). The other choices do not follow this logical order.

6. **B**—The sentence-to-be-placed follows logically from sentence 9 (B) because it builds on the idea that gravel or dirt roads can lend a rural atmosphere to an area. (Note that both sentences include the word "atmosphere.") The other choices are not logical.

7. **C**—Choice C presents the most logical order, moving from the causes of dying languages that are rooted in older generations or native speakers (who stop teaching the children their language and stop using it at home) to those that are rooted in the younger generations (who may be unwilling to learn the languages). The last sentence flows naturally from the one before it by explaining possible reasons for this unwillingness. The other choices do not follow this logical order.

8. **A**—The sentence-to-be-placed follows logically from sentence 7 (A) because it says that the "smaller groups" described in sentence 7 form a "large one." Understanding that this portion of the larger passage uses time order can help you determine the logical placement for the new sentence. Note also similar wording in sentence 7 and the new sentence ("smaller groups" in the former and "small groups" in the latter). This wording shows a connection between the sentences.

9. **B**—The description of the manatees' "bristly 'kisses'" in the sentence-to-be placed follows naturally from the statement, in sentence 4 (B), that sailors may have mistaken these creatures for beautiful women. The other choices are not logical.

10. **D**—Understanding that the entire passage uses time order can help you determine the logical order for the sentences in question. Choice D is the best because it begins with the selection of "Patriotic Song" as Russia's national anthem, then describes how the song didn't catch on. The passage then moves to the most recent change in the national anthem. The other choices do not follow this logical order.

3.1D USING EFFECTIVE TRANSITIONAL DEVICES

1. **B**—"Not surprisingly" provides a logical transition between the problems with the Beetle and the fact that young VW drivers gave up these cars as they aged. The other choices, which signal additions or examples, would not provide effective connections.

2. **A**—"Best of all" provides a logical connection between sentences 7 and 8, setting up the most important advantage of the bartering arrangement: the fact that neither

Jonathan or Shamila had to lay out cash to get their work done. B signals contrast, C comparison, and D a conclusion, and sentence 8 does not fit any of these patterns.

3. **C**—"Finally" is the best choice because it signals the last point, and that's just what sentence 13 is. None of the other choices would provide a logical transition.

4. **A**—"Soon" is the best choice because it provides a time transition connecting sentences 6 and 7. Choices B and C are addition transitions that do not fit logically, and choice D ("thus") suggests that sentence 7 is an effect flowing from a cause in sentence 6. This is not the case.

5. **C**—"Unfortunately" is the best choice because it signals a negative effect of the phenomenon described in the previous sentence. Choice A signals addition, B a concluding statement, and D an example, and none of these apply.

6. **C**—"Also" is the best choice because it signals an additional disadvantage of dirt roads. Choices A and D indicate contrast, which does not apply, and choice B is not a logical choice.

7. **B**—"Unfortunately" is the best choice because it signals a negative effect of the loss of endangered languages. Choice A is illogical because it suggests positive consequences. Choice C does not make sense. Choice D suggests an example, when in fact sentence 10 describes an effect.

8. **A**—"On the other hand" shows contrast; therefore, it's a logical set-up for sentence 9, which presents a different view of flash mobs. Choice D indicates that something in sentence 9 happened after something in sentence 8, and that's not the case. Choices C and D suggest addition, which does not apply.

9. **D**—Sentence 4 calls for a transition of contrast because it indicates that manatees were mistaken for beautiful women despite their whiskery faces, rough skin, and so on. "Although" suggests such a contrast while the other choices don't, or don't do so logically. ("Nevertheless," choice A suggests contrast, but it does not make sense.)

10. **D**—Sentence 9 calls for a transition that signals a time period, which D ("For a while") provides. It follows sentences that indicate a time line of anthems. The other choices do not signal time periods and are illogical.

3.2A CHOOSING APPROPRIATE WORDS AND EXPRESSIONS

1. **B**—*Complained* means "reacted negatively." "Even though" provides a clue that the guests reacted this way although the wedding took place in an attractive setting. The other choices are not logical in context.

2. **D**—*Boastful* means "given to bragging." This characteristic would make the other lawyers feel resentful. The other choices don't make sense in context. (You might be tempted to pick "greedy," but it's not the right word because it means "an excessive desire to acquire things." Therefore, it does not apply logically to a lawyer winning her first major case.)

3. **A**—*Revised* means "changed" or "improved," so it is the most logical choice. The other choices do not make sense in context.

4. **B**—*Encouraged* means "inspired," so it is the best choice. The other choices have negative meanings that are not logical in context.

5. **C**—*Peeling* is the best choice in context because it describes a negative, and logical, result of not applying primer. "Designing" (A) is not relevant to the context. "Breaking" (B) and "sagging" (D) also indicate negative consequences, but they are too extreme.

6. **D**—*Consulted* means "conferred with" or "checked with," so it is the best choice. The other choices are not logical in context.

7. **A**—*Compensation* means payment for a loss or injury, or for work done; therefore, it is the best choice. The other choices are not logical in context.

8. **D**—*Promoted* means "advertised," so it is the best choice. You might be tempted to pick "highlighted," but that is not the best term in context; a stronger expression—signaling the spa's interest in getting attention for the gourmet meals—is called for. The other choices are not logical in context.

9. **B**—*Imported* means "brought in from another country," so it is the best choice. The other choices are not logical in context.

10. **A**—*Disappointed* suggests that positive expectations were not met, so it is the best choice to describe the boss's reaction to his workers' slow progress. The other choices are not logical in context. You might be tempted to pick "unnerved," but that means "deprived of strength or vigor" or "seriously upset"—not quite the meaning that's called for here.

3.2B IDENTIFYING COMMONLY CONFUSED AND MISUSED WORDS

1. **C**—*Loose,* an adjective that means "not fitting snugly," should replace "lose," a verb that means "to suffer a loss."

2. **A**—*Effects,* a noun that means "outcomes," should replace "affects." Affect is a verb that means "to influence."

3. **B**—*Quiet,* an adjective meaning "calm," should replace "quite," an adverb that typically means "completely" or "very."

4. **A**—*Used* is correct here because "used to" indicates something done regularly or habitually (every Sunday) in the past.

5. **A**—*You're* is a contraction of "You" and "are" and should therefore replace "your," which is a possessive adjective.

6. **A**—*Weather* pertains to the climate or atmosphere and should thus replace "whether," which indicates a choice or alternative.

7. **A**—*A* is used before words that begin with consonants (like b, c, d, f, and g), and *an* is used before words that start with a vowel (a, e, i, o, and u) or y. Therefore "a" should replace "an" because "pounding" begins with a consonant.

8. **A**—*Ideal,* an adjective meaning "perfect," should replace "idea," a noun meaning "a thought."

9. **C**—*Alone* means "left without aid" and should therefore replace "along," which means "near" or "extending the length of."

10. **C**—In this sentence, *plane,* meaning "aircraft," should replace "plain," which typically means "unadorned."

1. **B**—Choice B shows the logical placement of the modifying phrase "while I was on my vacation." The placement of similar words in the other choices is potentially confusing. For instance, choices A and C give the impression that the camcorder was on vacation.

2. **C**—Choice C shows the best placement of the modifying phrase "while driving and playing loud music on the radio." (It logically modifies "the student driver.") The placement of the modifying words in the other choices is potentially confusing. For example, choice B suggests that the pole was on the radio.

3. **C**—C shows the best placement of the modifying phrase "watching a documentary at their uncle's house." (It logically modifies "the teens.") The placement of the modifying words in the other choices is potentially confusing. Choice A gives the impression that wild animals were watching a documentary. Choice B indicates that the teens were watching wild animals and saw a documentary, as separate activities.

4. **C**—C shows the best placement of the modifying phrase "wearing a crisp white shirt and black pants." (It logically modifies "the bartender.") The placement of the modifying words in the other choices is potentially confusing because it gives the impression that the drinks were wearing a shirt and pants.

5. **C**—C shows the best placement of the modifying phrase "lost in a new city." (It logically modifies "the tourists.") The placement of the modifying words in the other choices is potentially confusing because it gives the impression that the maps were lost in a new city.

6. **A**—A shows the best placement of the modifying phrase "after we turned on the water." The placement of this phrase in other choices is potentially confusing. For instance, choice C gives the impression that the bathtub was fast. In choice B, separating the subject/actor ("the bathtub") and the verb/action ("filled") serves no purpose.

7. **A**—A shows the best placement of the modifying phrase "stuck in the tree." (It logically modifies "the little boy.") The placement of the modifying words in the other choices is potentially confusing because it suggests that the firefighter was stuck in the tree.

8. **A**—A shows the best placement of the modifying phrase "waiting for the tea kettle to boil." (It logically modifies "the waitress.") The placement of the modifying words in the other choices is illogical. Choice B states that the order was waiting for the kettle to boil and choice C gives the impression that the tea kettle was waiting for the waitress to check her table's order.

9. **C**—C shows the best placement of the modifying phrase "dangling before a colorful fish." (It logically modifies "baited line.") The placement of the modifying words in the other choices is potentially confusing. Choice A indicates that the diver was dangling before the fish and choice B is not logical because it gives the impression that the diver was somehow before (in front of?) a colorful fish.

10. **B**—Here there are two modifiers to juggle: "shortly after accepting the position" and "without explanation." "Without explanation" refers to how the employee broke the contract, so it should appear next to (specifically, right after) the fact of

her breaking the contract. So what can be done about the other modifying phrase? The placement of modifiers in choices A and C are not as effective, although they are not grammatically wrong. Choice B presents an elegant solution by turning it into an introductory phrase.

3.3B USING COORDINATION AND SUBORDINATION CORRECTLY

1. **B**—The two parts of the sentence are equally important, and the coordinating conjunction "but" expresses this relationship best. The other choices would create an illogical sentence.

2. **C**—The two parts of the sentence are equally important, and the coordinating conjunction "nor" expresses their relationship best. The other choices would create an illogical sentence.

3. **D**—The first part of the sentence is subordinate to the second, so the subordinating conjunction "although" expresses the relationship between these parts best. The other choices would create an illogical sentence.

4. **C**—The two parts of the sentence are equally important, and the conjunctive adverb "however" expresses their relationship best. The other choices would create an illogical sentence.

5. **A**—The two parts of the sentence are equally important, and the conjunctive adverb "moreover" expresses their relationship best. The other choices would create an illogical sentence.

6. **C**—The phrase " ____ bit my neighbor's son" is subordinate information that is correctly introduced by "that." ("That" is preferred to "which" because the phrase is essential to the meaning of the sentence.)

7. **A**—"However" is the correct word to join these equally important sentences, but a semicolon is needed to connect the sentences, and it must appear before "however."

8. **B**—The phrase " ____ is one of her favorite restaurants" is subordinate information that is correctly introduced by "which." ("Which" is preferred to "that" because the phrase is not essential to the meaning of the sentence. "Who" is an illogical choice because the Cheesecake Factory is not a person.)

9. **A**—"But" is the right word to join these equally important sentences; however, a comma must precede it. Choice B is incorrect because "but" is not typically used after a semicolon, and this word shouldn't be followed by a comma.

10. **B**—The subordinating conjunction "because" provides the most logical connection between the two parts of the sentence. The other choices are illogical.

3.3C UNDERSTANDING PARALLEL STRUCTURE

1. **C**—Choice C uses parallel verb forms to list Virginia's activities: "to prepare," "(to) make," and "(to) decorate." The other choices begin the list with one form—"to prepare," "(to) make"—and end with another ("decorating" in choice A and "decorated" in choice B).

2. **B**—Choice A has two elements that are not parallel ("which is also famous for its varied architecture" and "and has a lot of great restaurants") as does choice C ("which is also famous for its varied architecture" and "and it also has a lot of great restaurants"). B is in parallel form.

3. **B**—"Patience" is a noun that is parallel to the other qualities listed ("firmness" and "persistence"). The other choices would cause an error in parallel structure.

4. **C**—Choice C uses parallel verb forms to list what the warehouse manager made the workers do: "restock the shelves," "clear out the old boxes," and "work overtime." The three similar elements in the other sentences are not parallel.

5. **C**—"Gardening" is a noun (specifically, a verb turned into a noun through the addition of *ing*) that is parallel to the other hobbies listed: "sewing" and "cooking." The other choices would cause an error in parallel structure.

6. **C**—Choice C uses parallel noun forms to list what John is looking for in a girlfriend: "kindness," "brains," and "good looks." The three similar elements in the other sentences are not parallel.

7. **B**—"Conjugating" is a noun that is parallel to the other tasks: "fixing run-ons" and "eliminating fragments." The other choices would cause an error in parallel structure.

8. **B**—Choice B uses parallel verb forms to list what the band has done: "toured Europe," "recorded two CDs," and "planned to release songs in Portuguese." The three similar elements in the other sentences are not parallel.

9. **B**—Choice B uses parallel noun forms to list what the gardener is planting when: "herbs," then "carrots," then "nothing." The three similar elements in the other sentences are not parallel.

10. **C**—Choice C uses parallel noun forms to list what makes Mom angry: "laziness," "sloppiness," and "tardiness." The three similar elements in the other sentences are not parallel.

3.3D **AVOIDING FRAGMENTS**

1. **C**—Choice C fixes a fragment by joining the word group beginning with "and" to the previous sentence.

2. **A**—Both word groups are fragments. Choice A fixes the problem by joining the groups to form a complete sentence.

3. **A**—Choice A corrects the fragment by joining the two sentences. In this case, no punctuation is needed to make the connection (in fact, it would be incorrect).

4. **C**—The final word group (beginning with "To make") is a fragment that choice C corrects by connecting this word group to the previous sentence.

5. **A**—The first word group (beginning with "Since raising") is a fragment that should be joined to the following sentence with a comma. The comma is needed because the first word group is an extended introductory clause. Because a semicolon, like a period, would separate the two word groups instead of joining them, choice C is incorrect.

6. **D**—The original sentence is correct.

7. **A**—The first word group (beginning with "Before I") is a fragment that should be joined to the following sentence with a comma. The comma is needed because the first word group is an extended introductory clause. Because a semicolon, like a period, would separate the two word groups instead of joining them, choice C is incorrect.

8. **A**—The second word group (beginning with "Since my") is a fragment. Choice A corrects the problem by connecting the word group to the previous sentence.

9. **C**—"And a great place to live" is a fragment. Choice C corrects the problem by connecting this word group to the previous sentence.

10. **B**—The second word group (beginning with "Because") is a fragment. Choice B corrects the problem by connecting this word group to the previous sentence.

3.3E AVOIDING COMMA SPLICES AND FUSED SENTENCES

1. **B**—This is a fused sentence that choice B corrects by adding a comma and a coordinating conjunction ("but").

2. **B**—This is a comma splice that choice B corrects by adding a semicolon followed by a conjunctive adverb ("therefore") and a comma.

3. **D**—The original sentence is correct. Note that a comma is the correct way to connect these two independent clauses joined by "and."

4. **B**—This is a fused sentence that choice B corrects by adding a comma and a coordinating conjunction ("but"). Using a colon (choice A) would be incorrect because the second part of the sentence doesn't explain or elaborate on something introduced in the first part. Choice B is better than C because "but" suggests something that, ideally, would have happened but didn't (getting the takeout food).

5. **B**—This is a comma splice that choice B corrects by adding a semicolon followed by a conjunctive adverb ("however") and a comma.

6. **B**—This is a fused sentence that choice B corrects by creating two sentences separated by a period. Choice A is an illogical choice because "but" suggests it's surprising that the three of them would meet for coffee. Using a colon (choice C) would be incorrect because the second part of the sentence doesn't explain or elaborate on something introduced in the first part.

7. **B**—This is a comma splice that choice B corrects by adding a coordinating conjunction ("but").

8. **B**—This is a comma splice that choice B corrects by replacing the comma with a semicolon.

9. **A**—This is a fused sentence that choice A corrects by adding a semicolon followed by a conjunctive adverb ("however") and a comma.

10. **A**—This is a comma splice that choice A corrects by adding a semicolon followed by a conjunctive adverb ("therefore") and a comma.

3.4A USING STANDARD VERB FORMS

1. D—The original sentence is correct.

2. A—The sentence is in simple past tense, so the form "fell" is correct. (Choice C—"felled"—is not the correct past tense of "fall.")

3. C—"Hurt" is already a past-tense form and thus does not need the *ed* ending.

4. A—The subject, "they," is the third-person plural; therefore, the correct present-tense form is "prefer."

5. A—The past participle of the verb "go" is "gone" (see the chart in the instructional text); therefore, "have gone" is correct.

6. C—The correct past-tense form of "wake" is "woke."

7. B—"Spend" is an irregular verb whose correct past-tense form is "spent." "Spended" is not a real word.

8. C—"Frozen" is actually the past-participle form of freeze. "Froze" is the correct form to use in this sentence.

9. A—Remember from the chart in the instructional text that *lay* means "to put or place" and lie means "to recline." Because the sentence refers to reclining on a couch, "lay" should be replaced with "lie."

10. B—"Shrank" should replace "shrunk" in this sentence because "shrank" is the correct past-tense form of "shrink."

3.4B AVOIDING INAPPROPRIATE SHIFTS IN VERB TENSE

1. B—This sentence shifts from present to past tense. Choice B puts the entire sentence in the past tense.

2. B—This sentence shifts from past to present to past. Choice B puts the entire sentence in the past tense.

3. C—The first part of the sentence refers to the future "After . . . this coming August," so the future tense is called for in the second part: "will go."

4. A—This sentence refers to something that happened in the past; therefore, "was" should be substituted for "is."

5. D—This sentence is tricky. It is correct as is, even though it starts with a present-tense verb ("likes") and then uses past-tense verbs ("spit out" and "was"). The first part is correctly in the present tense because Paolo continues to like bananas, even though he spit one out during a grouchy phase.

6. C—This sentence begins with the past tense, so the second part should also be in the past tense; therefore, "was" should be substituted for "is."

7. B—This is another tricky item. The first sentence correctly begins with the present tense because grandfather continues to like to tell stories. However, the second sentence discusses something that happened years ago. Therefore, "sings" should be changed to "sang."

8. C—The first part of the sentence refers to a past event (grandfather's joining of the club in 1964) and a past condition (the fact that most club members were French at that time). Therefore, "are" should change to "were" to refer to this past condition.

9. **A**—This sentence shifts from past to present tense. Changing "goes" to "went" puts the entire sentence in the past tense.

10. **C**—This is another tricky item. You might think that because George Washington has been dead for more than 200 years, the whole sentence should be in the past tense. However, he continues to be well known, so the first sentence correctly uses "is." The second sentence correctly uses "don't realize" because people continue not to realize that Washington was a good soldier as well as an excellent leader. However, the last underlined verb, "is," should change to "was" since Washington's soldiering is in the past.

3.4C MAKING SUBJECTS AND VERBS AGREE

1. **B**—The second underlined verb must agree with its plural subject: "banking and regulatory agencies." Thus, the proper form is "make." The other verbs in the sentence are correct. (For more details on standard verb forms, see section 3.4A.)

2. **A**—The first underlined verb, "has taken," must agree with its plural subject: "graduate students." Thus, the proper form is "have taken." The other verbs in the sentence are correct. (Note that "physics," as a term that refers to a single discipline, is singular and thus takes the singular verb form "has been.")

3. **C**—Because "aerobics" refers to a single discipline, it correctly takes the singular verb form "is."

4. **C**—Though "news" ends with an *s*, it is a singular entity and thus takes the verb "sensationalizes." The other verbs in the sentence are correct.

5. **B**—It is incorrect to conclude that "was running" should agree with the singular word that precedes it: "who"; rather, this verb should agree with "candidates." Thus, B is the correct choice.

6. **A**—You might encounter trouble here because you can't tell what subject the verb "stand" goes with. In cases like this, try changing the order of the troublesome part of the sentence: "A shadowy figure *stands* at the end of a long, dark hallway." Yes, the verb must agree with "shadowy figure," so the form "stands" is correct. The other verbs in the sentence are correct.

7. **D**—This sentence is correct as is. You might think that "make" should agree with "one" and thus should be changed to "makes." But the verb actually needs to agree with "students," so this change would be incorrect. See the guideline and example on p. 180 of the instructional text.

8. **B**—Here is another case where just looking at the word right before a verb could fool you. The subject of the underlined verb is not just "coach"; it's "cheerleaders and their coach," a compound (plural) subject. Thus the right answer is "have."

9. **A**—"has filled out" needs to agree with the plural subject "organizations." Thus, "have filled out" is correct. The other verbs in the sentence are correct.

10. **B**—Remember from the instructional text that "everyone" is one of those tricky words that you might think is plural. In most cases, including here, the meaning is singular. Thus, the right verb is "loves."

11. **A**—The subject of the first part of this sentence is not just "spending quality time" but also "studying for final exams" and "taking care of elderly parents." It is a

plural subject and, thus, "have taken" is the correct verb form to go with it. The other verbs in the sentence are correct.

12. **C**—Remember that when a compound subject is joined by "or," the verb must agree with the part of the compound subject that is closest to the verb (in this case, "five-dollar bill"). Thus, "is" is correct.

13. **A**—You might think that the first underlined verb is correct as "is," but try changing this part of the sentence around: "The passport and entry visa . . . are on the table." Yes, "are" is the correct form in this case because the verb must agree with the plural subject. The other verbs in the sentence are correct.

14. **B**—The underlined verb must agree with "grandparents," not "grandchild"; thus, "face" is correct. (Here is a case where crossing out words that come between the subject and the verb might help you on the test.)

15. **D**—The original sentence is correct. All subjects and verbs agree.

16. **A**—When a compound subject is joined by "or," the verb must agree with the part of the compound subject that is closest to the verb. The same rule applies to compound subjects joined by "nor." Because "sister," a singular word, is closest to the underlined verb, the singular form "has decided" is correct.

17. **B**—"Were" must change to "was" to agree with the singular subject "cost." The other verbs in the sentence are correct.

18. **B**—This is another case of a verb needing to agree with a compound subject, "Julie and Karen." This compound subject is plural and thus takes the plural form "have both quit."

19. **D**—The original sentence is correct. You might think that the last underlined verb ("was described") should change to "were described" to agree with "designs," but in fact, this verb needs to agree with "problem."

20. **B**—It might seem that the underlined verb is correct as "was," but try changing this part of the sentence around: "six tables . . . were at the book fair." Yes, "were" is the correct form in this case because the verb must agree with the plural subject.

3.4D MAKING PRONOUNS AND ANTECEDENTS AGREE

1. **A**—The underlined pronoun must agree with the singular antecedent "instructor." Thus, "his or her" is correct.

2. **C**—The underlined pronoun must agree with the singular antecedent "chamber of commerce." Thus, "its" is correct.

3. **B**—"Couple," the antecedent, is being used in a plural sense here because it refers to the couple driving in separate directions. (A single entity couldn't drive in separate directions.) Therefore, "their" is the correct pronoun in this case.

4. **A**—The underlined pronoun must agree with the singular antecedent "proposal." Thus, "it" is correct.

5. **C**—Remember the rule about compound antecedents joined by *or* or *nor*. In this case, the antecedent is "the campus center or the libraries." Because the pronoun is closer to the plural word "libraries," it must agree with that part of the antecedent. Thus, "their" is correct.

6. **D**—The pronoun "her" correctly agrees in person and number with the antecedent "Patricia."

7. **A**—The antecedent "toddlers" is plural and thus calls for a plural pronoun "their."

8. **D**—All the underlined pronouns correctly agree with their antecedents.

9. **B**—The underlined pronoun "it" must be made plural to agree with its antecedent ("warts"). Therefore, "them" is correct.

10. **B**—The underlined pronoun must agree with its singular antecedent ("one"). (Note that "buildings" is not the antecedent.) Thus, "its" is correct.

11. **D**—This sentence is tricky. Two elements ("every planet" and "every star") are connected by "and," but they do not form a plural, as you might expect. Rather, the word "every" suggests that the elements are regarded as individual entities. Thus, "its" is the correct pronoun.

12. **A**—Remember the rule about compound antecedents joined by *or* or *nor*. In this case, the antecedent is "Neither skateboarding nor soccer." Because the pronoun is closer to the singular word "soccer," it must agree with that part of the antecedent. Thus, "its" is correct.

13. **B**—The underlined pronoun must agree with its singular antecedent ("wolf"). Thus, "its" is correct.

14. **B**—"Audience" is plural in this case because individuals are getting up from their seats, presumably not in unison. Therefore, "their" is the correct pronoun to refer to "audience" in this sentence.

15. **D**—In this case, the antecedent is "Ling Phong or her cousins." Because the pronoun is closer to the plural word "cousins," it must agree with that part of the antecedent. Thus, "their" is correct.

16. **C**—The underlined pronoun must agree with the singular antecedent "company." Thus, "It" is correct.

17. **A**—In this case, a singular word ("one," not "gymnasts") is the antecedent. Therefore, the singular pronoun "her" is required.

18. **D**—"Its," a singular pronoun, correctly refers to the singular antecedent "mouse."

19. **A**—In this case, a collection of people (a mob) is acting as one: rallying, crossing the park, and demanding admittance to the statehouse. Therefore, "mob" must take a singular pronoun: "its."

20. **C**—Because the underlined pronoun refers to a feminine singular antecedent, the pronoun must also be feminine and singular: "her."

3.4E   AVOIDING SHIFTS IN PRONOUN PERSON

1. **A**—The sentence begins in the first person ("we") but then shifts to the third person ("they"). Choice A makes the sentence consistent by changing "we" to "they."

2. **D**—All of the pronouns ("his") are in the third person.

3. **A**—The sentence begins in the first person ("our") then shifts to the third person. Choice A makes the sentence consistent by changing "our" to "their."

4. **B**—The sentence begins in the first person ("we") then shifts to the second person ("you"). Choice B makes the sentence consistent by changing "you" to "we." (Note that the last part of the sentence appropriately uses "her" to refer to Morrison's work. Other choices would be illogical: the work is "hers," not anyone else's.)

5. **C**—The sentence begins in the third person ("they" and "their") then shifts to the second person ("you"). Choice C makes the sentence consistent by changing "you" to "they."

6. **B**—The sentence shifts from the third person ("they") to the first ("we'd") then back to the third ("their"). Choice B makes the sentence consistent by changing "we'd" to "they'd." (Note that "we'd" is a contraction of "we would," and "they'd" is a contraction of "they would.")

7. **D**—All of the pronouns ("his," "he," and "his") are correctly in the third person.

8. **C**—The sentence shifts from the third person ("their") to the second person ("you"). Choice C makes the sentence consistent by changing "you" to "they."

9. **C**—The sentence shifts from the third person ("they" and "their") to the second person ("you"). Choice C makes the sentence consistent by changing "you" to "they."

10. **C**—The sentence shifts from the third person ("they") to the second person ("you"). Choice C makes the sentence consistent by changing "you" to "they."

3.4F   MAINTAINING CLEAR PRONOUN REFERENCES

1. **A**—In the original sentence, it's impossible to tell whom "she" refers to: Regina or Mary. Choice A clarifies the meaning by specifying that Regina needed to pick up the cake.

2. **B**—"They" is often used this way in everyday speech, but writers need to be more specific. Choice B clarifies that "they" refers to "instructors."

3. **C**—What caused Jackie to lose the race—the fact that her parents called out to her or the breaking of her shoelace? Choice C clarifies that both actions were the cause.

4. **C**—Who is being told to fill out the accident report, Bob or the man who caused the accident? Choice C clarifies that Bob is being asked to fill out the report.

5. **C**—In the second sentence, "this" is vague. What, exactly, does it refer to? Choice C specifies "casual clothing," leaving no doubt.

6. **D**—All the pronouns refer clearly to either Marco ("his," "he") or his roommates ("they").

7. **A**—The first use of "they" in this sentence is unclear. Who are "they"? Choice A clarifies that "they" means "articles." Note that the second use of "they" clearly refers to "readers."

8. **C**—In the second sentence, it's not perfectly clear what "this" refers to. Choice C clarifies the meaning.

9. **B**—Is Bernadette giving Mary an order, or is Bernadette assuming responsibility for finishing the report? Choice B clarifies that Bernadette is the one who will have to stay late. Note that "he" in the second sentence clearly refers to the women's boss.

10. **A**—The use of "it" is unclear. What does it refer to? Choice A clarifies that the house's price is meant.

3.4G USING PROPER CASE OF PRONOUNS

1. **C**—The original sentence uses "whomever," apparently because the writer thought that it was the object of the preposition "to." In fact, the object of the preposition is the entire clause "whoever correctly answered the puzzle." The verb of this clause is "answered," and the subject is "whoever" (C).

2. **D**—You might think that "whom" should change to "who," but it is the *object* of a clause, so the objective case ("whom") is correct.

3. **D**—This is another tricky sentence. You might have chosen B, thinking that "who" should be used instead of "whom," but this pronoun is actually the *object* of the second clause; therefore, the original sentence is correct. In cases like this, you might want to change around key words in the troublesome clause: "the couple adopted whom." Then, for "whom," substitute words that, like "whom," are in the objective case ("her," "him," and so on) and words that are in the subjective case (like "she" and "he"). Note that the subjective-case substitutes sound odd: "the couple adopted he." This is a clue that the objective case is correct.

4. **D**—The underlined pronoun is the object of the preposition "with" and is correctly in the objective case.

5. **A**—The first underlined pronoun ("I," along with "Rita") is the object of the preposition "between"; therefore, the objective-case pronoun "me" is correct.

6. **A**—The first underlined pronoun ("me") is part of a compound subject; thus, the subjective case is correct ("Lucas and I"). (If you crossed out "Lucas and," the first part of the sentence would sound odd: "Me would like to finish . . .".)

7. **D**—The original sentence is correct. "I" and "we" are being used as subjects, so they are correctly in the subjective case. "Them" is correctly in the objective case because it is the direct object of the verb "help."

8. **C**—"Who" is the object of the verb "see" and should therefore be changed to the objective case ("whom").

9. **B**—"I" (along with "Ming") is the object of the preposition "with," so the objective case ("me") is correct.

10. **B**—"Me" (along with "Paul") is the subject of the sentence, so the subjective case ("I") is correct.

3.4H USING ADJECTIVES AND ADVERBS CORRECTLY

1. **A**—"Real" must change to the adverb "really" to modify the adjective "happy." "Well," an adverb, is the correct modifier for the verb "performed," and "extremely," also an adverb, is the correct modifier for the adjective "cold."

2. **D**—The original sentence is correct. "Red," "bright," and "good" are all adjectives that are correctly used to modify the nouns "truck," "car," and "trade," respectively.

3. **A**—"Good" must change to the adverb "well" to modify the verb "did." "Proudly," an adverb, is the correct modifier for the verb "explained," and "very," also an adverb, is the correct modifier for the adjective "glad."

4. **C**—"Restless," an adjective, is the correct substitute for "restlessly" because the word being modified ("I") is a noun.

5. **A**—"Quick" must change to the adverb "quickly" to modify the verb phrase "get over here." "Done" and "undercooked," both adjectives, are correct modifiers for the noun "it" (lobster).

6. **B**—"Awfully," an adverb, is the correct substitute for "awful" because the word being modified ("pleased") is an adjective.

7. **B**—"Newly" must change to the adjective "new" to modify the noun "costume." "Old" and "white," both adjectives, are correct modifiers for the nouns "uniform" and "shirt," respectively.

8. **A**—"Beautiful" must change to the adverb "beautifully" to modify the verb "played." "Sweet," an adjective, is the correct modifier for the noun "voice." "Entranced" is part of a verb ("were entranced") and is used correctly in this sentence.

9. **C**—Be careful with verbs (like "feel") that concern senses or emotions. They must be followed by an adjective form (in this case, "bad" instead of "badly").

10. **D**—The original sentence is correct. "Long," an adjective, is the correct modifier for the noun "walk"; "warm," an adjective, is the correct modifier for the noun "day"; and "bad," an adjective, is the correct modifier for the noun "mood."

3.41 USING COMPARATIVE AND SUPERLATIVE ADJECTIVES AND ADVERBS

1. **D**—"Best" is the correct superlative form to use, as you can see from the table in the instructional text. (The implication is that Maria's drawing was compared with—and found superior to—more than one other drawing.)

2. **B**—When two things are being compared, "better" is the correct comparative adjective (see the table in the instructional text). Here, the implication is that two proposals are being compared: one from the Koreans and one from the French. Therefore, B is correct.

3. **C**—"Tallest" is the correct superlative form of this one-syllable adjective. Choice A ("taller") is not correct because more than two things are being compared.

4. **D**—Adjectives with two or more syllables form the superlative with "most." Therefore, "most beautiful" is the correct choice.

5. **C**—"Loudest" is the correct superlative form of this one-syllable adjective. Choice A ("louder") is not correct because the sense of the sentence is that more than two groups are being compared.

6. **C**—"Better interesting" is never used in standard English. The correct choice is the superlative "most interesting," because Cindy presumably has more than two gadgets. Because "interesting" has more than one syllable, the superlative is formed by adding "most." (You would not say "interestingest.")

7. C—"Reddest" is the correct superlative of the one-syllable adjective "red." "Most reddest" is illogical because "reddest" is an absolute expression: if something is reddest, there can't be anything that's more red than it. "Redder" (A) would be used only if two things were being compared—one redder than the other.

8. D—"Bigger" is correct because two elements are being compared: the new courthouse and, as a group, the other buildings. Because "big" is a one-syllable word, you would never form the comparative or superlative by adding "more."

9. D—"Better," in the original sentence, is correct because the comparison involves two people: Patricia and Sara. "More better" and "bestest" are never used in standard English.

10. B—"Best" is the correct superlative form, as you can see from the table in the instructional text. "Most best" and "bestest" are never used in standard English.

3.4J USING STANDARD SPELLING

1. C—The correct spelling is "responsibilities." The other words in the sentence are spelled correctly.

2. B—The correct spelling is "receive." (See the list of frequently misspelled words on pp. 201–2.) The other words in the sentence are spelled correctly.

3. A—The correct spelling for the underlined word is "hostile."

4. D—All the words in the original sentence are spelled correctly.

5. D—The underlined word is spelled correctly.

6. C—The correct spelling is "neighborhood."

7. B—The correct spelling for the underlined word is "awesome."

8. A—The correct spelling is "prosecuting."

9. C—The correct spelling is "brochure."

10. A—The correct spelling is "occurred." (See the list of frequently misspelled words on pp. 201–2.)

3.4K USING STANDARD PUNCTUATION

1. C—Choice C is correct because a comma is needed before the coordinating conjunction ("and") that joins the two independent clauses in the sentence.

2. A—A comma is incorrectly placed after "Even though." The proper placement of the comma is after the full introductory clause "Even though cellular phones are helpful in today's busy world."

3. D—This sentence is correctly punctuated.

4. A—"Childrens" is being used in the possessive sense in this case, so it must include an apostrophe ("children's"). Note that the word "children" is already plural, so the word takes 's, not s'.

5. C—Because "however" is a transitional word, it needs to be followed by a comma.

6. C—The sentence is clearly a question, so it needs to end with a question mark.

7. B—"That bit Jimmy's sister" is a restrictive clause. Thus, as you'll remember from the instructional text, it does not need to be set off with commas.

8. B—The semicolon is needed to join these closely related independent clauses into one sentence.

9. C—In this case, an apostrophe needs to be added to "parents" because the word is being used as a possessive. Remember from the instructional text that to form the possessive of a plural noun ending in *s*, you add an apostrophe after the *s*.

10. D—"Who has always liked fishing" is a nonrestrictive clause; that is, it isn't necessary to the sentence. Thus, as you'll remember from the instructional text, it needs to be set off by commas.

(3.4L) USING STANDARD CAPITALIZATION

1. C—This sentence is tricky. Although "do" doesn't start the practice sentence, it starts an internal sentence that is being quoted. Thus, it needs to be capitalized. "Junior class" and "saleslady" are not proper nouns, so it is not correct to capitalize them.

2. D—"Haitian" is rightly capitalized because it refers to a nationality, and "Third Avenue," as the name of a particular street, must also be capitalized. "Family," however, is not a proper noun and so shouldn't be capitalized.

3. B—The proper noun "I" is always capitalized. "You" must be capitalized because it starts the sentence. "Project" doesn't need to be capitalized because it is not the exact title of a specific project (for example, the Human Genome Project).

4. A—As you'll recall from the instructional text, names of specific courses are capitalized, while names of general areas of study are not. Thus, the first underlined word needs to be capitalized as "Accounting I." "Psychology for Teachers" is also the name of a specific class, so it is rightly capitalized; however, "mathematics" refers to a general area of study and so should not be capitalized.

5. A—"International" is being used as a generic adjective in this case, not as part of a proper noun (such as the International Monetary Fund); therefore, it should not be capitalized. "American Indian" and "Caucasian" are rightly capitalized because they refer to an ethnic group and a race.

6. D—"Vietnam Memorial" and "Lincoln Memorial" are rightly capitalized because they are proper nouns. "High school" is not capitalized because it is being used in a general sense. However, if a particular high school were named in the sentence (for example, Halleyville High School), it would be capitalized.

7. C—"French" and "Spanish" must be capitalized because they are language names. "American" and "Europe" are rightly capitalized because they refer, respectively, to a nationality and to a specific geographic region.

8. D—Specific geographic regions ("New England") and names of months ("October") are capitalized. Seasons ("fall") are not generally capitalized.

9. **A**—"Will" must be capitalized because it starts the sentence. "Daycare center" doesn't need to be capitalized because it is not the exact title of a specific daycare center (for example, Bright Beginnings Daycare Center). It is not correct to capitalize "you" unless it starts a sentence.

10. **A**—Remember from the instructional text that titles without a name are not capitalized. Because "aunt" does not precede the name of a specific person (Aunt Betty), it should not be capitalized. "Uncle Leonid" is rightly capitalized because the title "uncle" precedes a specific name. "Summer," as a season name, should not be capitalized.

K

K   Answer Key for Post-Tests

PART FOUR. SELF-CHECK POST-TESTS

4.1   READING POST-TEST

1. **A**—Choices B, C, and D are valid supporting details. (See section 2.1A.)

2. **B**—The answer is in paragraph 2. Choices A and D are false. Choice C is an incorrect choice because we have no information as to what other books, if any, were written and published by Boswell. (See section 2.1B.)

3. **D**—Choice A is wrong because this is not primarily a story about Boswell's entire life. It describes only specific aspects of his life. Choice B cannot be correct because the author states that Johnson's biography is "one of the greatest." In addition, this is not the primary purpose of the passage. Choice C is incorrect because the author is not merely telling one story about Boswell's life. (See section 2.1C.)

4. **C**—The author clearly arranges these two paragraphs in chronological (time) order. The second paragraph takes place in 1762 and the third in 1763. The author is not listing, illustrating, or comparing. (See section 2.2A.)

5. **A**—Boswell struggled because of his alcoholism, disease, and other problems. No time relationship (B) is expressed in this sentence, and no comparison (D) is made. The sentence gives examples (C) of Boswell's troubles, but these examples are provided as *causes* of his struggle. (See section 2.3B.)

6. **D**—Although the author admires Boswell's literary achievement, she does not admire his personal life, so choice A cannot be the overall tone. The passage is neither pessimistic nor sarcastic. (See section 2.3C.)

7. **B**—The word "seemed" makes this an opinion. (See section 2.4A.)

8. **D**—We have no information supporting either choice A or B. Statement C is false because Boswell's wife is described as "long-suffering." In the last paragraph, we are told that Boswell could never control his impulses. Therefore, statement D is the best choice. (See section 2.4B.)

9. **C**—The author claims James Boswell gained well-deserved recognition by writing one of the greatest biographies ever written. Choice A is incorrect because Boswell was a heavy drinker, but he did redeem himself with his writing. Samuel Johnson did not write an autobiography (a book about his own life), so choice B is incorrect. Answer D is much too broad. In addition, the biography of Samuel Johnson was written in the eighteenth century, which would have been the 1700s, so answer D cannot be correct. (See section 2.3B.)

10. **B**—Choice B clearly puts forth the defense of mimicry, which is the main idea of the passage. Choice A is too specific, and C and D are too general. (See section 2.1A.)

11. **A**—Statements B, C, and D are false statements. (See section 2.1B.)

12. **C**—Choice A is not the correct choice because although the author lists several defense mechanisms in the first paragraph, the primary purpose is to discuss the defense of mimicry, not define it. Choices B and D are not discussed. (See section 2.1C.)

13. **A**—The author is comparing and contrasting Batesian and Müllerian mimicry and does not use summary (C) or order of importance (D). Although the author illustrates with examples, the main pattern of organization is comparing and contrasting the two types of mimicry. (See section 2.2A.)

14. **B**—The author is showing how the two theories are alike. Therefore, the relationship is comparison. The author is not giving an example (A), clarifying (C), or giving additional information (D). (See section 2.2B.)

15. **C**—*Agile* means "quick" or "nimble." A clue to its meaning is the author's description of prey as "quick or agile." If you don't know the answer to vocabulary questions like this, eliminate the answer options you know must be false. For example, the answer "slow" (A) can't be the right answer in context. (See section 2.3A.)

16. **D**—The second sentence clarifies or explains the previous sentence. The relationship between the sentences is not one of cause and effect (A), time order (B), or contrast (C). (See section 2.2B.)

17. **D**—Choices A, B, and C are all false statements. (See section 2.4B.)

18. **A**—The author substantiates this claim with a thorough discussion of two types of mimicry and sufficiently explains how mimicry is a defense mechanism. (See section 2.4C.)

19. **B**—Choices A, C, and D contradict specific details stated in the reading. Statement B is correct because the paragraph directly states that Japanese corporate culture discourages women who work from having children. (See section 2.1A.)

20. **D**—Choice A is false because it contradicts the finding of the Economy Ministry that companies with a greater percentage of female workers earn more profit. The passage states that Japanese women achieve a high level of education, so B is false. The passage states that Japan is a "strongly traditional society." Therefore, C is incorrect. (See section 2.1B.)

21. **A**—The author, in the next-to-the-last sentence in the passage, takes the position that all competent Japanese, both male and female, should be gainfully employed. The rest of the passage explains the inequities that women in Japan face in terms of employment. (See section 2.1C.)

22. **A**—This paragraph states that working women in Japan are discouraged from having children. It proceeds to explain how that is accomplished or caused. (See section 2.2A.)

23. **D**—The author is giving an example of one study and then adding information regarding another study. The author is not showing differences or contrasting the studies (A), nor is the author showing that one study caused the other (B). There is no spatial relationship between the two studies (C). (See section 2.2B.)

24. **B**—The word *theoretically* means "supposedly, hypothetically, or in theory." The clue to the meaning is that the sentence expresses an ideal versus an actual condition: while maternal leave is (*supposedly*) permitted, many women report being illegally fired when they take leave for a pregnancy or to care for a new baby. (See section 2.3A.)

25. **A**—The author backs up this statement with many examples, facts, and figures. (See section 2.4C.)

26. **B**—Again, the author's next-to-last sentence in the passage shows a strong bias in favor of Japanese women having equal opportunities in the workplace. (See section 2.3B.)

27. **B**—The word "should" helps the reader identify this sentence as the author's opinion. (See section 2.4A.)

28. **D**—A is false. Mangeshkar was not a movie actress. She was a playback singer. Choice B is incorrect because her father trained her as a singer but had nothing to do with her actual professional career. Choice C is wrong because we have no information about Mangeshkar's feelings about her responsibility to provide for her family after her father's death. We do know that she had natural talent as well as training and was expected to support the family following her father's death. Therefore, D is the best choice. (See section 2.1A.)

29. **A**—Use *all* of your skills to successfully comprehend what you are reading. If Mangeshkar was born in 1929 and performed in her first film in 1942, the year her father died, she would have been 13 years old. Choice B is incorrect because she won the award in 1958. Choice C is incorrect because India produces approximately 800 movies annually. Choice D is wrong because her first song in 1947 did not sell well. (See section 2.1B.)

30. **D**—This passage deals primarily with Mangeshkar's successful vocal career. The author does not take the position that Mangeshkar is more talented than other vocalists in the world (A), nor does the author care whether the reader purchases recordings of Mangeshkar's work (B). If this were a biography of Mangeshkar's life, there would be more information about her family, her education, and her personal life. There isn't. Therefore, C is incorrect. (See section 2.1C.)

31. **C**—The author is impressed with Mangeshkar's career and could be said to be admiring. *Ironic* (A) refers to a contradiction between what is said or believed to be true and the actual truth, or it can refer to a difference between an expected and actual result. *Nostalgic* (B) indicates a longing for the past. *Reverent* (D) is close to *admiring* in meaning but indicates that the subject is being worshiped—not the right sense in context. (See section 2.3C.)

32. **B**—In 1947 Mangeshkar received her first "break," but in 1949 she "struck gold" with her first hits. Choices C and D are dates that correspond to accomplishments later in her career. (See section 2.1B.)

33. **B**—The phrase "brought to life" is a matter of opinion. It cannot be verified. (See section 2.4A.)

34. **A**—The word *stellar* means "outstanding" or "excellent." A clue to the meaning is that the sentence describes Mangeshkar as "the most famous playback singer of them all." (See section 2.3A.)

35. **C**—The word "but" indicates the author is showing a change in direction and contrasting the two parts of the sentence. The sentence does not express comparison (A), time order (B), or example (D). (See section 2.2B.)

36. **A**—The author backs up this statement with many examples. (See section 2.4C.)

1. **A**—Choice B is incorrect because the statement is too broad and doesn't address the details in the paragraph. Choice C is incorrect because the paragraph is not dealing solely with foods and cuisines based on the tomato. Choice D is incorrect because it refers to current uses of the tomato. Statement A is the best answer because the paragraph explores old beliefs about, and uses of, tomatoes to address the question posed in answer A. (See section 3.1A.)

2. **A**—In or after sentence 3 (option A), the author does not indicate—with specific details—why tomato plants were viewed with suspicion. Sentence 4 (B) is a simple fact that doesn't need additional details. Sentence 7 (C) is actually supported by sentence 8. Sentence 10 (D) is a concluding statement that does not need additional support. (See section3.1B.)

3. **A**—In the original passage, notice how one sentence seems out of place ("In other parts of Europe, however, tomato plants were viewed with suspicion."). Option A presents a more logical placement of the sentence, putting it before the discussion of the relationship of tomatoes to poisonous plants. (See section 3.1C.)

4. **C**—Although the statement in sentence 2 (C) may be true, the popularity of tomatoes in the United States is irrelevant to this passage, which focuses on facts and beliefs about the toxicity of tomatoes. Sentences 3, 7, and 8 do relate to the question of whether tomatoes (and its relatives) are poisonous. (See section 3.1B.)

5. **D**—"As it happens" is correct because this phrase joins the previous idea (the fact that the plant was viewed with suspicion) and the fact that the tomato is related to a toxic plant family. Answers A, B, and C do not make sense in the context of sentence 7. (See section 3.1D.)

6. **A**—*Infuriated* means "angered" and thus makes the most sense in this context. You might have chosen *tormented*, but that word means "tortured" and thus has too severe a sense for the situation described. (See section 3.2A.)

7. **D**—*Faded* means "diminished in color" and thus makes the most sense in this context. The other choices are not logical in context. (See section 3.2A.)

8. **A**—For underlined item A, "used" is the correct verb form to signal a habitual past action. (See section 3.4A.)

9. **B**—The phrase "swerving in front of him" refers to "car" and thus should be placed by this word. The phrase does not refer to Jim (A) or the accident that occurred (C). (See section 3.3A.)

10. **C**—The modifiers are placed most logically in sentence C. The incorrect placement of modifiers in the other two options (A and B) gives the wrong impression—that the angel is holding a horn to the left of the entrance. (See section 3.3A.)

11. **A**—The fact that Janet "likes to play tennis" is an *addition* to the fact that she knows how to swim. Thus, the coordinating conjunction "and" is correct. "But" (B) and "yet" (C) are conjunctions that indicate contrast, and "nor" is a conjunction that indicates a negative relationship. (See section 3.3B.)

12. **C**—The coordinating conjunction "yet" (C) is correct for the sense of the sentence, which is that *although* Louise's purse was stolen, it was soon recovered. "So" (B) and "for" (D) are incorrect because they suggest a cause-and-effect relationship between the two sentences when none exists. "And" (A) simply adds the fact that the purse was soon recovered, but it doesn't suggest the relationship between the sentences most logically. (See section 3.3B.)

13. **A**—In choice A, all the sentence elements are parallel ("*met* with her fans," "*read* from her latest novel," and "*signed* copies of her poster"). They begin with verbs in the same form. The three similar elements in the other options are not parallel. Choice B introduces "she" before the third element, and C uses a different verb form for the second element ("was reading"). (See section 3.3C.)

14. **A**—Choice A is correct because a comma is needed after the introductory word group "Exhausted from the hike." (See section 3.4K.)

15. **B**—The original is a fragment. The word group beginning with "For instance" does not contain a subject or verb and cannot stand alone as a sentence. Choice B correctly and logically joins the word groups to form one complete sentence. (See section 3.3D.)

16. **B**—The original sentence is a comma splice because two complete sentences ("My first trip to Colombia was an unforgettable experience" and "I learned a lot about my family's heritage in South America") are joined only with a comma. Choice B corrects the problem by adding a coordinating conjunction ("for") after the comma. This addition joins the sentences logically and grammatically. (See section 3.3E.)

17. **C**—*Conscious* and *conscience* are commonly confused words. *Conscious* means "aware," and *conscience* refers a person's sense of what is moral and fair. (See section 3.2B.)

18. **B**—Section B of the original sentence contains an error in subject-verb agreement: "have attracted" does not agree with the singular subject "boutique." Choice B corrects the problem by using the correct verb form for the subject: "has attracted."(See section 3.4C.)

19. **C**—Remember that when a compound subject is joined with *or,* the verb should agree with noun or pronoun closer to the verb. In this sentence, the two parts of the compound subject are "the coach" and "the members of the athletic board." Since the second part is plural, the correct verb form is "decide." (See section 3.4C.)

20. **C**—Be careful with expressions that include "one of the." "Cater" (C) is correct, because it needs to agree with "stores" not "one." (See secion 3.4C.)

21. **B**—This sentence shifts from the past to the present and back to the past. Choice B replaces "find" with "found" and makes the entire sentence consistently in the past. (See section 3.4B.)

22. **C**—"Has decided," a past-participle form, is the proper verb form to use in this case. "Be deciding" (A) is nonstandard usage. "Decide" (B), the simple present, is incorrect to indicate that a decision has been made. (See section 3.4A.)

23. **D**—"Went" is the past-tense form of "go" and is thus the correct verb to use in this sentence. "Gone" is a past-participle form used with "has" or "had." (The forms of "go" are irregular and so must be memorized.) (See section 3.4A.)

24. **B**—The pronoun "their" in the original sentence is incorrect because it is plural and refers to a singular antecedent ("company"). Choice B ("its") corrects the problem by substituting a singular pronoun that agrees with the antecedent. (See section 3.4D.)

25. **A**—The underlined pronoun is part of the subject of the sentence (along with "Carlotta" and "Monica"). Therefore, the subjective-case pronoun "I" should be substituted for "me," which is in the objective case. (See section 3.4G.)

26. **C**—The underlined pronoun is (along with "Jose") part of the object of the preposition "with." Therefore, the objective-case pronoun "me" should be used. (See section 3.4G.)

27. **A**—The problem with this sentence is the first underlined pronoun, "whom." If you isolate the clause that this pronoun begins ("whom works as a hostess"), you can see that the pronoun is the subject of the clause, not an object. Therefore, the subjective case ("who") is correct. (See section 3.4G.)

28. **C**—The original sentence is fused: it contains two sentences run together with no punctuation joining them. Choice C correctly separates the sentences with a period. Choice A would create a comma splice, and choice B is illogical. (See section 3.3E.)

29. **C**—This is a case of unclear pronoun reference. Is Leanne saying that she must move her own car, or is she asking April to move hers? Choice C clarifies that Leanne is asking April to make the move. (See section 3.4F.)

30. **C**—The original sentence shifts from first person ("I") to second person ("you"). By substituting "I" for "you," choice C puts the entire sentence in the first person, making it consistent. (See section 3.4E.)

31. **C**—Be careful when "feel" refers to one's emotions or well-being. In such cases, it is a linking verb that needs to be followed by an adjective. (See section 3.4H.)

32. **B**—"Smartest" is the correct superlative form. "Smarter" (A) is incorrect because more than two people are being compared. "More" (C) and "Most" (D) are not used to create comparative or superlative forms of one-syllable adjectives. (See section 3.4I.)

33. **B**—Because "beautiful" is an adjective of more than one syllable, "most beautiful" is the correct way to form its superlative. "Beautifullest" (A) is not a correct word, and "more beautiful" (C) implies that only two things are being compared, which is incorrect. "Best beautiful" (D), like A, is a construction that would never be used in standard English. (See section 3.4I.)

34. **A**—"October" is the name of a month and thus should be capitalized. Seasons (like fall, B) do not need to be capitalized. Halloween (C), a holiday, is correctly capitalized. (See section 3.4L.)

35. **C**—The second word group is a fragment that lacks a subject and main verb. Choice C attaches it to the previous sentence to create a complete sentence. The punctuation used in A and B does not join the word groups grammatically. (See section 3.3D.)

36. **A**—Choice A corrects a spelling error. The other words in the sentence are spelled correctly. (See section 3.4J.)

37. **B**—Choice B corrects a spelling error. The other words in the sentence are spelled correctly. (See section 3.4J.)

38. **A** — "Yours" is already possessive; thus, it's unnecessary (and incorrect) to add an apostrophe to it to form the possessive. "Her's" (C) is incorrect for the same reason. Choice B would create a pronoun-case error. (See section 3.4K.)

39. **A** — "Algebra I" is the title of a particular course and thus needs to be capitalized. Choices B and C (physics and economics, respectively) refer to general disciplines, not specific course names; thus, these words do not need to be capitalized. Note, however, that "Physics 100" and "Economics 100" would be capitalized because they are specific course names. (See section 3.4L.)

40. **B** — Remember that *lay* means "to put or place," while *lie* means "to recline." Because the sentence refers to reclining in bed, the past tense of *lie* — "lay" — should be used. "Laid" (in the original sentence) is the past tense of *lay*.

NAME _____ DATE _____

INSTRUCTOR _____ SECTION _____

For each question, write the letter that corresponds to your chosen answer. Check your answers against the key on pp. 240–41, marking an X on the key when you miss a question. (Marking your answers there will make it easier for you to see sections of the book you may want to review.)

1. _____	10. _____	19. _____	28. _____
2. _____	11. _____	20. _____	29. _____
3. _____	12. _____	21. _____	30. _____
4. _____	13. _____	22. _____	31. _____
5. _____	14. _____	23. _____	32. _____
6. _____	15. _____	24. _____	33. _____
7. _____	16. _____	25. _____	34. _____
8. _____	17. _____	26. _____	35. _____
9. _____	18. _____	27. _____	36. _____

NAME _____ DATE _____

INSTRUCTOR _____ SECTION _____

For each question, write the letter that corresponds to your chosen answer. Check your answers against the key on pp. 241–42, marking an X on the key when you miss a question. (Marking your answers there will make it easier for you to see sections of the book you may want to review.)

1. _____	11. _____	21. _____	31. _____
2. _____	12. _____	22. _____	32. _____
3. _____	13. _____	23. _____	33. _____
4. _____	14. _____	24. _____	34. _____
5. _____	15. _____	25. _____	35. _____
6. _____	16. _____	26. _____	36. _____
7. _____	17. _____	27. _____	37. _____
8. _____	18. _____	28. _____	38. _____
9. _____	19. _____	29. _____	39. _____
10. _____	20. _____	30. _____	40. _____

NAME _____ **DATE** _____

INSTRUCTOR _____ **SECTION** _____

Here are several copies of a form you can use to answer practice items in Parts 2 and 3. If you need more forms, duplicate one of these, or simply use notebook paper. If you use notebook paper and are asked to submit your work, be sure to include your name, the date, and other items you or your instructor will find helpful (e.g., skill practiced, class section, instructor's name). On the forms, write the letter that corresponds to your chosen answer. Check your answers against the key on pp. 243–75, which provides explanations for each item.

1. _____	6. _____	11. _____	16. _____
2. _____	7. _____	12. _____	17. _____
3. _____	8. _____	13. _____	18. _____
4. _____	9. _____	14. _____	19. _____
5. _____	10. _____	15. _____	20. _____

NAME _____ DATE _____

INSTRUCTOR _____ SECTION _____

1. _____   6. _____   11. _____   16. _____

2. _____   7. _____   12. _____   17. _____

3. _____   8. _____   13. _____   18. _____

4. _____   9. _____   14. _____   19. _____

5. _____   10. _____   15. _____   20. _____

F

NAME _____ DATE _____

INSTRUCTOR _____ SECTION _____

1. _____   6. _____   11. _____   16. _____

2. _____   7. _____   12. _____   17. _____

3. _____   8. _____   13. _____   18. _____

4. _____   9. _____   14. _____   19. _____

5. _____   10. _____   15. _____   20. _____

F

NAME _____ **DATE** _____

INSTRUCTOR _____ **SECTION** _____

1. _____   6. _____   11. _____   16. _____

2. _____   7. _____   12. _____   17. _____

3. _____   8. _____   13. _____   18. _____

4. _____   9. _____   14. _____   19. _____

5. _____   10. _____   15. _____   20. _____

NAME _____ DATE _____

INSTRUCTOR _____ SECTION _____

1.	_____	6.	_____	11.	_____	16.	_____
2.	_____	7.	_____	12.	_____	17.	_____
3.	_____	8.	_____	13.	_____	18.	_____
4.	_____	9.	_____	14.	_____	19.	_____
5.	_____	10.	_____	15.	_____	20.	_____

F

NAME _____ DATE _____

INSTRUCTOR _____ SECTION _____

For each question, write the letter that corresponds to your chosen answer. Check your answers against the key on pp. 276–78, which explains the answers and shows where you can get more help in this book.

1. _____	10. _____	19. _____	28. _____
2. _____	11. _____	20. _____	29. _____
3. _____	12. _____	21. _____	30. _____
4. _____	13. _____	22. _____	31. _____
5. _____	14. _____	23. _____	32. _____
6. _____	15. _____	24. _____	33. _____
7. _____	16. _____	25. _____	34. _____
8. _____	17. _____	26. _____	35. _____
9. _____	18. _____	27. _____	36. _____

NAME _____ DATE _____

INSTRUCTOR _____ SECTION _____

For each question, write the letter that corresponds to your chosen answer. Check your answers against the key on pp. 279–82, which explains the answers and shows where you can get more help in this book.

1. _____	11. _____	21. _____	31. _____
2. _____	12. _____	22. _____	32. _____
3. _____	13. _____	23. _____	33. _____
4. _____	14. _____	24. _____	34. _____
5. _____	15. _____	25. _____	35. _____
6. _____	16. _____	26. _____	36. _____
7. _____	17. _____	27. _____	37. _____
8. _____	18. _____	28. _____	38. _____
9. _____	19. _____	29. _____	39. _____
10. _____	20. _____	30. _____	40. _____